A COURT FOR CHILDREN

A COURT FOR CHILDREN

A STUDY OF THE NEW YORK CITY CHILDREN'S COURT

by ALFRED J. KAHN

ASSOCIATE PROFESSOR OF SOCIAL WORK

NEW YORK SCHOOL OF SOCIAL WORK, COLUMBIA UNIVERSITY

COLUMBIA UNIVERSITY PRESS

MORNINGSIDE HEIGHTS, NEW YORK   1953

Library of Congress Catalog Card Number: 53-11069

PUBLISHED IN GREAT BRITAIN, CANADA, INDIA, AND PAKISTAN
BY GEOFFREY CUMBERLEGE, OXFORD UNIVERSITY PRESS
LONDON, TORONTO, BOMBAY, AND KARACHI
MANUFACTURED IN THE UNITED STATES OF AMERICA

This study was carried out under the auspices of the
CITIZENS' COMMITTEE ON CHILDREN
OF NEW YORK CITY, INC.

with the generous support of
THE FIELD FOUNDATION, INC.

Publication was made possible by the
NATHAN HOFHEIMER FOUNDATION, INC.

The following served as a special Advisory Committee:

KENNETH D. JOHNSON, *Chairman*

HERSCHEL ALT	ANNA KEMPSHALL
MRS. MAX ASCOLI	MRS. DAVID M. LEVY
VIOLA W. BERNARD, M.D.	EDWIN J. LUKAS
MRS. SIDNEY C. BORG	MRS. JARVIS MAXIMOV
FRANK J. COHEN	PETER NEUBAUER, M.D.
MRS. MARSHALL FIELD	SOL RUBIN
ALICE V. KELIHER	ETHEL H. WISE

TRUDE W. LASH, *ex officio*
EXECUTIVE DIRECTOR, CITIZENS' COMMITTEE ON CHILDREN OF NEW
YORK CITY, INC.

CHARLOTTE CARR, *ex officio*
CONSULTANT ON COMMUNITY RELATIONS, CITIZENS' COMMITTEE ON
CHILDREN OF NEW YORK CITY, INC.

A group of consultants from courts, social agencies, the United
States Children's Bureau, and professional associations cooperated
with the Advisory Committee.

FOREWORD

The author of *A Court for Children* has written a controversial and provocative report of what he has heard, observed, and learned. It will, without doubt, produce discussion and differences of opinion, and these are all to the good. The New York City Children's Court, to which Dr. Kahn refers in particular, and the juvenile court movement and its supporters, who must consider some of the basic questions raised, cannot but benefit from the attention which will be directed to problems and issues.

This important report is presented by the Citizens' Committee on Children—an organization known for its devotion to better services for children. It has the backing of an Advisory Committee of experts in many fields—a committee of which I had the honor to be chairman—and the report's recommendations are theirs.

To Judge John Warren Hill, the Presiding Justice of the Domestic Relations Court, who made it possible for Dr. Kahn and his associates to move in and about the Children's Court with such freedom of action and inquiry as to give them the material which such a study as this requires, goes the gratitude of all persons who are the sincere and true friends of a court for children—be such a court in New York City or elsewhere. The report should strengthen the efforts of Judge Hill, who has constantly initiated improvements in staff and services. In his most recent report, he emphasizes the need for further preventive work and states that "the community may well be concerned about . . . the increased seriousness of these cases."[1]

The outstanding facts are: (a) there is so much to be done; (b) so far, too little has been done; and (c) the main responsibility is ours, as members of the community. Here is where this report makes a most valuable contribution. It gives us facts which are not sugar-coated and which are not pleasant to take. More important, we are advised as to what should be done to remedy the situation.

I urge very careful reading of Chapter X, "A Dream Still Unrealized." No friend of the juvenile court movement can read that chapter and rest content until something is done about what Dr. Kahn reports. Clearly, the Children's Court has a difficult task and needs many new resources, because it can never forget that "effective preventive work through these courts (juvenile or children's) requires looking into much more than the bad external conditions of a household, such as poverty or neglect or lack of discipline. Internal conditions, a complex of habits, attitudes and reactions, may have to be dealt with and this means administrative treatment of the most intimate affairs of life."[2]

As one who has been trained in the law and who has been privileged to serve both at the bar and on the bench, I am happy that this look at "A Court for Children" was taken by one who combines understanding of what was intended when the juvenile court came into being with an unusual awareness of the need for legal safeguards. Dr. Kahn, who holds the first, and thus far the only, doctorate in social welfare granted in New York State, is well qualified to look at a children's court and recommend ways of dealing adequately, intelligently, and understandingly with the problems that arise. He properly stresses the central role of a fully qualified staff. Certainly to those of us who are charged with the responsibility of educating and training social workers

[1] New York City, Domestic Relations Court, Twentieth Annual Report, 1952, p. 8.
[2] Dean Roscoe Pound in his Foreword to Pauline Young, *Social Treatment in Probation and Delinquency* (New York: McGraw-Hill, 1937), p. XXVII.

the report dramatizes the special obligation to see to it that the graduate schools do more to prepare the men and women who are needed for active work in the areas covered by this study. The court, which owes some of its concepts to social work, was more familiar territory to social workers in earlier decades.

As the dean of a school of social work I am proud of the opportunity to write the foreword to this unprecedented report. No such study of a children's court has ever been published. It is my fervent hope that the constructive results of which it gives promise will materialize, that the community will be willing to understand the needs and provide the necessary support. As Dr. Kahn himself writes: "The New York City Children's Court is . . . a community endeavor. To the extent that it is neglected by the community, it cannot be expected to work well. Only if court and community see it as a joint venture and strive truly to give form to the promise, will it become all that it was meant to be—a sensitive and effective court for children."

KENNETH D. JOHNSON
Dean, New York School of Social Work
Columbia University

New York, New York
July, 1953

PREFACE

A revolution occurred late in the nineteenth century, a revolution signalized by the founding, in Chicago, of a specialized court for children. This revolution represented far more than a change in the judicial handling of children. It marked a new social attitude toward the problems of the young. Because it let loose on the world a stirring ideal which can never be wholly actualized, this revolution has not ended—and will never end.

The New York City's Children's Court is a product of this unfinished revolution. In these terms, Dr. Kahn, studying the Court under the auspices of the Citizens' Committee on Children, weighs its work. He asks what the Court aims to do; reports how far it is from its goal; and suggests ways to close the distance.

Some friends of the Court may not approve of this approach. To them it may seem to involve too much adverse criticism, to undervalue what the Court has achieved, to stress too little the devoted efforts of many of its judges and members of its staff. They may declare, therefore, that this report demands perfection, and that such a demand, concerning anything human, necessarily becomes unfair and causes discouragement. But those comments will themselves be unfair. The report has but stated what the Court's leading sponsors have often hailed as its chief purpose: as an agent of the government in its "parental" role, to make the most complete study possible of each individual child in "trouble," in order sympathetically to comprehend and then to solve that child's peculiar problems.

To measure the Court's actual achievements by comparing them with its ideal is to take that ideal seriously. Not to evaluate any institution—a school, a church, a legislature, a hospital—in the light of its avowed ideal is to forget it, to embalm it in a verbal ritual, to allow the mere continued existence of the institution to be substituted for the ideal—and so to stifle it. But if the ideal is not dead, then, in its light, the institution should recurrently be examined. Such an examination usually will yield some adverse criticisms of the institution's performance. If not—if the performance fully matches the ideal—then that ideal is of a rather low order.

It follows that friends of the Children's Court should welcome this report's approach. I, for one, would applaud this sort of painstaking review of the work of the court on which I sit as a judge, although surely it would reveal many distressing shortcomings, many respects in which we judges have not lived up to the noble standard of democratically "administering justice." Such a critical examination of any court is healthy, since it exposes eradicable defects for study and correction. A survey of the Children's Court cannot but be especially critical: since its revolutionary aims are higher than the aims of ordinary courts, its achievements are bound to be more exactingly evaluated.

The question has often been raised, and may here be raised, whether a competent appraisal of any public agency can ever be made by an outsider. But a wise "outsider" often proves the ablest critic: the little boy, because, being young, he was an "outsider," saw, as his conforming elders did not, that the Emperor wore no clothes. All too frequently, the "insider," accepting the scheme of things as they are, grows insensitive to the faulty ways on the "inside"; what he mistakes for sophistication numbs his doubts. Such sophistication—really nothing but pleased acquaintance with the accustomed—recalls the general who remarked that he could defeat trained, but not untrained, enemy soldiers. Jeremy Bentham, who never "practiced law," uttered strictures on courthouse conduct which offended most of his contemporaries in the legal profession but brought about major legal reforms for which all intelligent lawyers now practicing are grateful. The creation of the juvenile court itself resulted from widely publicized criticisms by outsiders of the manner in which courts had previously dealt with children.

Undeniably, the fact that the revolutionary ideal which engendered the children's court movement is kept constantly before the reader will prompt some persons to say that the report has a perfectionist mood. It should be noted, however, that there are two kinds of perfectionists: The positive perfectionist, insisting that men meet his ideals even if they are unattainable, is unjustifiably impatient of any accomplishment this side of absolute perfection. At least, however, he is usually forward-moving. The negative perfectionist, objecting to any change in the status quo unless it will produce a flawless substitute, discourages all attempts at betterment, while the positive perfectionist goads men to improvements they might otherwise have deemed hopelessly impractical. Indeed, if sufficiently tempered, this type shows up not as a perfectionist but as an intelligent "improvist." Dr. Kahn fits into that category. And so, despite the many defects he finds in the New York Children's Court, he praises the leadership of Presiding Justice Hill, whose zeal has often led to the Court's progress, and notably Judge Hill's wholehearted espousal of that most significant burgeoning of the revolutionary ideal, the psychiatric clinic, an invaluable experiment, the influence of which may permeate all phases of child care.

Nevertheless, this report does point out some major deficiencies which it is essential to remove if the Court is not to remain tragically incapable of discharging its principal purported purposes. But it clearly appears in the report that no one engaged in the Court's top administration can be held responsible for failing to wipe out these major defects. The responsibility must be borne by the citizens of New York City. For the worst ills of the Children's Court are but symptoms of a central disease from which that city's government suffers, a disease which might be called "New York-itis." To be sure, such a court in any large American city must be seen as a political institution, unavoidably affected by political crosscurrents. In New York City, however, for some time a variety of factors has caused an unusual incompetence in governmental management that has recently boiled up into a grave crisis, budgetary and otherwise. Every part of the city's government reflects that crisis. The Children's Court is not alone in being sorely infected with New York-itis. Until the city as a whole throws off this disease, that Court cannot function half as well as it should. That, surprisingly, in some respects it functions better than children's courts in many other cities is something of a miracle, to be explained by the devotion of some of its judges.

All of which goes to show the importance of personnel. The juvenile court idea did not just happen to happen. Some particular men and women invented it. Similarly, the continued maintenance and development of that idea will not occur automatically but will require the constant attention of imaginative and trained men and women, backed up by an alert public, willing to aid the Court with sage criticism and sufficient resources and facilities.

Stressing the fact that, with the shortage of other facilities in the community, a good probation service is desperately needed, the report recommends, as indispensable, higher educational requirements in the selection of probation officers. Although to some extent this recommendation now is apparently about to be met, I have heard it said that here the report betrays an academic preference for educational background as against practical experience, a snobbish intellectualism which blinds it to the excellent work done by some of the Court's experienced but not too highly educated probation officers. The reader of this book will, I think, regard that critical comment as unjustified: (a) The report acknowledges that some of the Court's probation officers now do as good a job as is possible with the present understaffing and the resultant excessively heavy case load. (b) The report nowhere

suggests that education alone will do the trick. Everyone knows
that an ass remains an ass, no matter how excellent his schooling.
Skill in any profession calls for intuitive qualities,—"reasons of the
heart,"—that cannot be taught. In any profession, a man possessed
of such qualities may go far with a poor education; some of our
wisest, ablest, lawyers and judges were graduated from inferior
law schools; training in the best political science department will
not assure us an Abraham Lincoln or a Franklin D. Roosevelt.
Yet no one suggests that, relying on the innate gifts of exceptional
men, we should shut down our better professional schools.

Those who zealously seek the general improvement of courthouse government have a lively interest in the juvenile courts,
an interest which, all else aside, sparks the hope that those courts
will prosper. For even as the initial creation of a court for children
signalized a revolution which ramified and still continues to ramify
in many directions, the experience of that court has had important effects on courts which deal with adults, both in civil and
criminal cases. Among other things, as Dr. Kahn shows, children's
courts have helped to revitalize, in the judicial process generally,
the "equity" idea of "mercy," of "individualizing" lawsuits, of
employing many legal rules flexibly and with an eye always to those
distinctive "circumstances that alter cases." Also the practices of
the courts have lent encouragement to the belief that the conten-
tious or "fighting" method of conducting trials, although it has
immense value, has been overdone, and should be modified to the
end that a trial may come closer to being a search for the truth,
so far as it is humanly discoverable. To have those ideas founder
in the children's courts, where first they were vigorously used,
might unfortunately retard their use in other courts.

Far more direct and often far more significant than that of
the United States Supreme Court is the influence on thousands
of lives of the special courts for children. On that account, a
judge of a children's court ought to have much better equipment
than a judge of any upper court. For the former should be not
merely a highly competent lawyer. He should also have con-

siderable knowledge of psychiatry and a firsthand acquaintance with the actual workings of many social agencies, together with unusual skill, developed and sharpened by previous experience, in evaluating the stories told by the children and witnesses who appear before him. Since the educational background and experience of most lawyers do not equip them, the report wisely recommends unusual care in the selection of future Children's Court judges. New York's citizens should promptly get behind this proposal; without it, only happy accidents, which seldom occur, will give the Court the kind of judges needed for its success. Indeed, I incline to criticize the report for not going further, i.e., in not urging that no one shall become a judge of that court who has not passed an examination carefully testing his special aptitudes for the post.

The notion of the "individualization" of cases in court is an old one. Aristotle discussed it centuries ago; and, in part at least, the medieval church applied it. But its extension to the child in trouble waited, necessarily, on the advent of democracy. Many a harsh, undemocratic, regime—that of ancient Sparta, for instance —has recognized that its future was its children. But only a democracy, with its emphasis on the dignity and uniqueness of each person, will adequately recognize the dignity and uniqueness of each child. So the ideal of democracy and the ideal which issues in a children's court interlace. The character of that court in any community serves as a test of the democratic character of that community. Chesterton once said (exaggeratedly) of Christianity that it has not been tried and found wanting, but tried, found difficult—and abandoned. Much the same may be said of the democratic ideal in a community which neglects its children's court. If a city will not, or believes it cannot, afford to make many of those improvements in that court which this report suggests, that fact will stand as a sign of the city's decadence.

JEROME FRANK
United States Court of Appeals

New York, New York
July, 1953

ACKNOWLEDGMENTS

Particular mention should be made of the wise and skillful chairmanship of Kenneth D. Johnson, Dean of the New York School of Social Work, Columbia University, who led the Advisory Committee and consultants in their efforts during the course of this study.

Valuable suggestions were made, after completion of an early draft, by the following Columbia University colleagues: Dr. Nathan Ackerman, Dr. Eveline Burns, Dorothy Hutchinson, Dr. Philip Klein, and Dr. Herbert Wechsler.

Indispensable throughout was the active cooperation of Trude W. Lash, Executive Director of the Citizens' Committee on Children, who has worked closely with the author in the planning and analysis phases of the study in addition to playing an active role in editing.

Finally, the author acknowledges the devoted support and assistance of his wife, Miriam.

While the Citizens' Committee on Children has, as an organization, endorsed the study and adopted its recommendations for improvement of services, the author alone, of course, remains accountable for the basic research design, the assembling and analysis of data, and the picture presented of Children's Court in New York City.

A. J. K.

CONTENTS

TABLES

A COURT FOR CHILDREN

I. INTRODUCTION: PLANNING FOR

CHILDREN IN TROUBLE

The earliest child welfare programs did not distinguish sharply between categories of children needing service. In fact, early programs and agencies offered shelter and other assistance to adults and children together. Gradually, however, agencies and institutions became aware of, and began to emphasize differences between, "kinds" of children in need, to appeal to the sympathy of the community for specific groups of unfortunates, and to shape their services accordingly. Thus, many patterns of "special" programs and agencies developed. First, to separate destitute children from adults in almshouses, special institutions for mothers and children or for children alone were created. Soon programs were developed for the handicapped, for unmarried mothers and their children—and for young offenders. With the arrival of the nineteenth and twentieth centuries, there were established many types of specialized institutions and programs for placing children in foster homes. Efforts to provide financial aid for children living with their mothers followed; more recently, programs offering guidance, protection, and rehabilitation for specific groups of children, in and out of their own homes, have been developed.

It is clear, in retrospect, that there were many different bases for organizing programs, relating them to each other, and selecting children as eligible. At times, the degree of stigma determined where a child was served; for instance, different programs were organized for children born out of wedlock and for those born in wedlock but orphaned. At times, what was seen as the immediate "cause" of the disability became the basis for grouping agencies; for instance, there were programs for the physically handicapped and programs for children of widows. On other occasions, the circumstances under which need was manifested determined, and in the main still do, where services were to be provided; for instance, school clinics treated children whose problems became known in school, while court clinics became the treatment agencies for children whose needs were identified by judges or probation staffs.

As knowledge of the needs of children and the basic causes of their problems developed, there were corresponding changes in the bases on which services were built. Thus, at one time the fact that a child was an orphan seemed to be the key consideration, and he was to be served in a program for all orphans. Later, the fact that he was emotionally disturbed was paramount, and he could be served, along with children who lived with their own parents, in a clinic for emotionally disturbed children. None of the trends was simple, clear-cut, and absolute, but examination of current programs and professional literature indicates clearly that patterns of service—while still reflecting all the older determinants—are now increasingly being based on treatment specializations related to clearly defined needs for service. The growing body of knowledge and skill and this greater emphasis on treatment considerations make feasible for the first time a view of the entire range of child welfare services as a whole and a search for rational bases for grouping services, organizing programs, and providing for the interrelationship of agencies. In brief, it should gradually become possible to define the total range of needs to be met by children's services, and then to expect that each agency offer a well-defined (and in this sense, specialized) service, or a combination of services to some of the children, within a comprehensive plan of helping. Such service might consist of readiness to screen cases skillfully, make referrals, conduct case studies, provide residential care, or carry out specified treatment activities.

There are those who would hold that, currently, agencies are already distinguished by functions specialized in this sense. While it is true that most major agencies allude to allegedly specialized techniques for serving, closer investigation often reveals that in reality this uniqueness consists solely of using special devices for case identification or of paying attention exclusively to children manifesting specified symptoms—this without fully evaluating the needs to be met by the particular services which follow.

Sound planning in a field such as this can thus mean using reasonably validated knowledge about children and parents to analyze problems in their totality, to see each part in relation to the whole, and to determine whether a given agency can contribute in specific ways to some of the requisite action. It is possible to cut through outmoded practice by asking in what sense each agency is a community resource and what particular contributions it can be expected to make, and then to inquire whether the community is fully equipped to offer coordinated services or whether major gaps exist. This approach points up the futility of a referral service where there are no treatment resources to accept referrals. It shows diagnostic work-ups as pointless and extravagant where there are no channels to interpret and implement recommendations.[1] It does not necessarily negate the possible validity of multifunction agencies, combined family and children's services, and so forth to the extent that these represent sound bases for organization, from the point of view of either administration or techniques of service.

An agency offering well-defined (specialized) services will always be asked for help by, or receive referrals of, individuals better served elsewhere and must therefore retain an intake or screening staff equipped to answer inquiries, evaluate applications, and decide whether the agency's own services are the most appropriate.

[1] Bernard, "Adolescence—Its Implications for Family and Community," in Community Service Society, *The Family in a Democratic Society*, pp. 121-140.

If itself not the best possible resource, the agency must be capable of preparing the applicant to understand and consider use of more appropriate agencies and must take responsibility for making a referral or facilitating an application.

This approach would reject such labels as "neglected," "delinquent," "defective" because they do not differentiate between children in terms of how they can be understood, what their needs may be, or how they should be served. (Whether the labels must be retained because of legal requirements is a matter for separate consideration in Chapter X.) While labels such as these have, in the past, helped shape agencies and institutions for specified groups of children, they express distinctions based on community attitudes or methods of case-finding rather than treatment needs. Other methods of classification must now be sought. Whether psychiatric diagnoses are usable in this way or whether they also describe ranges of phenomena too broad to be seen as homogeneous treatment categories remains to be clarified.

Whatever the possible success in using diagnostic labels, there is little question that symptom-labeling is of only limited use. Symptoms which come to attention at one time or another may be transitory or strongly fixed, and children with basically different problems may display the same symptomatic behavior. Moreover, the observation or reporting of a given symptom is often a chance matter. Thus, there is considerable evidence that truancy, stealing, specific "conduct disorders," and "neurotic traits" are symptoms which either occasionally or regularly characterize a wide range of children with many different kinds of needs. The truant may prove, on further examination, to be a bright, normal child best served by a more stimulating school program, or a schizophrenic requiring hospitalization. Stealing may identify the economically deprived member of a gang of boys acting in terms of their community's codes, or the kleptomaniac who expresses in it his particular emotional conflicts. Eneuresis may be a transitory symptom in a child under stress, or a sign of one of several forms of organic or emotional disturbance. The child who runs away from home may prove to be a normally adventurous adolescent, or a severe psychoneurotic.

Symptoms suggest situations to be examined and understood; they may also (in the case of a court) form the legal basis for public intervention in a family situation. They cannot, however, define the nature of the service or treatment necessary. Symptoms alone can seldom clarify, for instance, which children may need the skills available in hospitals, and which are best served through school adjustments, clinic visits, public assistance for the entire family, foster care, or visiting housekeeper service. Each of the "treatment" programs (using the term "treatment" broadly) must expect to work with children identified initially through a wide range of symptoms and manifesting various reactions to problems and to the potential help of the program. But no matter how the children are identified or what their symptoms, each agency must become available to those who prove to need its particular service and who are, in the instance of authoritarian programs, eligible under the statutes.

If each agency provided well-defined specialized services or treatment skills (or suitable combinations of such services), the current impasse represented by fixed services for fixed categories of children, on the one hand, and by the attempt to transform each staff member into a psychotherapist, on the other, would be broken. Many kinds of services, some requiring highly trained personnel, are important to the total pattern. If they are to draw on the advantages of a rational community program, those who refer cases must come to know, for example, just what a juvenile aid bureau can offer; they would then not expect other services. The same would hold true with regard to attendance programs, family casework agencies, psychiatric clinics, psychological services, educational settings, and others. When a child is sent to a guidance clinic, there should be as much assurance that a specific kind of skill will be brought to bear on his problem as there is when he is referred to a pediatric service. Similarly, asking the help of a probation department for a youth should be predicated on as clear a notion of a probation officer's functions as is the assignment of a teacher to a classroom. Each service in the community pattern should thus have something distinctive to offer, by virtue of the specialization of its personnel, its philosophy, legal delegation, the nature of its setting, and so on. True, certain elements of philosophy or attitude may be common to many of the skills (for instance, the desire to individualize the service), but the particular contribution of each derives from its combination of elements.

The identification of an agency's specific functions may be a difficult and slow task requiring much professional discussion and appraisal, study of programs in operation, and job analyses. Planning will vary from place to place, depending on the availability of other programs. Patterns of services must be flexible and subject to change with experience. Yet, if family and child welfare programs are to accomplish their intent and if protective programs are to be more than gateways to adult correctional programs, the task must be undertaken. What is more, with each advance in understanding human behavior and in developing treatment services, the effort must be renewed. Sound planning, by its very nature, does not permit stagnation.

CHILDREN IN TROUBLE. The logic of this approach might well raise the question: Why differentiate a special field of services for children in trouble from the broader field of family and child welfare? To avoid theorizing out of the context of real operations, it is wise to begin planning efforts with specific cases and existing programs. Such programs, including those for children in trouble, are, as already noted, all considered specialized— on sound and unsound bases, both. Planning objectives can be safeguarded, however, if, while studying a so-called "specialized" program, evaluation and recommendations are propounded in terms of the total field. Thus, for example, in appraising programs for orphans, one must not necessarily assume a specialized and separate program for them and for no other children. In examining what are currently the so-called "protective" services or programs for children in trouble there is no need to postulate that in the future these will be separated from the remainder of child welfare programs or, for that matter, from family welfare services as a whole. It is necessary, in fact, to ask what services, if any, ought to exist particularly to serve children in trouble and exactly how these should and can be articulated with other services.

The concern in this and related reports[2] is with children who are "in trouble" and have become known to public bodies either because of their own behavior or because of the way their parents may have dealt with them. These are the children reported to police, to attendance bureaus, to societies for the prevention of cruelty to children, and to children's courts. They are often called delinquent, neglected, delinquent "due to neglect," "potential" delinquents, or "vulnerable children." They may become eligible for the services of the various agencies by virtue of specific acts defined as delinquency or neglect in the law or because of agency policies or administrative directives. They may be like many other children in the community who for reasons of chance, social, religious, or ethnic background, economic status, or availability of other resources are not reported to public bodies and are either helped at home, ignored, neglected, served by voluntary social agencies and religious counselors, referred to private psychiatrists, or sent to private schools.

Full review of New York City programs for children in trouble would require, in addition to the Citizens' Committee on Children's studies of the Attendance Bureau and the Police Department's Juvenile Aid Bureau and the present analysis of the Children's Court, surveys of the work of the Societies for the Prevention of Cruelty to Children, the detention and shelter programs, the New York State Training Schools for boys and girls, some services of the New York City Youth Board, as well as certain voluntary foster care programs. Some of these programs have recently been examined in reports by other groups. Others fall outside the present area of study, which includes all public

[2] Kahn, Lash, et al., *Children Absent from School*, and Kahn, *Police and Children*.

services to children up to the point of a decision to remove them from their homes or to refer them to treatment by voluntary agencies.

There are, in fact, many other institutions and agencies devoted to helping children and parents incorporate the values and standards of behavior required by the community, particularly the school, church, and recreation center. The concern with agencies which come into action only after deviation has occurred, or is believed about to occur, does not preclude careful consideration of the implications of findings for these aforementioned institutions. There is also that vast group of activities on behalf of children, generally described as child welfare programs and including services provided under the Social Security Act, state and local assistance provisions, specialized educational and rehabilitation services for various groups of handicapped children, special health programs, programs relating to guardianship, foster care, and adoption, as well as activities to abolish child labor. In addition, there are the efforts of public and voluntary agencies to conserve family life, supplement the family's resources, assure community-wide health, and generally enrich the lives of children by improving the total community. The concentration of the present inquiry on public services for children in trouble is not meant to minimize society's obligation to conserve and strengthen the home and to provide all those "social utilities" (from good public recreation to school nurse services) which contribute to healthy growth and adjustment. However, it is urgent to evaluate the pattern of services designed to locate and help deviant children and those who endanger both themselves and their communities. In so doing, it is important (a) to utilize the knowledge thus gained to assure that basic preventive activities accompany case-by-case treatment efforts; and (b) to consider whether children in trouble should actually be served by separate agencies or, once identified, treated together with other children in accord with individual needs.

Emphasis on the specialized services of treatment or case-finding agencies inevitably gives the erroneous impression that delinquency, neglect, and personality maladjustment can be fully overcome by clinical means alone. Although other aspects are by no means excluded, the fact that this study emphasizes the search for individualization, and therefore apparently stresses only the clinical orientation, requires comment. Personal behavior has meaning and is shaped on three levels: the intrapsychic (the elements of a personality and the balance they achieve); the interpersonal (the person in relation to those closely involved in his life); and the social (the individual in relation to his community). While the relationship of elements within his personality may make a person vulnerable or determine his motivation, controls break down and unwholesome motives are learned in interpersonal, group, and community contexts. There are also situations in which individuals become involved in delinquent behavior although their relations to their parents or close friends pose no problems; in many such instances, the family, as a deviant group, encourages unacceptable behavior. Full appreciation of these possibilities would affect the entire approach to preventive programs and to research, but immediately relevant is the broad conception of treatment which is implied. In this context one cannot assume that a delinquent child necessarily requires individual therapy—although he often does; for treatment may be directed toward a child's total interpersonal, social, and environmental experience as much as toward helping him reevaluate personal experience or achieve a new internal balance of elements in his personality. Sound individualization draws on clinical understanding but goes beyond it as necessary.

While the basic step in delinquency prevention may well be, as some have stated, "the strengthening of resources needed by all children," this study, like that of the attendance and police programs, is by choice more immediately concerned with protection of children subject to neglectful parents or showing deviant unacceptable behavior, with provision for their treatment and with measures for the control of harmful community influences. In urging that understanding of a total problem supersede mere listing of symptoms or concern solely with circumstances of case identification, it views "needs and not . . . categories of institutional or agency provision" as the starting point for planning.[3]

RESPONSIBILITY FOR SERVICES. Protective services, technically defined in the more limited sense as "those social services for children whose parents or guardians do not fulfill their responsibilities for care and protection," were primarily developed by voluntary agencies: once the societies for the prevention of cruelty to children and now, increasingly, social casework agencies serving children and parents.[4] More and more, in recent decades, welfare departments, police, courts, and attendance bureaus have concerned themselves with such cases. Police and courts, particularly, were always considered to have primary responsibility for "delinquency" cases, but until very recently (and, in many places, even at the present time) they drew heavily for case study, probation, and treatment services on voluntary groups and limited themselves to apprehension, adjudication, and administrative functions.

With the gradual broadening of public obligation to children in general, the division of responsibility between public and private agencies was also affected in this specialized area. Just as concern with universal needs assured publicly supported schools, recreational and public health facilities, government has begun to meet other needs of children through financial aid and social services. With respect, particularly, to children in trouble or in need of protection, the duty of public agencies might be seen as identifying children in need of help and protection, assuring competent evaluation of the needs of such children and their families, and making certain that the obligation of helping the child or family is assumed by a public or private agency or facility. What is more, whether there is concern with the "protective role" (in the narrower original sense) or with services to children legally delinquent, a program involving the exercise of authority as a phase of service or treatment should be a public program (i.e., compelling attendance at a treatment or diagnostic facility, sepa-

[3] Federal Security Agency, Children's Bureau, *Controlling Juvenile Delinquency.*

[4] American Association of Social Workers, *Social Work Year Book, 1951,* pp. 94-95.

rating parent and child, etc.). Only a public program can assure the use of authority in accord with legal procedures, the safeguarding of individual rights, and the right to appeal a decision. No matter how beneficent the intent of a voluntary agency to which authority might be formally delegated, or how skilled its staff, it cannot by its nature guarantee such protections.

This is not to suggest that a public body cannot or should not call upon the resources of voluntary groups, where appropriate, or refer cases to them for consultation, examination, treatment, or, eventually, for assumption of full and continuing service. Rather, the decision that a child's welfare requires outside intervention, and control over the nature and extent of that intervention, should remain in a public body, with legally defined procedures and responsibility, subject to challenge and review. The client referred to a voluntary agency must be made aware that it acts without legal sanctions and that at most it can petition for court action.

In addition to safeguarding individual rights, such division of functions between public and private agencies is in harmony with the role evolving for voluntary social welfare programs in this country and with increasingly prevalent viewpoints about organized society's obligations toward its members.[5]

VALUES AND ATTITUDES. At first glance, it might seem that an appraisal could be limited to completely objective measures of court activities.[6] But even the definition of goals involves a judgment factor. There is no completely value-neutral way to measure effectiveness, and a study such as this necessarily embodies value judgments as it develops and applies pertinent criteria. Although all its premises, explicit and implicit, can hardly be elaborated, a brief statement will indicate its general orientation.

Basic to its outlook are the canons of modern scientific method, including the standards of objective inquiry, systematic gathering and checking of data, appraisal of findings through the use of

---

[5] See Hamilton, *Theory and Practice of Social Case Work*, p. 271.
[6] The methodology of the study is discussed in the Appendix.

available quantitative and qualitative research and statistical tools, as well as the reporting of results in a manner facilitating independent checking and public consideration of implications. Central too are the concepts and insights of modern social science, particularly in its attempts to understand the nature and variety of human individual and group behavior, the sources of individual and social deviation and disorganization, the factors making for change, and the meanings of cultural variations.

As for the underlying concept of delinquency and of how individuals can be helpful, the statement by Miriam Van Waters more than a quarter of a century ago represents this study's viewpoint: "That human conduct is caused; that ordering and forbidding cannot change it; that in order to modify behavior one must understand it and deal gently and comprehendingly with the human beings who experience it." [7]

Particularly apropos is the most recent interpretation of the needs and rights of children and of the principles of democratic social welfare organization as affirmed by thousands of experts and lay citizens at the Midcentury White House Conference on Children and Youth. Among the major conclusions were those which recognized: need to develop effective patterns of partnership between voluntary and governmental agencies; in effective teamwork between all professions, the essential knowledge and skill for the promotion of healthy personality; that all professions working with children require as part of their preparation "a common core of experiences dealing with fundamental concepts of human behavior, including the need to consider the total person as well as any specific disorder; the interrelationship of physical, mental, social, religious and cultural forces; the importance of interpersonal relationships; the role of self-understanding." [8] Assumed in these statements, and surely basic to the value-decisions in the remainder

[7] Miriam Van Waters, "The Juvenile Court from the Child's Viewpoint," in Addams, et al., The Child, the Clinic and the Court, p. 223.
[8] Midcentury White House Conference on Children and Youth, Proceedings and A Healthy Personality for Every Child. Quoted and summarized in this and the subsequent paragraph is resolution 8 and propositions 6 and 7 from the "Consensus" in the Proceedings.

of this report, are the responsibility of the community for its deviants and its ability to develop ways of helping or controlling people in trouble.[9]

Finally, there is that combination of values, attitudes, knowledge, and experience on which social work as a profession has built its education and practice. As summarized by Gordon Hamilton, these concepts, more than any others, suggest the total professional orientation guiding the research of this volume:

1. Any ability to help others effectively rests on respect for the human personality—on the person's right to make his own life, to enjoy personal and civil liberties, and to pursue happiness and spiritual goals in his own way.

. . .

2. Help is most effective if the recipient participates actively and responsibly in the process.

. . .

3. Respect for others, acceptance of others, as they are and as potentially they can be, tends to induce between worker and client, between the one who seeks and the one who offers help, a relationship which is not only the medium for educational counseling, but for a therapeutic process.

. . .

4. Respect for others includes respect for their difference.

. . .

5. Self-awareness is essential in understanding others.

. . .

6. The individual has responsibility, not only for himself, but towards the society in which he lives.[10]

[9] Young, "Social Psychology and Social Casework," *American Sociological Review*, XVI (February, 1951), 54-61.
[10] Hamilton, "Helping People—the Growth of a Profession," in Community Service Society, *Social Work as Human Relations*, pp. 8-14.

II. THE CHILDREN'S COURT

CONCEPT

The first juvenile court statute, enacted in Illinois in 1899, sprang from the inventive genius of a small group of men and women. Putting together ideas, some ancient and some then fairly recent, they added their own to create a new social philosophy of treatment for children in trouble. The legal formulation of this philosophy was uttered in 1899 by a committee of the Chicago Bar Association:

The fundamental idea of the Juvenile Court Law is that the State must step in and exercise guardianship over a child found under such adverse social or individual conditions as develop crime. . . . It proposes a plan whereby he may be treated, not as a criminal or one legally charged with crime, but as a ward of the State, to receive practically the care, custody and discipline that are accorded the neglected and dependent child, and which, as the Act states, "shall approximate as nearly as may be that which should be given by its parents."

It does not detract from the originality of this philosophy to note that steps leading up to it had been taken earlier in several parts of the country. Some courts had begun to treat children differently from adults and had experimented both with special sessions for children and with probation. The nature of children's offenses was being reinterpreted, and it was generally becoming understood that young offenders must be seen and dealt with as individuals in trouble. In short, protection and treatment of children were being substituted for the earlier systems of retribution.[1]

BEGINNINGS AND PHILOSOPHY. While there is considerable evidence that as far back as the colonial period many of the harsh punishments imposed on children were not actually carried out, court, police, and institutional treatment of children remained inhumane even through the nineteenth century.[2] The children's court movement developed in a period when children's institutions were gradually being improved, when foster care had become more responsible, when public education was taking important steps forward, and when public concern with child health and child labor was becoming more articulate. Government, for its part, was increasingly assuming responsibility for the protection of children.

Some of the proponents of a special, noncriminal court for children urged development of a treatment (or helping) approach because they questioned the value or effectiveness of punishment per se; others were particularly concerned about the justice of punishing those whose life circumstances were so conducive to deviation; still others had arrived at a concept of only limited responsibility of the child for his actions. Most advocates of the court joined in the basic conviction that "the child, though tech-

[1] The following are particularly helpful in clarifying the problems faced by the Chicago pioneers, the reasons behind their decisions, and subsequent developments (see Bibliography for a more complete listing): Abbott, *The Child and the State*, Vol. II, Part 2; Chute, "Fifty Years of the Juvenile Court," in National Probation and Parole Association, *Yearbook*, 1949, pp. 1-20; *Federal Probation*, XIII, No. 3, September, 1949 (a special issue commemorating the fiftieth anniversary of the Juvenile Court); Lou, *Juvenile Courts in the United States*, pp. 19 ff.; Lundberg, *Unto the Least of These*; Rubin, "The Legal Character of Juvenile Delinquency," and Schramm, "Philosophy of the Juvenlie Court," in *The Annals*, American Academy of Political and Social Science, CCLXI, January, 1949, 1-8, 103-104, a special issue devoted to juvenile delinquency; Teeters and Reinemann, *The Challenge of Delinquency*, Chapter IX; Thurston, *Concerning Juvenile Delinquency*. Australian juvenile courts were begun ten years before the Chicago efforts, according to Barnes and Teeters, *New Horizons in Criminology*, p. 926.
[2] See the evidence reviewed by Teeters and Reinemann, *op. cit.*, pp. 69 ff.

nically an offender against law, is really primarily a neglected child" whose conduct and problems are the outcome of identifiable social, familial, and personal factors and who has the right to the State's protection and help.

The reorientation from punishment to individualized treatment of children, with cure as its purpose, gave rise to legal questions: How was a court to relate disposition of a child before it to factors other than the nature of the offense? On what basis could there be individualized planning for each child in each particular case? In other words, the new social philosophy had to have a legal theory to support it. It has been said that most men, and especially most lawyers, fear to espouse major novelties; the proponents of this legal theory asserted that it represented no more than a slight advance on old precedents of the chancery and criminal courts. Their argument ran thus: Responsibility of the State for minors who require its care and protection dates back to feudalism, when the crown assumed supervision over estates of minors in order to realize the fruits of obligations owing to the overlord. As feudalism waned, this supervision was transferred to the chancery court, through which the king, as *parens patriae*, "assumed the general protection not only of infant tenants but of all infants in his kingdom, through the keeper of his conscience, his chancellor." The chancellor was to put himself in the position of "a wise, affectionate and careful parent." The essential idea of "equity," which the chancery court administered, is "welfare or balancing of interests." As a famous sixteenth century English lawyer put it, "Equity is a right wiseness that considereth all the particular circumstances" and is "tempered by the sweetness of mercy." A modern writer says that equity "stands for flexibility, guardianship and protection rather than rigidity and punishment. The common-law doctrine that the crown is *parens patriae*, father of his country, is but the medieval way of expressing what we mean today when we say that the State is guardian of social interests."[3]

---

[3] In this section, the presentation follows Lou, *op. cit.*, pp. 3-7; the quotation above is from p. 4. The doctrine of chancery origins is disputed by Giles,

The modern equity court might have limited its concern to the dependent, the neglected, and the destitute child. But in adopting chancery principles and extending them to so-called "delinquent" children, the juvenile court was following those principles to a logical conclusion, because the delinquent child is often dependent, neglected, and destitute. At the same time, the juvenile court was continuing the common law principle that where there is no guilty mind there is no felony — and that a child of seven can have no felonious intent. In a penetrating analysis of the origins of the jurisdiction of juvenile courts, Lou clarifies its legal origins, concluding that:

The neglect or dependency jurisdiction of the court is largely based on the parental aspect of the English chancery law, but its delinquency jurisdiction arose mainly on the side of the criminal law. There may be some historical reason for ascribing the basis of delinquency jurisdiction to the legal fiction of the age of criminal responsibility, yet its logical justification seems to lie in the recognition of the failure of the older criminal courts to prevent crime and in the experimentation in judicial methods and procedure. It is an attempt to relieve juvenile offenders under certain circumstances from the rigidity of the law prevailing in courts of more general jurisdiction. The view that chancery jurisdiction is not a factor in creating the juvenile court is correct as to the delinquency jurisdiction, but it does not preclude the view that the chancery principle has been extended to the delinquency jurisdiction of the juvenile court as a legislative policy rather than as a legal dogma.[4]

who sees the emphasis on the chancery jurisdiction of the court as a tool for ignoring rights which an individual has in criminal court. Giles, *The Juvenile Courts*, pp. 105-106.

[4] Lou, *op. cit.*, p. 7. See also Abbott, *op. cit.*, pp. 323 ff. and Judge Julian W. Mack as quoted by Thurston, *op. cit.*, p. 88. This study does not review the legal issues involved in the question of custody of the child and its relation to the juvenile court movement. Lou discusses this (pp. 8-9) and certain constitutional principles (pp. 9-12).

The new concepts formulated by the juvenile court movement could also find support in well-established legal tradition: Roman law did not hold a child under seven responsible for delinquent acts (Cf. the Catholic Church, which does not permit Communion for children under seven). The Romans permitted punishment between age seven and puberty where insight and discernment could be demonstrated, while from puberty to age twenty-five, the age affected the type of punishment. The Code Napoleon assigned limited responsibility under the age of seven, but a child of eight could be found

Children's courts begin with the recognition that punishment does not stop crime. In seeking more effective means, they become concerned, in the first instance, not with the offense per se but rather with whether or not the child requires special care of the State and with the nature of his specific needs. This means that social and psychological factors enter the court's consideration at least on a par with legal factors. The court ceases to be a battleground between two individuals or between an individual defending self-interest and a state concerned with the general welfare.

The juvenile court movement combined in one court procedures which had developed separately and incompletely in previous decades (for example: separate confinement for children, separate trials, a probation system). But these procedures, coupled with a sound philosophy and a legal theory, did not suffice. New methods had to be contrived; for it was no small step to ask courts which were oriented to learning whether or not a child had committed a specific offense to consider instead whether the child before them was "a subject for special protection, care and guardianship by the community in the same degree as the child who is neglected or homeless," and to ask a judge to see himself not as umpire or arbitrator but as a community representative acting with and for parents to protect children and bring about more desirable behavior as well as more effective adjustment. Judges and other personnel called upon to individualize cases were now expected to exercise discretion, but "all discretion is liable to abuse, and the consequences of abuse, affecting the general security on the one side, and life or liberty on the other side, are . . . serious."[5] When each "offense" led to a specified "penalty," it was somewhat easier to know whether justice had been rendered. Now that "justice" was assumed to require an individualized plan,

---

guilty of a felony. Even today, it might be noted in passing, chronological age is still a determinant of responsibility. On this see Teeters and Reinemann, *op. cit.*, p. 42; Abbott, *op. cit.*, Vol. II, Part 3; Lou, *op. cit.*, Chapters I, II, and Klein, *The Treatment of the Delinquent Child in the United States*, pp. 4-11.

[5] Pound, *Criminal Justice in America*, p. 75.

means had to be sought both to individualize and to protect fundamental rights.

It was understood in a short time that the court could not fully realize its intent unless it added to the new orientation of the judge a total court atmosphere in which the promise of helping received its first demonstration and a probation system which drew on modern skills in understanding the child, referring him for treatment or undertaking that treatment within the court. How far the court's intent and requirements have been clarified from the time of the Chicago law in 1899 is seen in the statement of Presiding Justice John Warren Hill, of the New York City Domestic Relations Court, who wrote in 1948:

Children's Courts have been established for the purpose of diagnosing, treating and reclaiming for society those children who are found neglected and delinquent in this community, and who . . . will not respond to the voluntary services of other agencies in the community. The situation of every child who comes before the court is examined for the purpose of discovering and treating the causes for his neglect or those things which are disturbing him and causing anti-social behavior.[6]

LATER DEVELOPMENTS. The children's court idea has had wide acceptance in the United States but only incomplete implementation. The first Federal law pertaining to juvenile delinquency was passed in 1938. By 1945 all states had juvenile court laws of some kind.[7] The earlier laws followed no fixed pattern, were limited in scope to juvenile delinquency jurisdiction, and often represented appendages to existing judicial systems rather than fresh beginnings. Later, recommendations by the United States Children's Bureau and the National Probation and Parole Association provided guidance for states developing programs, but major variations continued.

[6] Hill, in New York County Lawyers' Association, A *Colloquium on Juvenile Delinquency and Its Socio-legal Aspects*, p. 63.

[7] An extremely useful state-by-state summary of juvenile court delinquency jurisdiction appears as Appendix I of Sussman, *Law of Juvenile Delinquency*. A chronological listing of state laws is presented in United Nations, Department of Social Affairs, *Probation and Related Measures*, pp. 37-38.

Despite the existence of enabling laws in all states, there are currently only about two hundred special courts for juveniles throughout the United States. In forty states juvenile court hearings constitute just a small part of the business of courts with many other responsibilities. Only in Connecticut, Utah, and Rhode Island is the juvenile court a state court organized on a district basis.[8] It is the larger counties in some other states which have found it possible to have special children's court judges and to avoid the common practice of assigning such cases to judges who preside over other matters as well, inevitably crowding children's cases into heavy calendars.[9] It was found as late as 1949 that "the juvenile courts as they function in fact display all stages of development out of the criminal court origins from which they have in large part sprung" and that few courts really direct their entire procedure to determination of what is best for a child.[10]

Definitions and procedures vary in different states.[11] For instance, unlike New York, most jurisdictions have an upper age limit of eighteen years for juvenile court cases, while some states limit jurisdiction to ages sixteen or seventeen, and a few extend it to twenty-one. What is more, the definitions of "delinquency," "dependency," and "neglect" are so written that the distinction is actually quite difficult to apply, and a condition described in one way in a given state may be differently classified elsewhere. For definitions of "delinquency," eight states substitute descriptions of cases over which the court is granted jurisdiction.

Experience in many parts of the country discloses several sources of difficulty in practice: (1) the mixed legal and philosophical foundations of juvenile courts; (2) the expectation in almost all states that these courts concern themselves with dependency and

[8] Social Work Year Book, 1951.

[9] Victor B. Wylegala, "Children's Courts, an Effective Aid to Social Agencies," Child Welfare, XXV (June, 1946), 6-9.

[10] Tappan, "Children and Youth in the Criminal Court," The Annals, American Academy of Political and Social Science, CCLXI (January, 1949), 131.

[11] See particularly Sussman, op. cit. Teeters and Reinemann present a valuable chart dealing with juvenile court jurisdiction in all states in op. cit., p. 312.

neglect situations as well as with delinquency; (3) the fact that the children's court movement grew at a time when communities everywhere lacked social services for children.[12] The continued growth of juvenile courts, paralleled by nationwide expansion and improvement in social agencies which serve children and families, has inevitably been followed, too, by basic differences as to the future direction of these courts. They are urged to become both more like and less like community social agencies. They are also criticized simultaneously for utilizing rigid judicial techniques which belie the intent to help and for being so eager to diagnose and treat that they forget the necessity of prior adjudication and infringe on the legal rights of parents and children. The fact is that while both these tendencies have developed, in all likelihood the former is more pervasive.

Even within the framework of the law of a given state, there are still major variations possible from one county to another in the definition of the court's role, with the result that children's

[12] Because of the absence of community resources to serve children they dealt with, the courts attempted to provide such services as part of their own organization. Once the courts were accepted as social service agencies, it was almost inevitable that they become responsible for the administration of additional measures enacted early in the century for the care and protection of dependent children. The prime example of this is Mothers' Aid, the precursor of Aid to Dependent Children under the Social Security Act. Mothers' Aid, though always recognized as essentially a form of family relief, was developed as a child welfare measure. Children's courts were in close contact with many of the conditions which Mothers' Aid was designed to correct. Many Midwestern and Northwestern courts already had jurisdiction over dependent as well as delinquent children. These sections of the country as well as the Southern states had no public agencies to undertake a new child welfare venture. Furthermore, the larger cities, at least, had probation staffs experienced in case study. It was logical, therefore, in certain of these states for Mothers' Aid to become a court program and remain such until the passage of the Social Security Act, even though some child welfare leaders thought it an error in principle. New York City, with its more elaborate system of public and private welfare facilities, did not assign jurisdiction over dependent children to its children's courts, and Mothers' Aid was not included in its court program.

In similar manner, juvenile courts have variously been given jurisdiction over filiation, children born out of wedlock, adoption, guardianship, commitment of the feeble-minded, payment of medical and other expenses for crippled and handicapped children, and also over adults accused of contributing to a child's delinquency. Lundberg, op. cit., pp. 119, 131-132, and Abbott, op. cit., p. 235.

courts can be and are used differently in different communities. Their case loads are affected, for example, by the nature of the programs of social agencies, schools, and police. Some courts take petitions on any case brought to them, whereas others have a controlled intake policy, accepting only those cases which cannot be served elsewhere. There is variation, too, in the informal handling of cases not considered to require petitions.[13]

Although the juvenile court is generally regarded as one of the great social inventions of the century, many thoughtful leaders of the movement have begun to express disappointment at the limited expansion of the court idea beyond large counties and at the inability of many of the larger and more important courts to attain levels of service implicit in the juvenile court concept. The critics point out that while today there is wide agreement about objectives, the vast majority of these courts are still not equipped for effective service.

The children's court pioneers saw clearly that children should not be treated as adults and that they should not be punished for their problems. They urged that young offenders be aided to become well-adjusted citizens. However, they could not, in the early days, foresee in any detail what it would take to realize the full possibilities of their dream. Looking at court failings today one expert states:

The shortcomings of the children's courts of today are . . . due to the refusal by some courts to employ . . . special skills for both diagnosis and treatment of maladjusted children, and the inability of other courts to secure adequate treatment resources because of lack of community support. Such resources must include not only the personnel required for correct diagnosis of the individual child's problems, but also treatment resources in the community which involve cooperation of parents, school personnel, social workers and psychiatrists, and, finally, institutions to which a child can, when necessary, be sent for treatment rather than custodial care.[14]

[13] New York State, Department of Correction, *Annual Report* (1948), p. 132.
[14] Polier, in a review of *Unraveling Juvenile Delinquency* in the *Harvard Law Review*, LXIV (1951), 1037-1038. See also Polier, "The Role of a Juvenile Court in 1948," pp. 8-9.

CRITERIA FOR EXAMINING THE COURT. This study involves a distinct and basic point of view concerning the persons —children and parents—with whom the court deals. It holds, in brief, that the conduct which prompts the court's attention to them should be regarded primarily as symptomatic of, and as an attempt to satisfy, strong and often unconscious personal needs which, in the case of each such person, grow out of his total life history, his physical and emotional make-up, his social and cultural environment, his interpersonal relations, his intelligence. To cope with the neglected or delinquent child, then, requires as full an understanding as possible of his needs as well as a knowledge of the general circumstances and precipitating situations that have encouraged the conduct occasioning his being brought to court. With this understanding and knowledge, the court's problem becomes that of determining the kinds of help— material, social, or emotional—necessary to bring about the desired adjustment. At times, individual clinical help may be adequate; more often, the remedy must take into account the child's total family situation in its particular social setting.

All this means that the court has a most difficult task. Its difficulty becomes the more apparent when one observes that even in those instances where the key determinants seem clearly to be in the child's personal disturbance rather than environmental causes, "delinquency is not the name of an illness, nor is there one simple specific psychological category for all delinquents and for them alone. For . . . juvenile delinquents do not fall into one simple homogeneous psychiatric or psychological category." A very wide diagnostic range is disclosed among Children's Court clients in New York City who are referred for psychiatric study in the court clinic or while at detention facilities.[15]

Ideally, a court should itself be equipped, or be provided with

[15] Bovet, *Psychiatric Aspects of Juvenile Delinquency*, pp. 8-9, and Peck, "Relationship of a Court Clinic to Plans for the Mental Health Needs of Children in New York City," *Journal of Educational Sociology*, XXIV (May, 1951), 544-545. See also Youth House, New York City, *Sixth Annual Report* (1950), pp. 8, 75, 76, 79.

necessary community resources, to understand the possible determinants and meanings of child and parental behavior and to
provide the manifold kinds of help possible. While this ideal is
never wholly realized, since knowledge is incomplete and im-
perfect and limited resources must be apportioned equitably in
any community, the court should make use of the best means
that have thus far been achieved and can be made available; and
this the community has the right to ask.

An important source of criteria in evaluating the New York
City court is the Standard Juvenile Court Act, a model statute
which embodies the ideas of the outstanding experts concerned
with child care and juvenile delinquency.[16]

This act recommends, first, that eighteen years be the age
limit for original jurisdiction (Art. I, Sec. 2), pointing to the general trend to raise the age and recalling the provision for transfer
of cases of youths sixteen to eighteen to a criminal court when
the juvenile court considers this desirable.

The act contains (Art. I, Sec. 3) the so-called "Missouri plan"
for appointment of judges but recognizes that no one plan could
be universally adopted. Generally, the plan provides for appointment by the governor from a list of three names, to be nominated
by a panel of seven (the presiding judge, two individuals designated by the welfare department, two designated by the organized
bar, and two by the board of education). The act also permits
the use of referees, whose findings must be reviewed by the judge.

In accord with the philosophy that in dealing with the child
as an individual, the labels "delinquent" and "neglected" are
unnecessary and often harmful, the act (Art. II, Sec. 7) prefers
to list the circumstances under which a juvenile court shall have
exclusive jurisdiction. These circumstances as listed include:

[16] In 1925, the National Probation Association, now the National Probation
and Parole Association, published the first *Standard Juvenile Court Act*, conforming with standards developed by the United States Children's Bureau and
prepared with its assistance. The act was revised in 1927, 1933, 1943, and
1948 to embody the best judgments based on developments in the child care
field and on better understanding of the meaning of juvenile delinquency. See
National Probation and Parole Association, *A Standard Juvenile Court Act*
(1949).

neglect (from the point of view of education, as well as that of medical, psychiatric, and psychological care); involvement in injurious occupation, environment, or behavior; being out of control of parents; being alleged to have violated laws or ordinances. The act suggests, too, that the court have jurisdiction in cases of custody, guardianship, adoption, and consent to a child's marriage, as well as the right to order treatment or commitment of a mentally disordered or emotionally disturbed child.[17]

The act calls (Art. V, Sec. 17) for informal hearings and states that stenographic notes shall be made only if the court so orders. The requirement of the presence of the child may be waived by the court at any stage. "The hearing should have the character of a conference rather than a trial. It is not difficult to see the incompatibility of formal procedure . . . with the informal conference which is necessary to give the court the confidence of child and parents, and to bring out pertinent facts not only as to events but also as to personalities, emotional states and causes, all of which are of the utmost importance to a wise disposition of the case."[18] The committee which revised the act cites the legal decisions upholding the constitutionality of this approach. The point is made regularly that since the juvenile court is not a criminal court, constitutional guarantees protecting persons accused of crimes do not apply.

The section dealing with disposition (Art. V, Sec. 18) allows the court broad discretion, with emphasis that none of the dispositions must be in the nature of criminal penalties. Children are not to be found "guilty" and "sentenced." The court's function, rather, is to find whether the child comes under its provision and proceed to make plans to help. Any plans made must "where practicable" involve steps (choice of agency, institution, etc.) to protect the child's religious affiliation (Sec. 19). In certain circumstances (Sec. 23), the child's welfare may demand a termination of parental rights.

Juvenile court jurisdiction is to begin from the time a child is

[17] Difficulties in this provision are described in *ibid.*, pp. 17-18.
[18] *Ibid.*, pp. 24-25.

taken into custody (Art. IV, Sec. 15). This is meant to cope in two ways with the problem of indiscriminate detention: by centralizing responsibility for detention and release and by assuring interagency coordination in detention matters.

Additional specific recommendations of the National Probation and Parole Association are also useful in suggesting criteria. Pointing to the experiences of many courts, the association states that an effective juvenile court requires exclusive jurisdiction over children as well as over adults in children's cases. The judge of such a court should be chosen for his sympathetic understanding of children and parents. He should be able to conduct private, friendly court hearings as part of an informal noncriminal procedure. The court must be staffed by a sufficient number of professionally trained probation workers with access to facilities for physical examinations and for psychiatric study of children and to well-equipped detention or boarding homes for their temporary care. The court requires an efficient record and statistical system as well as adequate clerical help. It must also develop patterns of cooperation with other agencies.[19]

These recommendations, the provisions of the Standard Act, and the review of the objectives of the juvenile court movement provide the framework for a study of a court in action. The examination of the New York City Court, reported in the chapters which follow, began with questions such as these:

What are the scope and nature of the Court's activities? (a) What attitude does the Court have toward the child and parent in trouble and how they are to be helped? (b) Has it given up all remnants of a punitive approach? (c) Is its philosophy compatible with the best of modern knowledge? (d) Does court atmosphere contribute to, or detract from, the Court's purpose?

Are the judges able to develop and conduct a court which is intended to help, in the sense of the ideals of the juvenile court movement? Is the selection of judges geared to their qualifications for such a role?

Are the procedures and general orientation of the Court such

[19] As summarized by Teeters and Reinemann, op. cit., p. 343.

as to assure both protection of the individual's constitutional rights and concern with determining what lies behind his court appearance and how he may be helped? (*a*) How is jurisdiction assumed by the Court? (*b*) How are the procedures at each phase related to the Court's basic purposes?

Does the court staff represent the skill required to arrive at sound plans for the children served, to inaugurate such plans, to treat children skillfully, and/or refer them for skilled treatment? (*a*) Are the Court's probation, supervisory, and administrative machinery adequate for the ends sought? (*b*) Has the community provided the Court with necessary facilities, resources, staff?

What is the Court's direction? Has there been progress in the recent past? What do those in the Court see as immediate and long-range goals?

III. THE NEW YORK CITY

CHILDREN'S COURT

The earliest reforms in programs for young offenders in New York State were concerned only with institutional treatment and aftercare, and it was not until the last quarter of the nineteenth century that substantial changes were made with respect to temporary detention of juvenile offenders and the organization and procedures of criminal courts dealing with children.

In 1877 a law (Ch. 428) was passed which provided that children under sixteen should not be confined, detained, or transported with adult criminals "except in the presence of proper officers." Probation had its beginnings in 1884 in a statute (Ch. 46) which permitted commitment of a child under sixteen to a person or institution in lieu of fine or imprisonment. An 1892 Penal Code amendment (Ch. 217) allowed separate trials, dockets, and records for children under sixteen, although still in a criminal court structure. Not until 1898 did the New York City Charter provide for separate children's courts in the Magistrates' Court system, and this provision was never implemented.

It was a Buffalo judge who in 1901, on his own initiative, launched the state's first juvenile court procedure by conducting special children's sessions twice a week. That same year, a law was passed authorizing probation for three-month periods. A year later, the borough of Manhattan was permitted to establish a special children's court in the Court of Special Sessions, and

New York County (Manhattan) was the first county in the United States to house a children's court in a separate building, although there was then no law giving it chancery jurisdiction. The other boroughs of New York City gradually followed suit: Brooklyn in 1903, Queens and Richmond in 1910, and the Bronx in 1914. With four Special Sessions judges sitting as Children's Court judges and a probation staff, created in 1912, working under them, the Children's Court was established as a special division of the Court of Special Sessions in 1915 (Ch. 531).

The jurisdiction of the Children's Court division continued, however, to rest on penal law after 1915, and children were accorded essentially the same treatment as were adults. Still other steps were requisite before New York State could have noncriminal courts to serve juvenile delinquents and other children. Study and recommendations by the Judiciary Committee of the legislature led eventually, in 1921, to a constitutional amendment permitting creation of special tribunals. A comprehensive Children's Court Act for New York City was not passed until 1924. In the years which followed, a series of amendments expanded the court's jurisdiction. The Family Court, a Magistrates' Court branch created in 1918, was combined administratively with the Children's Court under the Domestic Relations Court Act of the City of New York, effective October 1, 1933.[1] This act, as subsequently

---

[1] The history summarized is based on the following sources: New York City, Domestic Relations Court *Annual Report* (1938), pp. 17-20; *Annual Report* (1933), pp. 28-30; *McKinney's Consolidated Laws of New York*, Book 66, Part 3, pp. 70-71; Thurston, *Concerning Juvenile Delinquency*, p. 104; New York County Lawyers' Association, *A Colloquium on Juvenile Delinquency and Its Socio-Legal Aspects*, particularly McGrath, pp. 13-14; Report of the Joint Legislative Committee to Examine into, Investigate and Study the Existing Facilities for the Care and Treatment of Children, Fred A. Young, chairman, *Young People in the Courts of New York State*, pp. 24-25.

It should be noted that although the 1924 act gave the Court noncriminal jurisdiction (delinquency, neglect, defectives, material witnesses), jurisdiction over marriage of children from fourteen to sixteen was not added until 1930. In 1931 the Court was given the right to place handicapped children if parents did not provide satisfactory care. The Court received sole jurisdiction over Compulsory Education Law violations in 1932. The new 1933 law, in combining the Children's with the Family Court, assumed all these jurisdictions.

amended, provides the legal basis for, and governs much of the current procedure of, the Children's Court in New York City.

THE DOMESTIC RELATIONS COURT ACT. When the Domestic Relations Court Act of the City of New York went into effect, it created a unified administration for the Children's and the Family Court. Although, under a rotation plan, the same judges preside over both courts, and although each of these courts may refer clients to, and cooperate with, the other, integration between the two courts is actually extremely limited in practice. This study addresses itself exclusively to the Children's Court. The Family Court is largely concerned with support petitions and does not hear divorce or custody cases; but it may make temporary orders of protection, which include provisions for visitation in connection with support cases. Thus the court seems to be a "domestic relations court" in name only.

The Domestic Relations Court Act (subsequently referred to as the New York City law and also as the DRC Act) embodies the spirit of the juvenile court movement. Its intent is clear:

This Act shall be construed to the end that the care, custody and discipline of the children brought before the court shall approximate as nearly as possible that which they should receive from their parents, and that as far as practicable, they shall be treated not as criminals but as children in need of aid, encouragement and guidance.

The act gives the Court exclusive original jurisdiction in cases of children under sixteen alleged to be delinquent, physically handicapped, material witnesses, mentally defective, or neglected. A 1948 amendment limits exclusive jurisdiction to those up to age fifteen in offenses punishable by death or life imprisonment. Special procedure is provided for transfer of children between the ages of fifteen and sixteen to the Children's Court at the discretion of the criminal courts. Delinquency and neglect are broadly defined, and the Court is in a position to intervene in a wide range of situations involving deviant behavior by a child, parent-child difficulties, or questionable care of children by their parents. Where the Court has intervened on such grounds it may grant adoption orders and decide with whom a child is to live while under its supervision. When delinquency and neglect issues are before the Court, it may determine charges below the grade of felony involving adult offenses against children.[2] Its jurisdiction does not include custody, separation, divorce, or habeas corpus proceedings. Parents may not be required to make restitution for damages or stealing by their children, nor can children be required to make restitution.

In the exercise of its jurisdiction, the Court may, before or after a hearing, require mental, physical, or psychiatric study of an adult having or seeking responsibility for a child's care. Where considered desirable, and after proof of need, the Court may require similar examination of children as well as order treatment for the physically handicapped.

Justices of the Domestic Relations Court, who must be attorneys of five years' experience, are appointed by the mayor for ten-year terms. The law requires them to be "persons who because of their character, personality, tact, patience and common sense are especially qualified for the court's work." The justices of this court also have the powers of magistrates.

Following adjudication of delinquency or neglect, the Court may make one of the following dispositions:

1. Suspend judgment.

2. Place a delinquent child on probation or a neglected child under supervision while he is remaining at home or in the custody of a fit person.

3. Commit the child to a suitable institution or agency.

4. Continue the proceeding while the child is placed at home, in custody of a fit person, or on temporary commitment to an agency or institution.

[2] The following sections in the law contain elaboration and further specifications: Sec. 2, Sec. 61, and the decisions reported in McKinney's *op. cit.*, pp. 103-8. Also see Amendment L. 1948, c. 556. A particularly useful summary of the New York law and court structure is included in Sicher, *Socialized Procedure of the Domestic Relations Court of the City of New York*. The quotation in the previous paragraph is from Sec. 89 of the law. The paragraphs which follow are based on the following sections of the law: 61.7, 85, 83, 89, 77, 76, 83, 84, 88, 25, 85, 58, in the order given.

5. Discharge neglected or destitute children to public bodies authorized to provide for them.

6. Render certain other judgments within the law's framework.

Hearings are to be private, separate from those of adults, and the Court may dispense with putting children under oath. It may adjourn hearings to allow time to obtain such information and understanding of the child as is necessary to arrive at a disposition. Adjudication under the act is to involve no civil disqualification of any kind; the child is not to be considered as having been "convicted" as a "criminal."

The law requires that court dispositions protect the child's religious faith. Commitments to other than public agencies and assignment to probation officers, guardians, and foster parents must be determined by that faith "when practicable," a term strictly interpreted by the higher courts.[3]

The law also allows for modification, setting aside or vacating of judgments, and permits appeal through the Appellate Division of the Supreme Court. In various decisions, higher courts have stressed that the Children's Court is to be a civil rather than a criminal court and that it cannot assume powers not specifically granted to it. Their opinions have held that the major purpose of the court is to protect and rehabilitate children rather than to punish. They have also emphasized that investigations conducted by probation officers at the Court's request must go beyond the "bare and apparent facts" to an understanding of the "causative factors"; for only through "suitable therapy" for those in trouble can the community be adequately protected. Although the Children's Court is clearly not subject to the procedural rules of criminal courts, its procedures in settling jurisdictional issues must not ignore "the customary rules of evidence shown by experience to be essential in getting at truths in civil trials"; the findings of fact must rest on the preponderance of evidence adduced under such rules.[4]

[3] *Ibid.*, Sec. 88.5.
[4] The following are illustrative, on different levels, of the decisions referred to: *Zambroth* v. *Jannette* (1936), 160 Misc. 558, 290 N.Y.S. 338. *Singer* v.

From time to time, criticism has been directed at the upper age limit of the Children's Court jurisdiction and at the exclusion of certain offenses; there have also been attempts to expand jurisdiction to cover emotionally disturbed children. Questions have been raised too about the particular manner in which the law seeks to protect a child's religion. Nonetheless, it is commonly agreed that the law is basically sound and that the quality of service under it derives more from its interpretation and from the personnel and resources made available than from its provisions per se.

COURT STRUCTURE AND PROCEDURES. The program of the New York City Children's Court is the largest anywhere in the United States. Each year the court handles more than seven thousand children under sixteen; it considers more than fifty-five hundred delinquency petitions, twenty-four hundred neglect petitions, and several hundred other petitions. Its more than two hundred staff members in five boroughs include: eighteen judges; more than seventy probation officers; several psychiatrists, psychologists, and social workers; and approximately one hundred attendants, clerks, typists, custodians, and others in information rooms, petition rooms, typing rooms, waiting rooms, and in the courtroom itself. While the total budget cannot be readily prorated as between the two sections of the Domestic Relations Court, it is noted that the court as a whole was allocated $1,602,250 in 1950, $1,827,231 in 1951, and $1,961,230 in 1952. Additional millions of dollars of expenditures are involved in the detention and shelter services, the institutionalization, the diagnostic studies, and the hospital observation undertaken at court request or initiated by the Court.

How does the Court organize this large and complex "team" to fulfill the responsibilities delegated to it? Basic structure and

---

Singer (1941), 177 Misc. 76. In re: ZYX (1941), 24 N.Y.S. 2nd 456. In re: *Kingsley* (1944), 183 Misc. 727. *Moses* v. *Moses* (1948), 193 Misc. 890. *People* v. *Lewis* (1932), 260 N.Y.S. 171. *Bowman* v. *Cruz* (1947), 188 Misc. 826; N.Y.S. 2nd 413. *Kane* v. *Necci* (1935), 269 N.Y. 13.

procedures are determined by the law itself and by the Rules of Practice,[5] the latter an attempt, as the Court sees it, to conform "not only with the letter of the law but with the socialized spirit in which it was written and the social mandate which it clearly proclaims."[6] One or more Parts of the Children's Court are set up in each county, and each Part is served by one of the judges of the Domestic Relations Court. (The technical term "Part" designates the full section of the court, staffed by judge and all other necessary personnel.) The judges are scheduled for monthly rotation between the Children's and the Family Court and from one Part to another. At the time of this study, the Children's Court adhered to the following schedule:

Manhattan   Two judges sitting daily, in sections designated as Part I and Part II

Brooklyn   Two judges sitting on Tuesday, Wednesday, and Thursday (Part I and Part II); one judge sitting on Monday and Friday and carrying on both Part I and Part II duties

Bronx   One judge sitting daily

Queens   One judge sitting on Monday and Thursday

Richmond   One judge sitting on Friday morning

In addition, during the school semester, the School Part of the Children's Court met in Manhattan on Tuesday and Wednesday, in Brooklyn on Monday and alternate Fridays, in the Bronx on Thursday, and in Queens on the alternate Fridays when not in Brooklyn. The Children's Court judge in Richmond also heard School Part cases, i.e., cases brought by the Bureau of Attendance of the Board of Education.

The client or potential petitioner, arriving at the Court, presents his request to a clerk at an information window or desk. Here he is referred to another agency if the Court cannot deal with his case, to the Bureau of Adjustment, if his case falls within one of several categories in which adjustment may be possible

[5] New York City, Domestic Relations Court, *Rules of Practice.*
[6] John Warren Hill in "Foreword," *ibid.*, p. vi.

without formal petition, or to the petition clerk for a formal petition. A formal court case, in the technical sense, exists only when a petition has been filed.

While petitioners and children, if present, remain in the waiting room, the clerks examine files for previous petitions involving the same children. The case is added to the calendar (the list of cases to be heard on a given day) by an attendant, and the first hearing takes place on the same day unless the family exercises its right to employ counsel or unless individuals important to the case are not present and cannot be reached while the Court is sitting (for instance, a parent in the case of a child picked up for shoplifting and brought directly to court; a child who is incorrigible and whose parent has initiated a petition; a parent who has abandoned a child).

At the first hearing, after ascertaining that the parents are present or have been informed of the proceedings, the judge usually explains the allegations, cites the family's right to counsel and/or to call witnesses, and then proceeds to "hear and determine the facts, rendering a decision thereon." [7] The judge usually adjudicates the case at the first hearing but may ask for a Probation Department investigation prior to adjudication and sometimes does so.

Unless the case is discharged or dismissed at the first hearing, the child is usually paroled to parents or relatives or placed in a temporary shelter, as in neglect cases, or in a detention facility, as in delinquency cases, pending case study by the Probation Department.[8] In some instances, children have been taken the previous night directly to the New York City children's detention facilities, Youth House or Girls' Camp, or are on commitment to institutions at the time of petition; in these instances the judge

[7] *Ibid.*, Rule 7 (*d*).
[8] The term "parole" is used in the Children's Court and throughout this study to refer to children released in the care of parents and guardians during the Court's case study and/or (in the case of neglected children) after adjudication. Unlike the more usual use of the term, such reference in the Children's Court is not to individuals who have been institutionalized and are permitted to complete their periods of sentence in the community.

must decide whether to continue the child on remand pending case study.

The date for the second hearing is usually set at the first hearing, although when circumstances warrant, probation officers or others concerned may take specified steps to advance the date. Where the judge orders physical or psychiatric examinations of the child and/or his parents, it may or may not be possible to obtain these before the second hearing. With few exceptions, however, the probation officers are expected to have their investigations completed by the time of the second hearing or to request a later date. Generally, the judge who conducts the first hearing, where the emphasis is on establishment of jurisdiction and interim plans, is expected to conduct the second hearing, which is concerned with case disposition. If the judge reserved decision (adjudication) at the first hearing, he must hear the case again, unless the evidence is to be reviewed completely by another judge.

The monthly rotation plan means that, in boroughs which have two Parts, a judge usually hears new petitions when he sits in what is called Part I and, when possible, conducts the disposition hearings on the same cases when he sits in Part II. The Part II calendar generally consists of disposition hearings in cases initiated the previous month and all other cases (probation, parole, etc.) requiring court review, but which the judge may never have heard before. Because of the rotation system or the time necessary to secure diagnostic examination of child and parents or for the probation staff to complete the planning preliminaries, a case heard by one judge in Part I may appear before another judge in Part II. In other instances, judges' absences or uneven work loads may necessitate case reassignment, and sometimes, even though an investigation is completed when the judge who has adjudicated the case is still assigned to the borough, a second judge enters the case at the planning phase.

The second, or "disposition," hearing by no means invariably results in a plan. A series of court appearances may be necessary before examination reports are received, referrals made, or long-term placement plans arranged. Even where "final" plans for probation or supervision have been made, new developments or new petitions may bring the family and probation officers back to court. Institutions to which children have been committed may also petition for their transfer.

In arriving at a probation or supervision disposition, the judge may himself set a date for a progress report and review of developments or may leave it to the probation officer, in consultation with his supervisor, to set a calendar date when the situation may warrant discharge, favorable or unfavorable, a new disposition, or arrangements for new examinations and consultation.

Where children, parents, or others involved in cases do not appear in court when scheduled, or when other circumstances so require, the judge may issue summonses, subpoenas, and warrants to be served by a warrant officer assigned to the Court by the Police Department.

At any stage in the process the Court may decide to call upon its own physiological laboratory to perform tests, or may ask its Bureau of Clinical Services to conduct physical or psychiatric examinations. As one possible disposition, it may decide to place a child on probation, referring him to the Court's Treatment Clinic, which is staffed by psychiatrists, psychologists, psychiatric caseworkers, and graduate students being trained in psychiatric social work.

These steps involve substantial activity on the part of all court personnel. Files must be checked to determine whether a family has been previously known to the Court. Petitions must be drawn. The court calendar must be prepared and controlled so that the load for a given day is reasonable. Attendants are needed to keep the calendar moving. Arrangements must be made with Youth House, Girls' Camp, the Department of Welfare, or a hospital when detention, shelter, or observation are required. When necessary, physical, psychological, and psychiatric examinations must be scheduled in one of several possible places. Children must be transported to and from temporary or long-range institutional and foster home facilities, must be cared for while in the Court's detention rooms, and must be fed while waiting in the building. What is more, procedures must exist whereby new cases are equitably assigned to probation officers for investigation, probation officers are introduced to new clients and informed of what has transpired in the courtroom, and cases are scheduled for hearings on days when the assigned probation officers and others involved can be in court.

At present, the court staff is made up of a director of administration and two deputy directors who also serve the Family Court, a clerk of court in each borough, court attendants, assistant clerks of court, interpreters, and various custodians, nursery attendants, clerks, and stenographers. This staff, performing administrative, clerical, auxiliary, and adjunctive services, is essential to the work of judges and members of the Probation Department who are more directly responsible for activities and treatment measures which would carry out the intent of the law.

While the presiding justice sits in court when necessary, as administrative head of the Court he must devote most of his time to "superintendence of the business of the Court." He is the chairman of the Board of Justices which, by vote, makes the rules and regulations for court procedure. He assigns judges to the various divisions of the Court, sets work hours for all staff, selects and supervises the various record systems, and investigates complaints about the Court or its personnel. He also controls the entire staff, making appointments and setting salaries within the limitations of competitive civil service procedure and Board of Estimate authorizations. (A few exempt positions are filled by appointment of the Board of Justices.) The presiding justice also has responsibilities in connection with employee discipline for those in the competitive civil service class, while the board has similar obligations for the few in the noncompetitive class. (Judges may be removed only following a hearing in the Appellate Division of the Supreme Court.) By virtue of his official position, although not specified in the Domestic Relations Court Act, the presiding justice is also a member of two New York City commissions concerned with child welfare, undertakes planning with agencies working with the Court, and has regular contacts with the budget director and members of the legislature.

A considerable amount of administrative responsibility may be assigned under the law to the director of administration for the Domestic Relations Court, a position in the exempt class of civil service. The law also permits appointment of an administrative officer for each court; but the responsibility has, in fact, been carried by the clerk of court in each borough, who, as a result, exercises a combination of custodial, administrative, and clerk of court duties.[9]

Court activities take place in separate Children's Court buildings in Manhattan, Brooklyn, and the Bronx, and in buildings shared with the Family Court in Queens and Richmond. Planning for separate buildings is an outgrowth of the concern early in the century with separating children from adults; it is based on that part of the law which says that Children's and Family Court buildings shall "be located conveniently near each other, and where possible adjacent to each other, but the respective buildings shall be separated from each other where practicable except that they may connect by a passageway or bridge." [10] Court is open Monday through Friday from 9:00 A.M. to 4:30 P.M., except for the luncheon recess, and is closed Saturdays, Sundays, and holidays; court sessions, problems of arranging placements, and probation work schedules often result in late hours.

The many and complex procedures and staffing provisions are designed, as are the various court facilities, to contribute to the Court's fundamental objectives of protecting community interests and promoting the welfare of children. These goals are stressed repeatedly in all court directives, in public statements of court leaders, in the law, and in higher court decisions. The successes and failures of the New York City plan (in the light of such objectives) will be delineated in the chapters which follow.

[9] Further details of duties of the director of administration, administrative officers, clerks of court, as well as responsibilities of the presiding justice and Board of Justices, are recorded in *Domestic Relations Court Act of the City of New York*, Art. 2.

[10] DRC Act, Sec. 46.

STATISTICS. In the year March 1, 1950, to March 1, 1951, the Children's Court listed, in its own monthly report, 4,947 new official delinquency cases (see below re: *neglect*); it also reported 2,793 new Bureau of Adjustment cases, of which about one third resulted in petitions.[11] The New York City Youth Board's central

[11] Although, in many respects, accurate and comprehensive statistical data about court clients and operations are lacking, available sources do provide a reasonable approximation of the case totals, clients, and types of petition involved in the court's work load. The court's own monthly and annual reports, the annual reports of the New York State Department of Correction, and the reports of the Youth Board Central Register provide the main sources for the statistical data below.

Although the Domestic Relations Court has been able, for certain brief periods, to publish relatively complete annual reports, it is ordinarily quite limited in the range of data which it is able to compile and utilize. The lack of skilled research and statistical staff, adequate clerical help, tabulation facilities, and sound reporting procedures have been described in Kahn, *Proposals for the Development of a Statistical and Research Service in the Domestic Relations Court (Children's Court).* That survey, undertaken at the request of the court, which is concerned with developing more adequate statistics and research, also indicates the limitations and major inaccuracies of data currently available in the court and elsewhere.

In brief: (*a*) Shifts in statistics from year to year and differences in rates, from place to place or group to group, may reflect policy changes with regard to tabulation and apprehension, or differences in use of the court, rather than actual changes in delinquency rates. (*b*) Most tables report numbers of cases or petitions rather than numbers of children. (The Youth Board data reported provide one of the few child counts for the Court.) (*c*) Court statistics often report alleged delinquency or neglect rather than adjudication. (*d*) Inaccuracy or inconsistency in policy in relation to a primary source (such as the listing of allegations in petitions which, in turn, are the source of such court data) can invalidate elaborate or careful work at a later stage.

The Central Register of the New York City Youth Board is a research instrument designed to provide an accurate case count, a child count, indicators of agency overlapping, and data about client characteristics. For a two-year period beginning March 1, 1950, coded I.B.M. cards were prepared, representing the records of children and youths known to public and private agencies as being "in trouble," a term which each agency was permitted to define in accord with its own practice. Mimeographed reports have been issued for each year, and certain additional tabulations are available at the request of the agencies involved.

This study's field work took place between September, 1950, and September, 1951. An attempt has therefore been made to present operational statistics for the closest comparable period available, so that the appraisal may be seen in the light of case load data. For all other purposes, data are presented to the end of the 1952 calendar year, the time of the study's completion.

registration project found that during this period a total of 3,254 different children (8.7 percent of the Register total) were registered exclusively by the Court as the agency to which the case was first known during the year. An additional 1,500 children were registered by the Court but had been known to other agencies earlier in the year. Thus a total of 4,754 different children "in trouble," representing 5,261 official cases, was listed by the Court. (Comparable data are not available for neglect cases.) They accounted for 11.8 percent of the Youth Board's city-wide case total (of which the names of youths over sixteen constituted more than one fifth), or 11.3 percent of the children. Further analysis discloses that the Children's Court, including the School Part and the Bureau of Adjustment, had contact during the twelve-month period with 15.0 percent of all cases of children under sixteen known to public agencies as being "in trouble," and with 14.0 percent of the under-sixteen group known to any agency.

It is of interest that, contrary to widely held assumptions, court cases do not represent the major part of the total registered with the Youth Board by schools, police, voluntary agencies, Youth Board referral units, and the courts. The Juvenile Aid Bureau of the Police Department, in contrast, registers more than 40.0 percent of all the children reported, while the Bureau of Attendance reports over 20.0 percent of all names. Each of these agencies, however, refers only a small proportion of its cases for official court action.

Central Register data do not take account of most court neglect cases, but the latter group and cases in several minor classifications make up 30.0 to 40.0 percent of the total court load. Since criteria vary, it is not possible to estimate what portion of the total neglect group is brought to court; so the final weighing of the Court's case load, as related to the total problem facing the community, remains in this sense incomplete.

TABLE 1. *New Children's Court Cases, 1902-1952*
Classified by Year and Sex[a]

Year	Male	Female	Total	Year	Male	Female	Total
1902	1,870	149	2,019	1928	8,686	3,258	11,944
1903	7,640	838	8,478	1929	9,167	3,278	12,445
1904	9,173	1,221	10,394	1930	9,365	3,353	12,718
1905	11,388	1,337	12,725	1931	8,885	3,209	12,094
1906	11,646	1,465	13,111	1932	8,987	3,274	12,261
1907	14,436	1,513	15,949	1933	9,404	3,159	12,563
1908	14,368	1,516	15,884	1934	7,991	3,348	11,339
1909	14,176	1,494	15,670	1935	7,545	2,913	10,458
1910	12,298	1,717	14,015	1936	6,266	2,286	8,552
1911	12,455	2,143	14,598	1937	6,154	2,253	8,407
1912	12,991	2,147	15,138	1938	6,015	2,108	8,123
1913	11,924	2,507	14,431	1939	6,333	2,444	8,777
1914	11,452	2,464	13,916	1940	5,415	2,716	8,131
1915	11,413	2,722	14,135	1941	5,401	2,818	8,219
1916	9,549	2,876	12,425	1942	5,749	3,184	8,933
1917	11,322	3,197	14,519	1943	7,716	3,720	11,481
1918	11,010	2,975	13,985	1944	8,153	3,497	11,650
1919	10,668	2,959	13,627	1945	7,626	2,342	9,968
1920	8,937	2,645	11,582	1946	6,534	2,081	8,615
1921	7,950	2,495	10,445	1947	4,967	2,056	7,023
1922	7,755	2,531	10,286	1948	5,606	2,465	8,071
1923	7,804	2,912	10,716	1949	5,832	2,768	8,600
1924	7,794	3,064	10,858	1950	5,438	2,521	7,959
1925	8,477	3,035	11,512	1951	5,972	2,590	8,562
1926	7,262	2,885	10,147	1952	6,318	3,099	9,417
1927	7,621	2,897	10,518				

[a] Source: New York City, Domestic Relations Court, annual reports, 1938-1952.

Court statistical reports, which usually list petition totals rather than children, have recently shown relatively little variation except for two war years and the considerable rise in 1952 (Table 1). In addition to cases listed for official action, the Court has, through its Bureau of Adjustment, served between one and two thousand cases informally each year (Table 8). As might be expected, there are interborough variations in numbers of new cases (Table 2). There is reason to believe that these rates reflect police policy, attitudes of different groups in the population to use of the courts, availability of voluntary agencies to assist with family problems, as well as differences in the size of the borough populations.

TABLE 2. *New Children's Court Cases, 1949-1952*
Classified by Year and Borough[a]

	1949	1950	1951	1952
Manhattan	3,169	2,984	3,070	3,411
Brooklyn	2,897	2,628	2,769	2,904
Bronx	1,405	1,188	1,375	1,605
Queens	1,006	952	1,198	1,280
Richmond	123	207	150	217
Total new cases	8,600	7,959	8,562	9,417

[a] Source: New York City, Domestic Relations Court, annual reports, 1949-1952.

The Court's annual reports also record "rehearings" and add these to "new" cases for a grand total of cases. There were 37,319 rehearings in the Children's Court in 1949; 36,341 in 1950; 40,114 in 1951; and 45,586 in 1952. Rehearings are computed merely by adding all the case entries on court calendars for the entire year, while "new" cases involve counting petitions. Since a calendar entry can represent anything from a brief routine request to the judge by the probation officer, in the absence of child or parent, to a careful review of an investigation and elaborate discussion of plans with child and parent in the courtroom, the rehearing totals do not in themselves give any clear picture of court volume and the "new case" total is probably more useful.

The Court may consider a case formally only if a petition is filed. As might be expected, the bulk of the petitions presented to the Children's Court allege delinquency, although in recent years neglect cases have represented an increasing proportion of the case load (Table 3).[12] The other categories of petitions are relatively minor. Police, individual citizens, parents or relatives, school

[12] Material witness petitions are ordinarily employed in cases in which children are held so that they may testify against adults as needed in other courts. The limitations placed by the detention facilities on how long children will be kept, is currently a major safeguard against abuse. The marriage application procedure makes it possible, after investigation, to allow desirable exceptions to the law about marriage age, although the selection of criteria is complex. Adult proceedings were at one time used in large numbers for violations of the Compulsory Education Law, but this has changed with changes in the School Part of the Court (see Chapter V). The other types of minor jurisdiction are self-explanatory.

representatives, and social agencies account—in the order named —for all but a few delinquency petitions, with the police alone filing more than half. Social agencies, chiefly the Societies for the Prevention of Cruelty to Children, file nearly two thirds of the neglect petitions, while school representatives, parents or relatives, and the police—listed in order of importance during 1951—are the petitioners in almost all the remainder.

TABLE 3. *New Children's Court Cases, 1949-1952*
Classified by Type of Petition[a]

Type of Petition	1949	1950	1951	1952
Allegedly delinquent	5,269	4,805	5,538	5,762
Allegedly neglected	2,187	2,600	2,427	3,094
Material witness	179	175	161	164
Petition for release	49	37	31	13
Petition for transfer	97	68	79	63
Application for consent to marry	136	172	158	190
Mentally defective child	75	48	138	96
Adult proceedings	604	49	26	31
Others	4	5	4	4
Total[b]	8,600	7,959	8,562	9,417

[a] Source: New York City, Domestic Relations Court, annual reports, 1949-1952.
[b] Totals are for petitions, not children.

New York State Department of Correction statistics show that for 1951, the period when much of this study took place, burglary or unlawful entry was the most frequent delinquency allegation about boys (1,649 cases), while other stealing, except that of automobiles (516), acts of mischief (438), automobile stealing (361), robbery (321), sex offenses (307), truancy (296), injury to person (281), and ungovernable behavior (263), were also important. The major allegations in cases of delinquent girls were ungovernable behavior (265), sex offenses (223), running away (146), truancy (146), stealing (63), injury to person (48), burglary or unlawful entry (38), and acts of carelessness (35). Most neglect petitions alleged that the children involved were "without adequate physical care from parent or guardian" (1,929), "living under conditions injurious to morals" (284), had been abandoned or deserted (164), or were abused (71).

Another kind of classification is offered by the New York City Youth Board Register, which lists "reasons for referral" for all delinquency cases registered by the Bureau of Adjustment or the Children's Court proper. Since all reasons are tabulated rather than the immediate concern as reported at the time of court referral, the percentages represent 7,282 "reasons" listed in 5,261 cases for 4,754 children (Table 4). While the Children's Court sees only a minority of cases registered, there is little doubt from the data presented that it is confronted, through these case situations, with opportunity to serve many of the most serious child welfare problems in the community:

TABLE 4. *Reasons for Referral of Children's Court Cases as Compared with Reasons for Referral of All Cases Known to the Youth Board Central Register March, 1950-March, 1951*

(IN PERCENTS)

Reason	Children's Court Cases	All Agencies' Cases	Part Accounted for by Children's Court
Truancy	15.8	25.1	9.0
Stealing	30.0	16.3	27.0
Disobedience and conflict	12.6	8.3	23.0
Disorderly conduct	6.8	15.6	7.0
Incorrigible	11.7	3.7	48.0
Sex offenses	7.3	2.6	42.0
Destructiveness	3.6	6.2	9.0
Quarrelsomeness	3.7	5.3	10.0
Other	6.1	14.1	
Not reported	2.4	2.8	
Total	100.0	100.0	15.0

Data in the annual reports of the Domestic Relations Court also show that of the totals in Table 3, boys outnumber girls in cases of alleged delinquency in a ratio of three or four to one (1950—males 77 percent, females 23 percent; 1951—males 82 percent, females 18 percent; 1952—males 81 percent, females 19 percent). There is almost an equal number of boys and girls in the allegedly neglected group. For the New York City Children's

Court as a whole, the 1949 distribution of cases was 68 percent male and 32 percent female; the comparable 1950, 1951, and 1952 distributions differed by only one percent or less. The data for individual boroughs varied somewhat. Earlier in the history of the Court (Table 1) the case loads showed an even higher proportion of boys than girls. The material witness petitions consist largely of cases of girls who are to testify in rape cases. All marriage applications are filed on behalf of girls. Upstate children's courts tend to show a wider variation between boys and girls in delinquency petitions than do New York City courts and approximate equality between boys and girls in neglect cases.[13] The United States Children's Bureau's country-wide juvenile court statistics reports, which are computed somewhat differently, show males outnumbering females in a ratio of more than four to one in official and "unofficial" delinquency cases.[14]

As might be expected, age data compiled by the Department of Correction for cases disposed of in 1951 establish that children who come to court on neglect petitions are substantially younger than those allegedly delinquent. The median age for delinquent boys was 14.5 and for girls 14.7; in the neglect group, the median age was 8.1.

The filing of a formal petition does not necessarily mean a long court contact. In fact, from 20 to 30 percent of all cases are decided in the courtroom without referral for probation investigation (although an unknown number may have previous probation records, and the number so decided is rapidly decreasing). Most such cases are those in which one of the following occurs: the petition is withdrawn or dismissed, the client is discharged with a warning (with or without adjudication), judgment is suspended or immediate placement is indicated.

More than what can be said about the total court case load is known about how those cases of alleged delinquency and neglect which are referred for probation study are processed thereafter

[13] New York State, Department of Correction, *Annual Report* (1948), pp. 140-141.

[14] Federal Security Agency, Children's Bureau, *Juvenile Court Statistics, 1946-1949*, p. 4.

(Tables 5 and 6). In brief, somewhat more than 60 percent of all such cases are placed on probation or supervision after case study. Probation usually involves the child's brief appearance at a reporting center or office bimonthly and occasional contacts with parents or others (Chapter VII), but may include referral for more intensive help in the court clinic or other agencies. Supervision implies bimonthly home visits to the families of neglected children and occasional brief contacts with the children themselves; the Department of Welfare or other agencies may be asked to help with family problems.

More than a fifth of the total group of children in the delinquency and neglect group are discharged or their dispositions suspended after probation investigation, sometimes with the suggestion, or even under the condition, that child or parents receive the help and guidance of clinics, social agencies, religious counselors, or other sources of aid.

In 1950, 1951, and 1952, of all case studies completed in the Probation Department in instances where delinquency or neglect was alleged, 15 or 16 percent were followed by institutional commitment to one of many facilities (Chapter IX). While approximately the same proportion of boys as girls in the neglected group are sent to institutions or referred to other foster care programs, a higher percentage of the girls found delinquent are committed.

More specifically, the Court reported commitment of 230 girls and 724 boys (total 954) as delinquents in 1950, 283 girls and 782 boys (total 1,065) in 1951, and 266 girls and 733 boys (total 999) in 1952. Some of these commitments were ordered immediately at the time of the hearings (often on the basis of reports from previous probation investigations or psychiatric study); other commitments followed probation investigations. The comparable commitment totals for neglect cases were 266 boys and 223 girls (total 489) in 1950, 269 boys and 272 girls (total 541) in 1951, and 322 boys and 302 girls (total 624) in 1952. The neglect totals are minimal, since a substantial number of children adjudicated as neglected are "remanded" for long periods—theoretically, pending permanent plans; actually, as part of a long-term plan—and are

TABLE 5. New Children's Court Delinquency and Neglect Cases, 1950-1951 Classified by Disposition, Type of Petition, and Sex[a]

TYPE OF PETITION AND SEX

DISPOSITION	1950					1951				
	TOTAL CHILDREN	DELINQUENT		NEGLECTED		TOTAL CHILDREN	DELINQUENT		NEGLECTED	
		Boys	Girls	Boys	Girls		Boys	Girls	Boys	Girls
Total new cases (delinquency and neglect only)	7,405	3,931	874	1,358	1,242	7,965	4,558	980	1,231	1,196
Total referred for Probation Department investigation	5,379	2,859	702	898	920	6,542	3,352	873	1,129	1,188
Percent of total referred for probation investigation	73	73	80	66	74	82	74	89	92	99
Placed on probation (delinquents) or under supervision (neglected children)	3,399	1,736	402	621	640	4,021	1,920	497	793	811
Committed to an institution[b]	873	420	151	152	150	985	451	176	177	181
Discharged or disposition suspended	1,107	703	149	125	130	1,536	981	200	159	196

[a] Source: Table 2 and Table 8 in New York City, Domestic Relations Court, annual reports, 1950-1951. Note that only delinquency and neglect petitions are here included. Table 4 gives totals for other types of petition.

[b] Does not include institutional commitments made without referral of case for probation study. See Chapter IX.

TABLE 6. *New Children's Court Delinquency and Neglect Cases Referred for Probation Investigation, 1950-1951 Classified by Disposition, Type of Petition, and Sex*

(IN PERCENTS)[a]

TYPE OF PETITION AND SEX

DISPOSITION	1950					1951				
	TOTAL CHILDREN	DELINQUENT		NEGLECTED		TOTAL CHILDREN	DELINQUENT		NEGLECTED	
		Boys	Girls	Boys	Girls		Boys	Girls	Boys	Girls
Placed on probation (delinquents) or under supervision (neglected children)	63	61	57	69	70	61	57	57	70	68
Committed to an institution	16	15	22	17	16	15	13	20	16	15
Discharged or disposition suspended	21	24	21	14	14	23	29	23	14	17
Total referred for Probation Department investigation	100	100	100	100	100	100	100	100	100	100

[a] See footnotes to Table 5, the source of the raw data on which these percentages are based.

not included in the totals. All commitment totals have a small but untabulated amount of overlapping.

Summarizing, probation and supervision are the most common case dispositions; more than a fifth of the petitions are discharged or lead to suspended dispositions, and a smaller number are followed by the separation of child from parent. Boys who are found to be delinquents are slightly less likely than girls to be committed to institutions and are more likely to be placed on probation or have their cases discharged. In neglect cases, there is not so much variation in disposition as between boys and girls.[15]

While these data serve to introduce the Court and the people whose lives it touches, they communicate little of what happens to these people and of what is involved in the task of serving them. It is to these matters to which the discussion must now turn.

[15] Data relating to status on discharge after probation supervision are discussed in connection with the over-all review of probation (Chapter VII). Bureau of Adjustment case load data are reviewed in the context of the discussion of the Bureau (Chapter IV). Clinic case loads are discussed in Chapter VIII.

IV. DOORWAYS TO THE COURT

Those who meet clients initially must understand that asking for or taking an agency's help is an experience with complex and varied meanings to the individuals concerned. This is true whether the request is made by a relief applicant in a welfare center, by an individual asking the assistance of a counseling service, or by a parent requesting court action against an "incorrigible" child. Those who would help should know too that the problem or request as initially presented may take on other complexions as more confidence is engendered and better understanding created. They must recognize that it is easier to ask for a concrete thing or service ("I need relief"; "Put my son away") than for intangible help ("Can something be done about how we, in this family, get along together?"). They must realize that the emotion accompanying an application may be compounded of disgrace, despair, hostility, or dependence and that fuller comprehension of the meaning of the experience to the applicant is only gradually to be gained.

Where such contact is not with a person who himself comes to ask for the agency's intervention, but with a child brought in by parent, policeman, or other petitioner, the emotional interplay is even more complex and the difficulty of conveying a mood of helping rather than punishing is even greater. If the agency or institution is one associated in the public mind with punishment, revenge, or stigma, as it may be in the instance of a court, the resultant feelings of disgrace, failure, or hostility may be considerable and are manifested in numerous ways.

The various "helping" professions—psychiatry, social work, psychology—aware of how crucial a client's initial contacts with an agency are in determining its ultimate usefulness to him, have considered these matters in some detail. They have stressed the responsibility incumbent on a community service to recognize and meet the varied components in such situations, and in the course of such consideration they have developed a body of literature dealing with the theoretical and practical aspects of application and "intake," or initial, interviews.[1]

Particularly relevant to the court setting are, in brief, the following major components of a good first contact:

1. Mutual confidence must be established, for without it there will be sparring, not helping. (How does the client view the agency and its interest in him?)

2. A preliminary estimate is needed of the type of service the client requires and of the agency's ability and legal right (or, particularly in the case of the Court, legal responsibility) to offer that service. Consideration must be given to whether the needs are better met elsewhere in the community. (Does he need relief, a child guidance clinic, a family welfare agency, or court service?)

3. The interviewer must appraise accurately what the experience means to the client in order to gear the helping process to his ability to use help. (Is he humiliated? Does he come to court to seek revenge? Does he seek to relinquish his responsibility?)

4. The initial contacts should demonstrate just how the agency helps. Technically, intake must be a first "treatment" experience.

In the Children's Court, intake activities are represented by the work at the information desk, in the Bureau of Adjustment, and at the petition desk (see chart). The first of these is a center for answering questions and sifting cases; the second, a casework

---

[1] See, for example: Alexander and French, *Psychoanalytic Therapy*; Garrett, *Interviewing: Its Principles and Methods*; Hamilton, *Theory and Practice of Social Case Work*; Hollis, "The Relationship between Psycho-social Diagnosis and Treatment," *Social Casework*, XXXII (February, 1951), 67-74; Maeder, "Generic Aspects of the Intake Interview," *Social Casework*, XXIII (March, 1942), 14-23.

CASE FLOW, NEW YORK CITY CHILDREN'S COURT

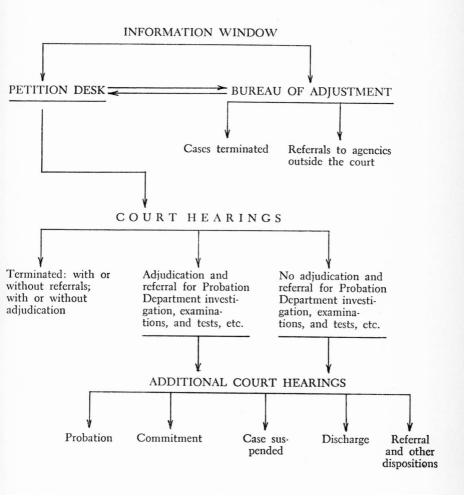

agency for settling specified situations informally or for making referrals; while the third is the channel through which formal courtroom action is initiated. Examination of these services must take cognizance both of current assignment of functions and of possible long-range goals and conceptions.

THE INFORMATION SERVICES. In each borough, a clerk at an information desk or window does preliminary case sifting for the Court. One day, when observations were recorded, the following situations were met by a clerk in sequence:

A man wished to be directed to the medical department.

A boy wanted to know his probation officer's room number.

A student asked whether he could observe in court.

A man and his son came, stating that they had been instructed to meet a police officer in court.

Parents, their daughter, and a young man to whom she was engaged came to obtain court permission for a marriage.

A man had been referred by the local police precinct to complain about his son, twenty-four, who kept late hours.

A man wished to see the Court about his children. Asked whether his wife neglected the children, he described a marital problem rather than neglect.

A mother came to the window and began to cry about the late hours and questionable companions of her fifteen-year-old daughter.

An agent of the Society for the Prevention of Cruelty to Children inquired about the status of a case.

There are no regular tabulations of activity at the information desk, and there is no reason to believe that they are needed. This study's sample tabulations in two offices for a brief, and possibly not fully typical, period suggest that approximately one out of four individuals who appear at the information desk is referred out of the court to other courts, the S.P.C.C., the Department of Welfare, etc. More than half are merely given directional information, i.e. how to find the courtroom, the clerk, certain probation officers, and so forth. Only about a quarter of those seen at the information desk actually require referral to the Bureau of Adjustment or to the petition desk for further service. Since formal channels are not consistently observed, some petitioners familiar with court structure appear both at the petition desk and at the Bureau of Adjustment without having been referred by the information desk. Some cases referred by the information desk do not arrive at the Bureau of Adjustment or at the petition clerk's desk at all.[2] Of particular importance is the fact that at least a quarter of all requests which were made during this study's tabulations took the form of presenting a problem and asking for advice. People usually come to the window describing the circumstances which have brought them to the Court, without knowing exactly by what procedure the Court can serve them.

The need to deal with many different kinds of situations at the information desk represents a complex challenge for the clerks assigned the responsibility. Faced by great difficulty in filling probation officer field positions and not at all certain that they are needed for this assignment, the Court has, of course, not been able to request professionally trained personnel for the information posts. It has, however, stressed the need for efficient clerical routine essential to answering inquiries, considerate listening, clear explanations, and proper referral.[3]

Limited in its resources and handicapped by its manpower situation, the Court makes various kinds of arrangements to staff the information desk. During this study, it was noted:

1. In two offices, manning the information desk is merely one of the functions of the docket room staff. This room contains dockets (petitions), docket books, and numerous other files. The clerks on duty (two in one borough's office, three in another) prepare all statistical reports, except those on probation cases,

[2] Marlene Seldin, of Bard College, undertook the tabulation of information desk data.

[3] In fact, directives were issued early in 1949 instructing information clerks to consult with probation supervisors when in doubt as to where to refer cases. However, the content of the directives was forgotten in the rapid staff turnover, and they were never implemented. Since information clerks remained responsible to clerks of court, it was in any case unlikely that they would accept the leadership of probation personnel.

and complete the daily court calendars and cards for the index files; number and enter petitions into the docket book; file and pull petitions; answer inquiries from authorized agencies and telephone requests; make records available to authorized persons— as well as serve the information desk. In one office, which had three clerks on duty, one clerk devoted himself largely, but not solely, to answering inquiries at the information window, and he demonstrated the highest level of skill observed. Currently, only two clerks are on duty in that office, and they must concentrate on other duties, moving to the information window only as clients appear. Not infrequently, other court personnel who happen to be present, particularly warrant officers or attendants, handle the information requests.

2. In each of two offices in smaller boroughs, two clerks handle these duties for both the Family Court and the Children's Court. In one of these borough offices, the clerk also operates the switchboard.

3. In another office, the information desk clerk also has typing duties.

The general impression, after a period of observation, is of quite uneven performance on the information desk job. For instance, in two offices with approximately the same numbers and types of requests at the information window, files are examined for prior record of the family almost three times more often in one than in the other. More important, people who tell their story are at times heard impatiently by a harassed clerk who must also answer the phone and make entries in a docket book, at times directed elsewhere by a court representative who enters into an argument as to what they should and should not have done, at times sent to the Bureau of Adjustment or to the petition desk without prior consultation of the Court or Bureau of Adjustment name index. In some boroughs, the information desk and window are so situated that very personal requests must be made perforce in the immediate presence of others waiting to approach the windows. Unfortunately, poor service is more typical of the Court than are instances where clerks listen sympathetically, efficiently check files or other information sources, explain to the petitioner why he should go to another court, or skillfully dispose of the situation as soon as it is clear what is called for.

An additional task of the information clerk is to assist the large number of authorized persons who inspect case lists in the docket book for one purpose or another. These include representatives of other courts in the city and of the FBI, Civil Service, the Army, Red Cross, Travelers Aid, and voluntary social agencies. Police precincts send officers to the Court to examine docket books and to copy disposition data on arrest cases. The Hack License Bureau, concerned with whether applicants have run afoul of the law, sends its representative to look at petitions. If the case is not over ten years old, and if they wish details, these agencies may also turn to records in the Probation Department, although psychiatric and psychological examination reports are not available to them without the examiner's permission. If the case is older, access is limited to petitions. In addition, Department of Welfare investigators regularly read Probation Department case records, and young men enlisting in the armed forces, who have been known to the Court, come to have certain necessary forms completed. (The Probation Department may make a more detailed statement.)

While the Domestic Relations Court Act refers to the "privacy of records" it permits their use by "authorized" agencies and institutions. Observation and discussion disclose varying interpretations within the Court as to the specific application of the law's intent and considerable lack of information by some judges and probation supervisors as to actual practice. This study is able to offer no detailed proposals for improvement, but calls attention to the urgent need for clarification of policy: Each agency involved may have convincing reasons why it can better help or evaluate a person after it receives a summary of the court contact. However, a petition which briefly records allegations, findings, dispositions, and a docket book which contains little more, can hardly provide an adequate picture. Furthermore, it is questionable whether even such disclosure is consistent with the spirit of the Court's purposes, for the law states clearly that "no adjudication under the provisions of this Act shall operate as a disqualification of any child." [4] Even if it is assumed that other courts do not use information about juvenile delinquency findings against a former client of the Children's Court, there is considerable evidence that some of the agencies listed above want the docket or probation records only because the existence of the offenses in the past makes a difference in whether a person will be employed, given a license, or permitted to enlist. The record made available has the result of stigmatizing the individual involved and introducing certain disabilities for him. Children's Court records may safely be shared only with agencies which have kept pace with the law's view of the Court's function, and this is hardly the case with some who currently call upon the Court.

THE BUREAU OF ADJUSTMENT. It was inherent in the philosophy of the juvenile court movement that procedures would be developed for informal adjustment of certain cases, and in almost all juvenile courts, some cases are now listed as unofficial (informally adjusted). In fact, in recent years about half the cases reported by courts throughout the country to the United States Children's Bureau have been handled unofficially.[5]

The Bureau of Adjustment in the New York City court was created on March 5, 1936, on the initiative of the Presiding Justice, since it had become apparent that specified cases were best treated unofficially and that some petitions were being drawn in the haste of immediate emotion. It was also intended to relieve the pressures on a too small staff of judges attempting to deal formally with heavy calendars. Despite considerable opposition and a lack of resources, the Presiding Justice continued his efforts on behalf of the Bureau. The New York Bar Association studied the Bureau in 1940 and found no basis to question its constitutionality. In 1941, the Attorney General ruled that an adjustment

---

[4] DRC Act of New York City, Sec. 84.

[5] Sussman, *Law of Juvenile Delinquency*, p. 35, and annual *Juvenile Court Statistics* reports of the United States Children's Bureau.

bureau may attempt to adjust "minor cases of neglect and delinquency by agreement and only with consent of all interested parties before the case comes before the Court." There is concensus that the Bureau's activity must in no way deprive a person of the right to present a petition if he elects to do so.[6]

According to Rule 6 of the court's Rule of Practice, the Bureau is to afford opportunity, where "desirable and possible," for case adjustment without court proceedings. It may offer its services to cases in the following categories:

1. All cases of children in which neglect or destitution is alleged.

2. Cases in which court action is sought for the first time by a summons for an alleged delinquency which if committed by an adult would be below the grade of a felony.

3. All cases in which delinquency is alleged for the first time and the complaint is made by a parent or guardian of the child or children involved.

4. All cases where truancy is alleged for the first time.

Also included in the Bureau's assignment are requests for help in making voluntary visitation arrangements, requests for conferences by agencies considering court action, and referrals from judges in the Family Court. In addition, the Bureau considers any case referred by the justice who is presiding, but sends for petition cases placed within its own jurisdiction by the rules but considered by individual justices to require formal action. Thus, at the time of this study, the Bureau was operating under instructions not to dispose informally of a case where severe alcoholism was alleged without first conferring with the judge who was sitting.

The Bureau has, since its creation, substantially reduced the number of petitions for formal action drawn in the Children's

[6] Hill, "Limiting Unofficial Casework" in National Probation and Parole Association *Yearbook*, 1951; also Brick, "A Study of Twenty Boys Who Were Committed to the New York State Training School for Boys through the Manhattan Children's Court," pp. 14-17. The Bar Association study is on file at the Welfare and Health Council of New York City. The Attorney General's opinion is cited in *McKinney's*, p. 125. See also, Hill, *op. cit.*, p. 2, citing DRC Act, Sec. 71.

Court (Table 1). However, the unofficial case rate in New York City is below that in some other centers, and proportionately fewer of the Court's cases have come before the Bureau in recent years (Tables 7 and 8). These latter trends may reflect qualitative changes in the case load as much as bureau staff size and court policy.

The probation officer in charge of the Bureau is expected to maintain close liaison with the justice who is conducting initial case hearings and to consult with him when in doubt about a case or where a complainant insists on a petition, despite the Bureau's contrary opinion. At the time of this study, the Bureau of Adjustment was staffed by a probation officer in each borough, who was designated as chairman, and by Juvenile Aid Bureau (J.A.B.) representatives in all boroughs except Richmond.[7] The rules permit the presiding justice to invite to the Bureau, on a liaison basis, representatives of public departments concerned with children. The police, through the J.A.B., and the schools, through the Bureau of Attendance, were represented in the Bureau on this basis, but withdrew their personnel during the Second World War. The J.A.B. of the Police Department reestablished its representation in 1949, assigning policewomen from the J.A.B. to the Bureau. Observations and case reading reveal that J.A.B. representatives did not, in the main, concentrate on the intended liaison function, although they did give valuable guidance in delinquency cases through conferences with police considering court action. They arrived at a time when the Probation Department was understaffed and could not spare enough workers for the bureau assignment. They were, in effect, used as full-fledged staff members and were never able to limit themselves to purely liaison functions. Since they were ultimately responsible not to the Court but to the J.A.B., which was free to call them from time to time for other police duties, and because they received higher salaries than the probation officers in the Bureau, their use as staff members was complicated. Nonetheless, the Court appreciated

[7] The Queens and Richmond Bureau of Adjustment chairmen had other duties as well.

TABLE 7. *New Applications in the Bureau of Adjustment 1938-1952*[a]

Year	New Applications	Size of Bureau Case Load as Related to Number of Formal Petitions before the Court
1938	5,867	.72
1939	5,776	.66
1940	5,013	.62
1941	3,799	.46
1942	3,682	.41
1943	3,592	.31
1944	2,630	.23
1945	3,037	.30
1946	2,961	.34
1947	2,798	.40
1948	2,785	.35
1949	2,789	.32
1950	2,539	.32
1951	2,396	.34
1952	2,420	.26

[a] Source: New York City, Domestic Relations Court, annual reports, 1938-1952.

their contribution and regretted that personnel shortages in the Police Department itself necessitated their removal in May, 1951.

With slight variation, the Bureau of Adjustment procedure is uniform throughout the city. Parents, with or without their children, are referred to the Bureau by the clerk at the information window. J.A.B. officers, S.P.C.C. agents, and representatives of social agencies usually telephone or come of their own accord. (Data on sources of referrals are not tabulated as part of the Bureau's regular reports; this study's tallies, based on a case sample, appear in Table 10.) A receptionist makes sure that the person involved has been properly sent to the Bureau, telephones an information request to the Social Service Exchange (S.S.E.) to learn whether the family is known or has been known to other agencies, and fills out a "face sheet" with basic identifying information. When the S.S.E. clearance has been received and the probation officer or J.A.B. representative is free, he interviews the client. In some instances, only one interview is necessary to complete the Bureau's planning and action. In other cases, the

TABLE 8. *Cases Terminated by the Bureau of Adjustment, 1948-1952, Classified by Disposition* [a]

Case Action	1948	1949	1950	1951	1952
Referred for petitions	719	883	923	885	966
Referred to public agencies	427	476	344	308	332
Referred to private agencies	325	268	236	213	248
Closed within the Bureau of Adjustment (major service)	1,143	1,143	1,000	1,173	1,032
Consultation service	47	70	118	48	68
Information service	448	194	139	139	92
Closed by action of another agency		32	19	5	6
Total terminated during year	3,109	3,066	2,779	2,771	2,744
Cases pending from previous year	191	135	171	223	150
New applications	2,785	2,789	2,539	2,396	2,420
Reopened cases	268	316	292	302	300
Cases pending at close of year	135	171	223	150	126

[a] Source: New York City, Domestic Relations Court, annual reports, 1948-1952.

parent may be asked to return with child or spouse. Quite often, where parents are separated and one parent has come to complain that the other is neglecting the children or to ask for a voluntary visitation agreement, a letter and a second interview are necessary. In the instance of a neighbor complaining about a child's conduct it is usual to send a letter to the parents, asking them to come in.

Agency representatives who come to the Bureau usually seek clarification of court policy and procedure or ask the Bureau to interview a family; in the latter instance, the agency representative or the bureau worker sends an appointment letter. Where one or more agencies have known the family in the past or are still active in the case, the worker may telephone the agencies before, during, or after the contact with the client in an attempt to clarify the situation and determine what other help may be available to the family. In some instances, reports are requested by letter.

The study's sample tabulations, summarized below (the Court makes no regular tabulations), show that most cases are disposed of after one or two interviews, and that practically none requires more than three interviews. By its very nature, the Bureau is what is known as a "brief-contact" agency. If it cannot make an informal adjustment or close a case after giving information, it will refer outside the Court for help or initiate a petition to inaugurate formal court action. (Table 8 summarizes disposition data.)

When the Bureau of Adjustment worker refers a client to the petition desk for formal action, he forwards a statement of allegations which becomes the basis of the official petition. In most instances, the Bureau's contact with the case ends at this point. If the family is referred to outside health, counseling, or welfare agencies, arrangements may be made by telephone, but more often referral is in writing and a report of action is requested.

The Bureau of Adjustment worker dictates a brief report of his contacts in each case, and this record is kept in a case folder along with the face sheet, correspondence, and other data. The Bureau also maintains an alphabetical index file to facilitate answering inquiries. (In the larger offices, there is also a duplicate file in the information room.) A standard docket book serves, along with the receptionist's diary and the worker's desk sheet, as the source of monthly statistics.[8]

THESE ARE THE PROBLEMS. The full "flavor" of Bureau of Adjustment activity is best conveyed by summaries of a few typical cases[9] as they appeared before one of the better trained staff members one day:

Two parents who spoke little English came in with their 14-year-old son, complaining that he refused to go to school. Careful questioning by the Bureau of Adjustment probation officer revealed that the boy had been in trouble with the police and now attended a special school for "difficult" boys. A telephone call to the school adviser disclosed that the lad had recently been at Rockland State Hospital, a mental institution. A history of strange and uncontrollable behavior, truancy, and occasional unprovoked violence was conveyed. Learning that the boy was on parole from the institution, the bureau repre-

---

[8] The procedures involved in compilation of Bureau statistical reports and their limitations have been discussed in Kahn, *Proposals for the Development of a Statistical and Research Service in the Domestic Relations Court (Children's Court).*

[9] Throughout this report names and case details have been disguised to protect the individuals involved without distorting the picture from the point of view of the issues under consideration.

sentative telephoned the social worker and found that this disturbed child was not considered a proper subject for either Rockland State Hospital or the New York State Training School but had been referred to the hospital because no suitable intermediate facility was available. The social worker agreed, however, to see the boy sooner than originally planned and to consider his return to Rockland, in view of the parents' and the school's indications that the boy was endangering himself and others. This plan was explained to the parents, and the boy was encouraged to attend school until his appointment with the Rockland worker.

The Bureau of Adjustment representative explained to the observer that in a case such as this, the agency which has contact is encouraged to continue; the Court, moreover, could do little more than send the boy to Bellevue Hospital for observation, which could only lead to his eventual return to Rockland.

A small, chubby man, whose manner was rigid and hostile throughout the interview, brought in his youngest son, one of seven children. He said that he had given his son "lots of breaks" but now wished him sent away, to avoid more serious difficulty. The boy had stolen at home, caused trouble, did not go to school, and would not listen to his parents. The 15-year-old was "sharply" dressed and had the surface mannerisms of a "man of the world," but his relations with his father, as revealed in the interview, were full of infantile spitefulness. He admitted most of the misconduct but denied keeping late hours, except during week ends. At this, the father took out a diary and began a day-by-day recital of the boy's late hours and other offenses, including his suspicion that his son was a gang member and a marijuana addict. The boy was seen alone and gave a picture of great unhappiness at home with a very strict parent and a mentally ill older brother. He reluctantly agreed to a referral to the Police Department's Juvenile Aid Bureau. When seen again the father, however, was insistent on court action, now revealing for the first time that the boy had been threatening his brother with a knife. The case was referred for formal petition, and a court hearing took place that day.

A father, a veteran receiving a disability pension, had come to the Bureau of Adjustment the previous week to ask for the privilege of regular visitation of his daughters, aged 16 and 15. He agreed to stay out of the home but wanted to see his children from time to time. The police, to whom he turned, referred him to the Children's Court.

The Bureau of Adjustment worker had previously explained that this court could not compel visitation, but could attempt to arrange a voluntary agreement. A letter had been sent asking the mother to come to the Bureau on this day. In the course of the initial interview, the Bureau had tried unsuccessfully to get a report about the man from the Veterans Administration Mental Hygiene Clinic, to which he was known.

The interview which followed revealed that the mother was willing to permit visitation, but the younger child refused to see her father, who had been unfaithful to his wife and whose peculiar conduct had caused him to be known in the neighborhood as "crazy." The bureau worker, stressing the father's right to see his children, urged that all "try" visitation, and a time was set once a month at a "neutral" place. The younger daughter left upset and hurt.

A man of about 40 came in to ask for help in caring for his two young children. His wife, an alcoholic who for ten years had been going off every few weeks on a "binge," had disappeared again. On her return, she was always abusive. The man believed his wife's neglect caused the death of their first child. In the past, when his wife would leave, he would place the children in the care of his mother, aged 70, or with his sister-in-law; but now the sister-in-law had children and the mother worked. This time he had lost several days' work while caring for the children. Friends had urged him to commit his wife, since her behavior had long been strange, but he delayed for fear people would say he wished to be rid of her. The bureau representative obtained the details about the children necessary for temporary placement, and the father agreed to come to court with them the next morning. He stressed that any arrangements made were to be temporary since he did not wish to give up the children. Placement could not be made the next day, and another day of waiting in the office proved necessary.

THE BUREAU IN STATISTICS. Well over two thousand new cases came into the Bureau in 1951 and 1952, and several hundred cases were reopened (Table 8). The bureau routine is a busy one, since workers are constantly interviewing, making or receiving telephone calls, conferring with judges or agency representatives, and dictating case summaries. Nonetheless, tabulations made in the course of this study, on the basis of the Court's monthly reports for 1950, indicate that the pressure does not derive so much from average case load size as from an unstable staff situation.[10] What happens to cases appearing before the Bureau varies somewhat from borough to borough, as does the percentage of situations leading to petitions (Table 9). It is not possible, because of the many factors involved, to know whether this is primarily because the problems presented to the Bureau in the different boroughs are somewhat different, the philosophies and skills of the workers are not the same, or because at any given moment each borough is under the supervision of a different judge.

TABLE 9. *Relative Proportions of Cases Terminated by Petition in the Bureau of Adjustment in the Different Boroughs, 1949-1952*

IN PERCENTS

Year	Manhattan	Brooklyn	Bronx	Queens	Richmond	City-Wide
1949	31	30	27	24	20	29
1950	33	35	37	23	34	33
1951	39	31	35	19	20	32
1952	44	30	40	24	40	35

In the Court as a whole, there has been gradual increase in the proportion of bureau cases referred for petitions (Table 9). This may signify an increased readiness to refer for petitions, but may also reflect a change in the kind of service required by those coming to the Bureau. The latter explanation is suggested by the fact that, at the same time, fewer cases are closed as "information" cases.

Analysis of a representative sample of 225 bureau records provided detail not regularly available relative to the Bureau's case

[10] This is elaborated later in the chapter. Tabulations based on the court's monthly reports for 1950 indicate that the "average" Bureau of Adjustment worker terminated 28 cases during an "average" month in 1950. Excluding J.A.B. staff, the monthly average of cases terminated is 26.6 Computation of a median figure instead of the mean for the total group results in a lower average, 20.7. (This figure is based on the possibly arbitrary estimate that the Richmond worker gives half-time to her duties in the Bureau and the Queens worker two-thirds time. Revision of these estimates would result in only minor changes in the totals. As is the practice in such estimates, no allowance is made for illness or vacations. The individual staff member's average work load is, therefore, probably about 15 percent higher than the figure indicated—making the mean number of cases disposed of per month of actual work closer to 32.)

load and practice.[11] The largest single source of cases in the group was the Police Department (Table 10); police officers on posts who were approached for advice and precinct desk officers were actually responsible for more case referrals than the Police Department's Juvenile Aid Bureau, although it is recognized that the J.A.B. may have had a role in these referrals not apparent in the records. Large numbers of referrals were self-referrals of parents or relatives who sought court help, or neighbors who wished to make complaints. The latter cases can be distinguished from instances in which agency representatives themselves came to discuss cases in the Bureau. As a rule, they were acquainted with court structure and had deliberately decided to suggest

TABLE 10. A *Sample of 225 Representative Bureau of Adjustment Cases, Classified by Borough and Source of Referral*[a]

SOURCE OF REFERRAL	TOTALS				PERCENTAGES			
	Total	Borough			Total	Borough		
		A	B	C		A	B	C
Self								
Parent, etc.	48	22	16	10	21	18	32	20
Agency representatives	37	25	8	4	17	20	16	8
Police (other than the Juvenile Aid Bureau)	37	18	10	9	17	14	20	18
Juvenile Aid Bureau	19	18		1	8	14		2
Society for the Prevention of Cruelty to Children	9	3	3	3	5	2	6	6
Court (other than the Family Court)	8	2	1	5	4	2	2	10
Family Court	13	6	2	5	6	5	4	10
Private social agency or institution	6	2	1	3	2	2	2	6
School system	29	18	8	3	12	14	16	6
Other	19	11	1	7	8	9	2	14
Totals	225	125	50	50	100	100	100	100

[a] For discussion of the sample see footnote 11 and also the Appendix.

[11] A total of 268 Bureau of Adjustment records in *all* boroughs has been reviewed. After establishing the relatively small range of variation in level of professional competence among the workers involved, it was decided to complete the case analysis form only for records from the Bronx, Manhattan, and Brooklyn courts. A total of 225 such schedules was completed, and they provide the basis for the tabulations in this section. The work of eight different Bureau of Adjustment staff members, three of them from the J.A.B., is involved.

bureau activity, to utilize it as a required or desirable channel to a formal hearing, or to consult about next steps. Most of these were S.P.C.C. and J.A.B. cases, but various categories of school personnel and Department of Welfare staff members were also well represented. The category "other" includes such referral sources as friends, other public departments, and the Legal Aid Society.

The referral analysis shows interesting variations from one borough to another. Perhaps of greatest interest is the higher rate of self-referrals in Borough B, the less frequent use of the Bureau by agency representatives in Borough C, and the fact that the J.A.B. is credited with a large group of referrals in only one of the boroughs. Whereas the school system does not refer as often in Borough C, other courts there seem to know and use the Children's Court. It seems highly likely that these differences may be ascribed to the ethnic, religious, and economic differences in populations from borough to borough, as well as to differences in the patterns of social welfare services.

While in the Court as a whole boys predominate (since they predominate in the largest single category of cases, the delinquency group,) the Bureau of Adjustment case sample shows slightly more girls than boys in the cases referred to the Bureau. It is not surprising that once the "serious" offenses are omitted, as they are by the bureau rules, as many girls as boys are involved. Moreover, parental petitions and neglect allegations are in many instances channeled through the Bureau; the latter involve girls as often as boys, while the former frequently are cases in which parent charges that a daughter is "incorrigible" and sexually delinquent.

The largest single group of applicants in the cases studied (37 percent) were mothers, fathers, guardians, and relatives who wished help with regard to a child's conduct (Table 11). A smaller but significant group (15 percent) of parents, relatives, and guardians wished intervention by the court because they felt that the parent or guardian caring for the child was doing it badly and might harm the child. A considerable number of neighbors also came to court (13 percent) complaining of a child's conduct, usually alleging that the child had hurt their children, had insulted them, or damaged their property. Other important groups were the cases in which the police or other agencies suggested the need for bureau action because of the conduct of the children involved (12 percent) or because parents were believed to be neglecting their children (8 percent).

Many motivations and as many different objectives were revealed by the interviews: some wished the child in question punished or placed in an institution; others thought that he merely needed a "talking to" by a court representative; while still others came for advice as to proper handling of a problem. Many of the complaints entered by neighbors about children proved to be merely vehicles for quarrels between adults who saw the children as convenient targets. A surprising number of the complainants in this group are eccentric people who move from court to court in quarrels with their neighbors.

Bureau of Adjustment interviews may involve seeing a parent, then a child, then seeing both together—or perhaps seeing several participants in a neighborhood quarrel, both separately and together. Of the 225 cases tabulated, there were 107 in which the Bureau's service was completed after one in-person contact with the

TABLE 11. *A Sample of 225 Representative Bureau of Adjustment Cases, Classified by Problems Presented on Referral*

Type of Problem	Number	Percent
Child's conduct		
Parent, relative, or guardian concerned	84	37
Police, agency, or institution concerned	25	12
Neighbor's or landlord's complaint	30	13
Parental care and treatment of child		
Agency concerned	17	8
Parent, relative, or guardian concerned *re* other		
parent, etc.	34	15
Request for court help to obtain custody of child		
or effect reconciliation	11	5
Parental request for clarification of law, rights,		
procedure, etc.	5	2
Other	19	8
Total	225	100

client. (Telephone calls were necessary before and after most
of these cases, usually to agencies which had had some experience
with the family.) A total of 68 of the cases were closed after two,
and 33 after three or more, in-person interviews. Finally, 18 of
the cases were closed after single interviews with the representative of the agency alone rather than with the family involved.
Four cases were completed on the basis of extensive telephone
consultation provided to agency representatives without office
interviews. (The Bureau does not keep a record of the many
telephone inquiries which it handles, representing, in its view,
services too minor to be tabulated as "cases.") Conferences within
the Bureau between the J.A.B. worker and the chairman, and
conferences between the judge and the bureau representatives,
are not reflected in these statistics.

The clients in these 225 cases were offered many different kinds
of service (Table 12). Almost a third (32 percent) were referred
to public or voluntary agencies which may or may not have known
the family previously—often in connection with the very problem
occasioning the referral to the Bureau. The 15 percent of the
cases which were completely served within the bureau recorded
activities such as effecting a reconciliation between quarreling
neighbors or arranging for a father to see his child once a week
in the home of his estranged wife. More than a third of the
cases (37 percent) in the group were eventually referred for
formal court action.[12]

[12] Since there were some differences from borough to borough in the way
Bureau of Adjustment cases were tabulated in accord with the Court's own
disposition categories (see Table 8), it was necessary to recode dispositions
for the sample of 225 cases in accord with one consistent system. Apart from
the explanations given in the text, it might be noted that this explains why
the totals for cases referred for petition are higher in Table 12 (the special
tabulations) than in Table 8 (bureau statistics). It should be noted too that
the cases tabulated under "Consultation" are those in which agency representatives came for advice and were given suggestions other than to file a
petition. The "Information" category is used only in those few instances
where a client asked for factual information and was given just that—rather
than, as is the practice in some boroughs, to include cases where this is all
the worker manages but where he really attempts referral. The dividing line
between these two categories has to do with whether the bureau considers
that the client has taken a positive step.

TABLE 12. *A Sample of 225 Representative Bureau of Adjustment Cases, Classified by Borough and Disposition* [a]

(IN PERCENTS)

Disposition	Borough			Total
	A	B	C	
Petition	40	46	22	37
Referred to a public agency	20	14	16	18
Referred to a voluntary agency	13	14	14	14
Within the Bureau (includes "advice" cases)	11	12	30	15
Consultation	4	2	2	3
Information	1	2		1
Client rejected service	6	4	8	6
Client made own plans or withdrew request	5	6	8	6
Total	100	100	100	100
Number of cases	125	50	50	225

[a] See footnote 12 for explanation of these categories and the differences between these totals and those in Table 8.

It is sometimes asked whether there is a constant relationship between the source of referral and the kind of service rendered in the Bureau of Adjustment. In all probability an agency tends to refer one type of case more often than another, and each is more or less consistent in the approach it brings to bear on a case. Thus, in this group of cases, the bulk of J.A.B. referrals resulted in petitions; this is to be expected since the J.A.B. itself operates a screening and referral program and brings to court only those cases likely to require petitions. Police other than those in the J.A.B. are not equipped for such case evaluation and referral, and their cases were often referred elsewhere or closed after "advice," although more than a third eventuated in petitions. Agency representatives who come to court seem to wish either to seek advice from the Bureau or to present cases on which petitions tend to be necessary. Many different categories of school personnel are involved in school referrals, and a sizable proportion of the cases which they referred required the services of other public and private agencies—to which, technically, the schools might have referred them in the first instance. The self-referrals included a wide range of situations and, therefore, of dispositions; and the other categories of referral sources represented too few cases in the sample for a clear trend to be discerned. Examination of the relationship of the problems presented at the first contact to the Bureau's ultimate disposition showed that the bulk of the cases representing agency (usually police) concern with a child's conduct or with parental neglect resulted in petitions (28 of 42 cases) and most of the remainder, in referrals to other agencies. In contrast, fully half of the complaints by neighbors were handled within the Bureau, and relatively few led to petitions.

HOW WELL DOES THE BUREAU DO ITS JOB? Statistics of the Bureau's operations thus show:

1. It is keeping a substantial number of cases out of the court-room by making referrals or effecting settlements.

2. It limits its activity to cases over which it has been assigned jurisdiction.

3. It serves as an information center for agencies and individuals and tells them about their rights in the Children's Court and in other courts.

4. It handles different cases in different ways—an absolute necessity where the need to individualize is central.

5. It renders these services on a brief-contact basis, which is precisely what is needed in an essentially "intake" or application agency of the court.

Statistics cannot, however, tell whether the special type of service offered to a client is based, as would be desirable, on his need as skillfully evaluated, or determined instead by routine acceptance of recommendations by the referral source. In short, statistics indicate that the Bureau of Adjustment serves the clients designated as properly within its function, but analyses of individual case records and observations are necessary to disclose whether it serves them well.

In establishing criteria for evaluating bureau service, one must recall, first, that the Bureau, while it is eager to have a fully qualified staff of caseworkers, is not staffed by graduate social workers. Its probation officers are college graduates who have had thirty course credits in related social science areas and a year of experience, often in agencies demanding lesser qualifications than does the Court. They have usually been assigned to the Bureau after successful work in the Probation Department. Although they may discuss doubtful cases with the judges, these staff members have to work without regular intensive casework supervision and, therefore, have very limited opportunity for training on the job. While one can expect that staff with such qualifications will adhere to court rules, follow court procedures, interview reasonably well, know and use community resources, and demonstrate an elementary conception of what is involved in evaluating problems in a case, it would be unrealistic to require of them the competence of fully trained social workers.

This does not mean that the Bureau of Adjustment is not in need of staff prepared for more skilled service. Its staff members interview or are consulted about families who, in the main, have been known to many public and private agencies which have been unable to change the situation basically or, in some instances, serve them at all. Social Service Exchange clearance and summaries of agency contacts in most of these cases record disappointing beginnings and inadequate service. For some, the Court seems either a final station in a downward course, or a last opportunity for a new beginning. In view of all this, it seems reasonable to ask that such professional skill be made available at this key spot in the Court as is necessary to conduct the intake process in the most effective fashion known. As indicated, Bureau of Adjustment staff members and Probation Department leadership agree that such performance, though impossible for staff as currently qualified, represents the Bureau's goals.

In fairness to staff members, this study therefore asks, first, whether their work is satisfactory in the light of their current qualifications. The more important long-range question remains, however: *Is the service currently rendered adequate to help children, in the light of knowledge of their needs and of the helping process?* More specifically, are the Bureau's interviews, or agency and community contacts, conducted so as to give comprehensive understanding of the problems; or does the worker appraise the client superficially, alerted only to what the interviewee can say, rather than revealing ability to apply knowledge of behavior and of family relationships? Do the staff members reveal a diagnostic sense as well as interviewing skills? Are they acquainted with other community agencies and their services, and able to refer clients for such services where proper? In making such referrals, are they able to help the client to understand the agency and its service and to interpret the client's need to the agency? Do they know which cases should properly be sent back to the original agency and not be considered by the Court at all? If a court petition is required, is the Bureau of Adjustment worker able to prepare the child and parent for the procedure in the courtroom, explain what might be expected and just how the Court might help? The broad general question, then, is whether the probation officers in the Bureau of Adjustment are able to render with competence the services required in their special setting.

The 225 cases which were analyzed were grouped into three classes, determined by the degree to which either minimal service was rendered or more exacting professional standards of helping clients were met. In about one sixth of the cases the recording was too brief to permit classification. The remainder of the cases, no matter how brief the recording, provided sufficient detail for judgment.[13]

A small group of cases, approximately 10 percent, received services which could be characterized as *good* or *very good* in the sense that many of the criteria for well-conducted intake work were met. In the best of these cases, the work with children and parents compared favorably with that expected of an average graduate social worker with one year of experience after school. Since it was accomplished by staff members without full professional training and without skilled supervision, this record is all the more outstanding. Roughly, half (55 percent) were considered *acceptable* in the light of court expectations of staff and their limited qualifications upon employment. Bureau of Adjustment staff members rendering such service are considered

[13] The question may be raised as to whether the brevity of the recording affected the types of judgment made. It might be noted that the observation of more than forty full interviews in the Bureau of Adjustment served to establish the fact that the case records properly reflect the quality of the work.

satisfactory workers by judges and probation supervisors. While these cases did not represent skilled service as known to the helping professions, staff members showed some understanding of the problems and arrived at dispositions consistent with court program and policy. Many of the cases required only agreement that the S.P.C.C. might file a previously planned neglect petition or the J.A.B., a delinquency petition. A large group were neighborhood complaints which could be resolved by calling a conference of all parties concerned and effecting agreement. These cases all revealed useful, although limited, ability to grasp the essential elements of the case and passable interviewing skills. Routine rather than imaginative use was made of community resources, and little was done to prepare families and children for the court experience.

Almost two thirds of the Bureau's cases were thus found receiving service ranging from *acceptable* (the Court's expectation of staff as now trained) to *very good*, the achievement in a few cases reflecting devotion, innate ability, and particularly good use of experience and limited training. Over one third (35 percent) received *unsatisfactory* service, failing to meet minimum standards (even for partially trained workers) for interviewing, case appraisal, or skill in making referrals.

A few examples will illustrate the standards applied, suggest some of the problems found in the Bureau, and indicate specific areas where more skill and training are necessary.

1. These cases received "good" or "very good" service:

A mother was sent to the J.A.B. by the Bureau of Attendance, since her 13-year-old son was said to be associating with a delinquent gang. The J.A.B., in turn, sent the mother to court. Consulting the Social Service Exchange clearance slip, the Bureau of Adjustment worker asked about the mother's two contacts with private family service agencies and learned that she did not wish to return to them. A phone call revealed that the Bureau of Attendance case was still active, that an attendance hearing was scheduled, and that, if necessary, the Attendance Bureau would bring the case to court. The Bureau of Adjustment referred the case back to the Bureau of Attendance, recognizing that the referral to court at this time only confused the mother and that it was preferable for one agency at a time to work with the child.

A child, age 6, placed by an agency in foster care, was choked by a 10-year-old neighborhood boy who tried to push him into a yard where there was a vicious dog. The 10-year-old boy and his mother were called in, and the boy admitted grabbing little boys by their necks, not realizing he could thereby kill them. He seemed guilty and regretful as the worker impressed him with the seriousness of the matter. The mother, when seen alone, described a series of habit and conduct disorders manifested by her son. Although the referring agency pressed no complaint, the worker saw the need for referring the family for help, and the mother agreed to go to a guidance agency. An attempt to obtain information about a Youth Board contact with the family was unsuccessful until after the mother had left, when it was learned that the school had asked for help because of the boy's behavior problems.

The Bureau of Adjustment in this borough is careful to follow up on cases; when the guidance agency returned the case because of the mother's apparent hostility, the worker obtained Youth Board agreement to follow through with a new referral, called the mother in, and dealt with her resistance to going to the Youth Board referral unit.

In the case of a 5-year-old boy, a grandmother had come to court out of concern for her grandson, who was exposed to the neglectful, irrational conduct of a mentally deteriorating mother. In addition to conducting a skillful interview to obtain needed background history, the Bureau of Adjustment worker gave the grandmother emotional support and helped her to begin the difficult process in the course of which she would be called upon in court to describe her daughter as a neglectful mother.

A Bellevue Hospital social service worker telephoned about a one-year-old girl who had been in the well-baby clinic from the time her mother, a schizophrenic of long standing, had jumped from a window and fractured her skull. The father rejected the hospital suggestion that his wife be committed to a state hospital and signed his wife out. Indications were that he was disturbed, probably psychotic. Not wishing to discharge the child to these parents, Bellevue Hospital referred the case to the Department of Welfare, but the father exercised his legal rights and claimed the child two days before the case was called to the Bureau's attention. The Bureau of Adjustment worker lost no time in consulting with the judge and effectively interpreting the problem; the judge ordered an immediate court petition by the Department of Welfare.

A neighbor complained that a 10-year-old boy broke her window, killed a cat and threw it in front of her property, molested younger boys, etc. She said, too, that his mother was an overprotective and improper guardian. The bureau worker checked with the J.A.B and learned that the police had received and dismissed the complaint. He called in the boy and his mother, who depicted the complainant as an eccentric troublemaker against whom they themselves had filed a disorderly conduct complaint in the Magistrates' Court. The Bureau's "mediation" led to agreement by the boy and his mother to avoid their neighbor and her collection of animals. After a quarrel in the office, all complaints were dropped.

2. The following cases were found "acceptable" in that useful service was rendered. Far more might be done for the clients, however, given more adequately qualified personnel and regular skilled supervision. The summaries seek to illustrate just how better trained personnel might improve the Bureau's performance:

Referred by the school, a mother came to court with her 11-year-old daughter, the fourth of ten children, many of whom have court records. The mother reported that the child was beyond her control, having remained away overnight twice without explanation, having associated with older girls, and probably having had sexual intercourse. The Bureau of Adjustment worker tried to talk to the girl alone but received no response. Upon calling the Bureau of Child Guidance, the worker obtained a long list of conduct complaints about the girl. Because the mother insisted on a petition and placement and because the girl would not talk, the case was referred to the petition clerk.

One can only speculate as to whether a more skilled worker might have found out what led so many children of this family into court and made the mother so eager to be rid of her daughter. Would a more skilled interviewer have made it possible for the girl to talk?

The mother of a 14-year-old girl came to the Bureau of Adjustment at the suggestion of the police. The child was often out until 10 or 11 p.m. and once stayed out until 2 a.m. She talked back to her mother and spoke of leaving school to work. The mother reported that her daughter was better behaved when the father, a taxi driver, was at home. When brought to the Bureau the next day, the girl stated that her mother's complaints were correct. She gave the worker a picture of her active recreational interests. The worker urged her to keep better hours and listen to her parents; the mother was instructed to be less strict.

From the Court's point of view this complaint was satisfactorily handled, since a "minor" case was informally adjusted and a court hearing was hardly necessary. The record reveals, however, that the worker had no real grasp of what was going on in the family. Six months later, when the mother returned to report her daughter's conduct worse and to insist on placement, the factors operative were still not clarified. The worker could only agree to permit a petition to be drawn, and the question then became whether or not the Probation Department, or other services on which the Court might call, would get beneath the case surface.

In case after case in this group, one finds the Bureau handling complaints either by serving as a channel to the petition desk or by effecting a verbal agreement for improvement without obtaining, in the course of the interview, leads as to the meaning of the misconduct and, hence, as to the possible effectiveness of proposed disposition plans.

3. The following cases received "unsatisfactory" service. That all the Bureau of Adjustment staff members are represented by cases in this category itself suggests the general need for improvement of performance in the Bureau. No matter how many are served satisfactorily, a "last-resort" agency concerned with people and their problems, and to which they *must* come, either for lack of resources or because authority tells them to, cannot afford to let them down as much and as often as is manifested in the Bureau's records or observed in interviews. As the case material shows, the lacks are in all areas of skill essential to intake or brief-contact interviews. Standards reasonably expected even of the Court's partially trained staff are not attained:

An attendance officer came to the Bureau with a 15-year-old high school student and her mother. A chronic truant since her entry into high school, the girl contended that writing was her only interest. At an Attendance Bureau hearing that morning it had been learned that she had been away from home four days without her mother's permission and was said to be keeping late hours with undesirable companions. The mother said she could not account for this since her daughter was well behaved at home. She wished help before serious consequences resulted. Although the daughter had been reported to the police as missing, she actually proved to be in a friend's house. When spoken to, the girl evidenced guilt. She had stayed away to avoid the truancy hearing, slept in a parked car, and ate at the home of a friend, who eventually telephoned her mother. She did not attend school, the girl said, because the commercial course did not satisfy her interest in writing.

The Bureau of Adjustment worker referred the case for a delinquency petition. It is reasonable to ask whether the problem of school placement, the girl's guilt, and the mother's eagerness for help did not suggest the wisdom of avoiding the court experience and attempting case evaluation and help through a voluntary social agency.

In a number of cases in this group, action was taken without full use of Social Service Exchange information. The Bureau of Adjustment worker relied completely on the interview and inevitably had more limited insight than would have been possible had the experience of other social agencies in contact with the family been drawn upon. This was the situation in the case of a 9-year-old girl whose mother was referred to the Bureau by the S.P.C.C. after the child had admitted sexual experiences. The mother stated that her daughter, being retarded mentally, was poorly oriented and unable to learn. An older sister had overheard the child tell how a mentally defective boy and an adult had played with her, sexually, in a hallway. The mother indicated that she had previously asked for a social agency's help but had withdrawn upon being told that the child was normal but lacked affection. They offered placement in an institution for epileptics, which the mother rejected, although she acknowledged there had been convulsions until three years before. The girl cried when talked to in the Bureau and admitted frequent hallway sexual experiences. Although three social agencies (one of them a guidance clinic) were listed on the S.S.E. clearance slip, the worker made no attempt to learn about their contacts prior to referring the case for a delinquency petition. There was obvious need for action to protect the child, possibly placement, but this could best be determined by clearance with the agencies involved in lieu of, or at least prior to, a court hearing.

In several cases, the Bureau of Adjustment worker decided on the basis of superficial, one-interview contacts that children had to be placed away from their parents and made referrals to the Child Place-

ment Division of the Department of Welfare. In one instance, the
worker pursued a suggestion of a private social agency which had
been rejected by the mother several months before; in another
instance, referral for placement followed a girl's remark that she was
unable to get along with her family and that she liked boarding school.
Even assuming that the Department of Welfare would evaluate the
case, much damage can obviously be done by initiating a procedure of such consequence as placement without more thorough
consideration.

The S.P.C.C. called to refer a mother and her 10-year-old son to the
Bureau of Adjustment. The mother had previously received services
from many public and voluntary agencies. She said the son was born
out of wedlock, the result of her having been "raped." She described
the child as stupid, difficult in school, a truant, and a liar. He damaged things in the home and did not listen to her instructions, and
hence she wished him punished by the court. The Bureau of Adjustment interviewer recognized that the mother was a punishing and
rejecting person who "investigated" her son's friends and gave him
little freedom. She talked to the mother about the boy's needs. When
she called the school, the worker was told that the boy's record was
satisfactory, but the mother was sure this was incorrect. When the
mother insisted that the boy be "put away" for a week, the worker
explained there was no basis for a delinquency petition but that a
voluntary placement through the Department of Welfare was possible.
The frightened child welcomed the offer of referral to the J.A.B.
as an alternative to placement. A month later the J.A.B. reported that
since its investigation revealed no delinquency, it could not continue
to serve the case; the mother did not wish voluntary placement. There
is evidence in this latter report that the frightening experience made
the child even more compliant. Despite the mother's role in the problem, the worker had made a J.A.B. referral and the J.A.B. considered
possible action in regard to delinquency, while no initiative was taken
anywhere to cope with the obvious pathology in the mother.

The Family Court referred a father who had left his family after the
latest in a series of quarrels. He stated that his wife neglected and
beat the children and that she was becoming a "mental case." The
wife was called in, and the worker repeated the charges and counter-
charges on each side, asking for replies. Only after permitting a violent
scene to develop did she refer the parents to a family counseling
agency. In a similar case, the worker made no referral at all and, after
recognizing that there was marital discord rather than neglect, tried

to solve a marital problem of long standing by "advice" to the parents to "arrive at an understanding that would eliminate quarreling."

THE BUREAU, A CHANNEL TO THE PETITION DESK? As already noted, approximately one third of the cases which come to the Bureau of Adjustment are referred for formal court action. Some cases so processed in the Bureau represent situations in which it is highly likely that a petition will subsequently be necessary, but in which court rules insist on prior bureau interviews. There are other cases in which public and private agencies are in a position to file petitions directly but consider it best to have the parent serve as petitioner; these, too, by court rules, come to the Bureau. Finally, there are the situations in which the desirability of formal court action is not at all clear prior to bureau evaluation.

The question arises as to why the Bureau of Adjustment sees some cases in which formal petitions are almost certain to follow and does not, under its rules, see others. If the purpose of such procedure is to advise agencies considering petitions on whether they are making appropriate use of the Court, why are the parents and children brought to the Bureau? If, on the other hand, it is felt that the Bureau is offering valuable service as it helps clients see how the Court can serve them—and in obtaining data useful to the judge as he hears the case—should such service not be made available to all cases and not just those currently processed in the Bureau? What of the Bureau's original purpose, i.e., to provide informal case disposition? Would it be lost in an expanded function in which cases were seen even if no informal adjustment were possible? In short, what is and what should be the relationship of the Bureau to the petition desk, the channel for formal court hearings? Fundamental decisions are essential to the Court's planning.

Whether the Bureau is ultimately conceived of as a case screening service, a consultation agency, or both its value to the courtroom process is to considerable degree dependent on the data it forwards. Unfortunately, valuable material is at times assembled but not made available at the appropriate point. The following case may serve as illustration:

The mother of a 10-year-old boy came to ask for temporary placement at a detention facility while the Wiltwyck School considered
a social agency's recommendation for commitment. The boy admitted
a long history of misconduct, and the mother insisted on a petition.
In accord with current procedure, the Bureau of Adjustment worker
forwarded to the petition desk a brief statement of allegation. Nothing
was said of the diagnostic picture which the Bureau had obtained
from the interview and from telephone conversations with representatives of Wiltwyck, the J.A.B. and the Bureau of Child Guidance
about the mother's apparent need to be rid of the boy and the boy's
feeling for the father from whom his mother was separated.

Just what can and what cannot be presented in a petition is a
complex matter, since adjudication must be based on an examination of facts relating to allegations, whereas the Bureau of Adjustment case study is also concerned with opinions about the family
situation and with possible corrective measures. However, while
the law may assert that the "petition shall state such facts as will
bring the child within the jurisdiction of the court," it is nonetheless true that following the determination of jurisdiction and at the
same hearing the judge makes temporary or long-range plans for
the child.[14] There would thus be great advantage in making available to the judge (who in some instances discusses the case with
the Bureau's representative before the hearing), whatever social
data and preliminary appraisal may be at hand at the time. If legal
considerations exclude such data from the petition, why should not
the Bureau provide a supplementary summary to be used upon
establishment of the Court's right to intervene?

STAFFING THE BUREAU. Most professional personnel in the Children's Court carry heavy work loads and operate under pressure;
the Bureau of Adjustment is no exception. It is self-evident, however, that specific estimates of the Bureau's personnel needs are
intimately related to the levels of performance considered acceptable.

To some extent, the sense of pressure observed in the Bureau,
even when less intensive work was being done routinely, developed
out of the Court's inability, despite repeated efforts, to obtain

[14] DRC Act, Sec. 71.

funds and authorization to replace staff members at once as they were transferred or resigned, inability to cover positions during vacation periods, and inability to rely on J.A.B. representatives at certain times. Were it not for such factors, the assignment as generally interpreted at the time of the study might well have been carried out by the authorized staff members in each borough. The withdrawal of J.A.B. personnel and the inability of the Court to replace them with probation officers has, since that time, left the Bureau seriously understaffed. Currently, daily case quotas are required to keep a worker's load to a reasonable size; except in extreme emergency, clients representing cases above these quotas are given appointments for the next day. Thus, even assurance of status quo in the Bureau requires that the Court be permitted immediate staff replacements, the addition of some staff, and adequate vacation coverage. However, the Court's purposes are not fulfilled when some of the staff members invariably miss or avoid leads in the interviews and hover close to the surface of the case. Clearly, the Bureau's screening function demands the more intensive work that other members of the Bureau's staff demonstrate. Unskilled staff members must therefore be replaced, standards must be raised, and the staff *must* be substantially expanded.

Long range, there remains the problem of the nature of the liaison function to be performed in the Bureau by representatives of outside agencies. Obviously, staff positions must be filled from within the Court. An attempt must be made to differentiate just what a liaison worker does from the regular duties of a staff member and to determine whether he functions best as part of the Bureau or in his own agency. And, if the liaison function ought to exist in the Bureau, should not the schools also be represented once again? [15]

[15] It has been said that J.A.B. and Board of Education personnel were not really intended for liaison and that the Court was only taking an available opportunity to staff the Bureau at a time when it was not permitted to add to its probation staff. Whether or not this was the case, it is obvious that in the future the Bureau must be provided adequate staff as part of the Court's regular budget. It may well be that liaison workers are not needed at all, but they should be evaluated on the basis of their legitimate functions, not in the light of an indirect and unsatisfactory effort to staff the Bureau.

Even if the Bureau were to be fully staffed to do more intensive work with a broader group of cases, it would still lack means of obtaining home and community studies of certain cases before it. Often, particularly where neglect is alleged, the Bureau's disposition is a referral to the S.P.C.C. The S.P.C.C., in turn, may subsequently file a neglect petition, and because the S.P.C.C. report is not official the Probation Department has to repeat the investigation—duplicating effort. Sometimes the delays attending the referral of such cases have serious consequences:

When a maternal grandfather came in to complain of his daughter's severe neglect of her year-and-a-half-old child, the worker called in the mother. The family shared a substandard furnished room with several relatives; the child was said to be sleeping in a dresser drawer in a dirty room and was not being taken out for fresh air. The mother indicated the child was ill and that although she was seeking an apartment in a housing project nothing better was possible at the time. She rejected the idea of temporary placement but promised to secure medical attention for the child. Between the time of the Bureau's referral of the case to the S.P.C.C. and the first visit of an S.P.C.C. agent, the mother and child disappeared.

It is by no means clear whether such cases would be better served by assuring prompt referrals from the Bureau to the J.A.B. or the S.P.C.C., when a home investigation is needed, or by making probation officers available to the Bureau for field investigation service. Choices must, however, be weighed as part of a long-range plan.

THE RECEPTIONIST. The receptionist is a key person in the Bureau in the three larger boroughs. It is she who greets clients sent by the information clerk, interviews them to obtain identifying data, checks the file for previous records, clears with the S.S.E., prepares the Bureau's statistical reports, types the records, and directs clients to the worker's office for interviews.

Almost inevitably, receptionists become involved in case handling and exercise what amounts to professional judgment, despite the fact that they have only clerical training and are not necessarily oriented to the Court's outlook. The extreme situation is illustrated by the following case:

A mother came in with her children. She explained that she was not living with her husband, and that he wanted a divorce, to which she would not agree. A conference, at which both parties and their counsel would be present, was scheduled for the next week. The husband had threatened to run away and end his support if his wife would not cooperate in the divorce proceedings. She came to the Bureau of Adjustment because she wanted help.

The receptionist advised her to go to the conference. The woman responded that she was concerned that her lawyer would not respect her interests and that her husband would bribe him. The receptionist reassured her that her lawyer was not likely to permit himself to be bribed and informed her that if her husband refused to support her, she could resort to the Family Court. The woman continued to be skeptical and the receptionist reassuring.

Since the receptionist must determine whether the information clerk has sent clients and whether they have come properly to the Bureau, must obtain basic identifying data to check her own files for previous records and to clear with the S.S.E., some discussion is necessary. She must also, at times, determine the urgency of a case. Because of the stress of the situation and because they of course do not know bureau procedure, many of the Court's clients, understandably, begin to tell their story to the receptionist. Cognizant that certain clients will have to wait for the bureau worker, and recognizing the difficulty of stopping troubled people from describing their situations, the receptionist often listens to the story and tries to provide reassurance and advice. In so doing, she inevitably encourages considerable elaboration and emotional outpouring.

While several of the receptionists are truly reassuring, diligent, and efficient, and while the more questionable practices described above are readily understood, their continuance is fair neither to clients nor to receptionists. This problem area derives from understaffing in the Bureau, as well as from ill-defined concepts of the Bureau's function and of roles within it. Solution must, therefore, be sought in adequate staffing of the Bureau, job definition, orientation of receptionists, and in procedural improvements at the information desk. Recep-

tionists must learn increasingly to say what is necessary
to reassure a client and yet not create confusion of roles:
"I'll just take a few facts, like your name and address, and
Mr. ——— will see you in a little while to get the whole story."
This would lead to fewer complications if efficient case sifting
at the information desk assured that only clients who should be
interviewed by a bureau worker entered the Bureau. At the same
time, it would become feasible, during the interview, for the
bureau worker himself to complete all identifying data on the
bureau face sheet, except that portion which is necessary for
prior S.S.E. clearance.

PHYSICAL FACILITIES. Inadequate physical facilities can pose serious obstacles to placing clients at their ease and assuring relaxed and
confidential discussion. It is therefore important to note that the
facilities available to the Bureau of Adjustment in Brooklyn
(where construction of a new building has been authorized) and
Manhattan are particularly inadequate. In both of these boroughs
the floor plan of the Bureau is such that the receptionist cannot
control access to interviewers' offices. In addition, the Brooklyn
interviewers are separated only by partitions which do not reach
the ceiling. By contrast, the more adequate and cheerful Bronx
quarters seem to influence worker and client morale as well
as assure smoothness of operation. Seemingly small matters, such
details of physical plant clearly affect the Bureau's efficiency.

THE PETITION DESK. The Bureau of Adjustment offers complete service to only a minority of court cases, and most situations
coming into court result in formal petitions because (a) such processing is required for all "serious" offense categories under court
rules, or (b) the case has been to the Bureau of Adjustment but
the complainant or the Bureau's staff member regards a petition
as the proper next step. Except for cases channeled through the
Bureau, those involved in situations to be served formally go to
the petition desk directly or are referred there by the information
clerk. (See Table 2 for case totals, which represent numbers of
new petitions.)

The clerk prepares a standard petition form, copies being made for later use of the reporting officer, probation officer, and others. It provides for name, sex, birth date, place of birth, residence, and religion of all children involved in a case. By custom, race is added. Space is also designated for a listing of allegations, for various orders and adjournments which may follow in the course of the child's contact with the Court, and for "Justices' Memoranda." In each instance, the petitioner must sign the petition and be prepared to swear to the allegations in the courtroom.

All parties in a case gather around the petition desk while the clerk, sitting at his typewriter, obtains the essential data, completes the petition, and presents it for the petitioner's signature. He also lists on the petition the Court's code numbers for the various offenses involved. The petition is then delivered to an attendant and the case is placed on the court calendar. The petitioners, respondents, and some of the children sit in the waiting room until the hearing. Many of the younger children wait in the nursery, in the two boroughs so equipped. Children who have been in detention overnight, or have been brought to court by the police, often wait in a detention room until the hearing.

The petition desk is responsible, too, for completion of necessary forms and notification on remands, commitments, summonses, warrants, subpoenas, and other legal "process." In most of the offices, petition clerks have some responsibility for dispatching buses and station wagons to detention facilities and for scheduling other necessary transportation of children.

Petition clerks are, by civil service designation, assistant clerks of court who have passed an examination requiring knowledge of the Domestic Relations Court Act and the Criminal Code. As has been seen, they must know how to complete the various forms and how to translate a petitioner's complaint into a statement of allegations on the petition. As members of the clerical section of the court, petition clerks are responsible, locally, to the clerk of court, and, ultimately, to the director of administration. In two of the boroughs, the same clerks are responsible for Children's Court and Family Court petitions.

Within the limits of court policy, each of the petition clerks tends to develop his own style and approach to petition writing. Some provide more detail than others by giving a more complete statement of allegations (e.g., one clerk is particularly careful to differentiate between what a detective saw and what he was told). The typical delinquency petition gives detail about the circumstances of the offense, such as what was stolen and its worth, the source of knowledge, and so forth. A neglect petition may take the following form, giving more or less detail:

The child is under such improper guardianship and control by his custodian as to injure and endanger his health and general welfare in that the respondents reject the child and neglect to provide the necessary control and supervision needed by this child; that the child is permitted to roam the streets at will and has on numerous occasions slept in hallways and on roof tops and due to these conditions the child has been absent from school five days this term.

In addition to exercising judgment in coding offenses and in the formulation of allegations, the clerks at times enter into discussion with an agency representative who presents a petition as to whether the objectives are best advanced by a delinquency or by a neglect petition. Unlike the Bureau of Adjustment interviewer, the petition clerk is not expected to consider what lies behind the petition request and whether the petition is in fact appropriate to the needs of the child. He is required and trained only to prepare such a statement of allegations as will facilitate the determination of whether the Court may assume jurisdiction. The instances in which a clerk goes beyond this, frequent occurrences in at least one borough, therefore represent what might be characterized as needless confusion.

As everywhere else, the physical facilities surrounding this function set the tone of the petition-writing process. In Manhattan the petition desk is located in a room off the waiting room. It consists of a long counter behind which sit two clerks equipped with forms, directives, and typewriters. The petition desk telephone is used by many other staff members on the courtroom floor, and there is a constant stream of messages for attendants and probation officers on the floor, with the result that petitions are seldom completed in privacy and without disturbance. The Brooklyn petition "desk" is located in two small offices opposite the waiting room, and the clerks are able to close their doors for privacy, although this is not always done. The Bronx clerk also has a counter, located on the floor below the courtroom. There is a small waiting room outside and a door which can be, but is usually not, closed for privacy. The Queens and Staten Island clerks work behind counters which also serve the Family Court and behind which other court clerical operations are located. With few exceptions, little attempt is made to achieve privacy during the petition-writing process in the court even in those instances where physical facilities permit. In all boroughs, several clients may stand together as petitions are typed; people on near-by benches or in the corridor listen in; at times, the "accused" child gives certain of the necessary information.

Such emphasis is placed, as a matter of tradition and law, on how the allegations are worded, in contrast with what it might mean to a child, that the clerk perforce cannot do more than ask detailed questions about an incident, the value of stolen property, and so on. Thus, while present personnel carry out their assignment in accord with tradition and with their preparation as technicians, the operations centered about the petition desk do not generally help translate Children's Court philosophy into practice. Instead, the lack of privacy and the traditionally clerical definition of the undertaking conspire to make the procedure more akin to that in adult criminal courts than to what might be suggested by Children's Court intent. For many families the petition-writing process is the first contact with the Court, but it certainly does not provide any preparation for what will transpire in the courtroom.

An example of a not unusual situation underscores the need for another concept of the place of the petition desk:

A J.A.B. policewoman came in with a 15-year-old girl who had fainted in church. When she said she had no place to live, the girl was taken to Bellevue Hospital. From there she was sent first to a shelter and then to Girls' Camp. At the shelter she reported that she was pregnant. At Girls' Camp she told the following story, which she repeated to the petition clerk: She had flown to this country from Puerto Rico two or three months before with a man with whom she had lived until a few days previous, when he put her out on the street and left her, in her second month of pregnancy. The police-woman and the petition clerk attempted, while others waited near the petition desk, to get the man's name and further details from the child, but to no avail. They decided that there was no way to have her appear before the judge except on a delinquency petition. After asking a few questions about her parents, who were said to be in Puerto Rico, they completed the petition and gave it to the attendant, who then put the case on the calendar.

About an hour later, as policewoman and child were still sitting in the waiting room, the policewoman came in to say that the child had admitted that the story was fabricated. Having become friendly with the policewoman, who had taken her to dinner the night before and breakfast that morning, the girl decided against telling her a falsehood. There followed a joint interrogation of the child by the policewoman and the petition clerk, and it developed that the child was living in New York City with her mother and sister. She had had one sexual experience in the park several months previously and had decided that she was pregnant because she had been fainting. She told her mother, who said that this was probably so and suggested that she get a job for a while. When she lost her job after one day, she felt she could not go home and had taken to sleeping in doorways and on roofs and not eating. When she fainted in church, she felt she could not tell the truth.

The original petition was torn up, and the policewoman called the local precinct. The mother promised to come to court immediately. Policewoman and child waited for three hours, but nobody appeared. At that point, the petition clerk and the policewoman decided that the case had to go before the judge. A new delinquency petition was completed, and the case was heard.

Even the current rather narrow definition of the role of the petition clerk allows scope for improvement by the introduction of privacy and of consideration for the feelings of clients. Beyond these obvious steps, however, children and parents about to go before the Court require preparation for the significant experience and an indication of what to expect. They need to know about procedures, legal rights, possible dispositions, the meaning of remand. They often require considerable reassurance that their rights will be respected, their story heard, and their wishes seriously considered. The Court's helping intent needs to be explained time and again. Currently, the petition procedure is not expected to provide any of this. While it is understood that, except for the judge at the hearing, no one can properly enter into a determination of the truth of the allegations, there are serious grounds for concern that a completely clerical conception of the responsibilities assigned to, or assumed by, petition clerks may, at its doorway, negate the very intent of the Children's Court.

THE REMEDY: A UNIFIED BUREAU OF APPLICATIONS. Under present rules and division of responsibility in the Court, some clients are sent by the information clerk to the Bureau of Adjustment while others go directly to the petition desk, a procedure which flows from court traditions, concern with individual rights, and the desire to assure formal processing of "serious" cases. Technically speaking, most cases are correctly served through the assigned channels; but in effect, whether the introduction to the courtroom is via a clerical procedure or an individualized interview and evaluation becomes a matter not of a person's needs but rather of the category into which he is placed by procedures, rules, or the understanding of petitioners.

From a broader perspective, the information-giving function, informal adjustment of cases, and the petition-writing process are part of one central phase of the Court's work: intake. Just as individuals and agencies may at times err in calling upon the Court to aid in certain cases, they may also fail to come to court in other instances when it would be proper to do so. Whatever the exact frequency of such situations, their common occurrence is verified by Bureau of Adjustment records and statistics, observation of the petition desk and courtroom, and examination of cases discharged after investigation by a probation officer. Since the community cannot possibly do its own case screening and interpret the Court's purpose to all potential clients, the doorways to the Court must remain open and competent advice, consultation, interpretation of the Court, case evaluation, and preparation of all referrals be assured. Questions must be answered, clients interviewed with skill, and situations carefully weighed if the Court is to make itself fully available to those who should use its facilities, while referring all others elsewhere for appropriate service.

The Court has increasingly come to recognize how crucial in the entire helping process are these first contacts of clients with court representatives. Yet the Bureau of Adjustment still does not serve the majority of Children's Court cases, and the information and petition desk assignments have remained largely clerical in nature and basically unrelated to the Court's program. As long as these continue as separate functions and fail to reflect a unified helping philosophy the total effect of these services will be inadequate for people under stress.

Clearly, the time has arrived to extend the helping concept and to unify all the intake activities of the Court in a single, professionally directed Bureau of Applications. This can be accomplished while protecting the right to formal court action for those cases best served formally. It assumes basic agreement about objectives, the provision of a sufficiently large and properly qualified group of skilled workers in the Probation Department, and the readiness of the judges to accept the validity of such a plan.[16]

[16] Details are specified in Chap. XI.

V. IN THE COURTROOM

By its very nature, the Children's Court can never be a happy place. At any given moment there are present in the corridors and waiting rooms parents whose children have been picked up for one offense or another, or who, themselves taking the initiative, have decided they need court intervention in their difficulties with their children; children in all manner of trouble and at various stages of disturbance—as well as police officers, S.P.C.C. officers, and other complainants. In the midst of all this, one can ask only that the physical facilities and conduct of official personnel reduce tensions and permit real understanding of problems preliminary to the inauguration of corrective measures.

It must be concluded, after scrutiny, that the New York City Children's Court, admirable in its exclusion of the public and the press, is not, in the main, successful in creating such an atmosphere. In more than one borough the Court has not been provided with the necessary physical facilities to achieve comfort and confidence. The building in Manhattan is old and formal. It was built in an era when the Children's Court was thought of as a criminal court, and its waiting rooms and courtrooms tend to inspire fear and, perhaps, suggest dignity rather than create ease for parents and children. Moreover, the waiting room is overcrowded and poorly maintained. There is, fortunately, an attractive nursery on the floor below for young children whose parents are on the courtroom floor. The Brooklyn building, soon to be replaced, is in even worse repair and has a far too small waiting room, which obliges clients to crowd into the corridors; it too provides a very useful nursery. The facilities in Queens are adequate and brighter, particularly in the provision of a more friendly courtroom, but the Bronx is the only borough in which a sense of light and adequate space attends the waiting room and the courtroom. However, the Court in this borough lacks a nursery, and the steel protectors on the waiting room windows add an inappropriate note. The Staten Island quarters are small, informal, and satisfactory. In Queens and Staten Island, the Children's Court now shares space in one building with the Family Court; these buildings were originally meant only for the predecessor Children's Court and, particularly in Queens, are now overcrowded because they must include extensive Family Court activities as well.

Similar differences between the boroughs obtain with respect to the judge's bench. In Manhattan, the judge who conducts the adjudication hearings sits on a high formal bench in a large, dark, awe-inspiring courtroom. By contrast, the room for disposition hearings is small, and the judge sits at a desk on a level with those in the courtroom. The Brooklyn courtrooms, though smaller, are rather formal, and the judges' benches are raised even higher. Despite raised benches, the Bronx courtrooms create a more relaxed atmosphere by virtue of better lighting and simpler *décor*, and the Queens and Richmond courtrooms are quite similar except for minor details. A few of the judges wear robes during proceedings; the majority do not.

The physical aspects of the court buildings as a whole and generally poor maintenance facilities handicap most of the boroughs in the attempt to convey to those who enter an atmosphere very different from that which prevails in adult courts. Some court personnel do not seem overly concerned about this, but the Court's leadership has made many efforts to obtain more adequate and appropriate facilities.

From the perspective of the clients, the court attendants are an important part of the total waiting room and courtroom atmosphere. The several attendants in each court divide among themselves such tasks as: posting the calendar; adding names to the calendar; calling cases; presenting petitions to the judge as he hears the cases; seeing to it that all personnel involved, including probation officers, are in the courtroom at the proper time; accompanying children to or from the detention rooms (usually not adjacent to the courtroom); occasionally assisting in transporting children from the Court; and numerous other responsibilities involved in maintaining order and assuring the flow of courtroom activity.

The potential ability of each attendant to contribute positively to the court mood is seen in the fact that some of the attendants are reassuring, considerate, and gentle, but by no means neglecting to maintain order when necessary. However, an equally large group of attendants add to the confusion and fear of clients by the manner in which they fulfill their responsibilities, while they fail to use available opportunities to interpret the Court and relieve some of the tension. Although some of the failure results from pressure of multifarious duties, questionable performance seems due more to the tradition in courts governing the conduct of attendants and the lack of conviction about the Court's mission. Some attendants are often unkind or indifferent as they answer waiting room inquiries; their courtroom announcements too often create the mood of a formal adult court as they "herd" people in and out of the courtroom. Children and parents are ordered how, where, and when to sit, and petitioners are given instructions in such a manner as to create tension and fright.

Proper civil service selection and court training would result in a more consistently helpful group of attendants within a short time. This would improve the situation but would not solve the basic problem of creating a calm, reassuring, helping atmosphere in the courtroom itself. There would still be the continuous (and to the client, confusing and frightening) coming and going. In addition to judge and court stenographer, who are always present, and one or two attendants who move in and out during hearings, generally present in each courtroom are a court reporting officer, interpreters, and probation officers participating in cases. Police Department warrant officers may also come in several times during a morning.

When not performing his main function, the interpreter usually assists the attendants with clerical details which follow the Court's disposition of a case, such as marking the calendar, checking the judge's entry for date and disposition, filling out forms, forwarding petitions, and so forth. In the two largest boroughs, probation officers have no choice but to wait around in the courtroom until their cases are reached. To the clients, all these people convert the court hearing into a formal and semipublic affair. The judge can conduct intimate discussions only by overcoming great obstacles. While this fact colors all stages of a proceeding, it is a particularly serious problem (although not all those listed above are present) in the disposition phase of case handling where long-range plans are being reviewed.

THE JUDGES AT WORK. The importance of the work of the judges can hardly be overemphasized. Theirs is the role which sets much of the Court's tone, and they carry the delegated responsibility to promote both community protection and individual welfare. They embody power and prestige which can be used in the Court per se and in the community to protect, to help, and to rehabilitate. In short, they are the leaders of the court "team." For the majority of parents and children the significance of the entire court is largely decided on the bench.

Judges are appointed for ten-year terms by the mayor and paid at the rate of $19,500 a year (including the increase of $2,000 granted after the completion of this study). Political configurations in New York City in recent decades and the tendency to consider religious "balance" in such appointments create a situation in which, at the time of a vacancy, the struggle is often between civic groups seeking to promote qualified candidates and the political and sectarian groups promoting "their own." The personality, integrity, and judgment of the mayor, as well as the nature of accumulated "debts," determine the outcome. Good advice may or may not be ignored. The results, sometimes favorable to the Court and often not, are illustrated below.

The majority of the judges were observed from one to four days each, and their case dispositions, as recorded in several hundred case records and petitions, were also studied. The basic purpose of such observation and study was not to evaluate the individual performance of the eighteen Domestic Relations Court judges who serve in the Children's Court, but to discern the philosophies embodied in courtroom proceedings, the concept of what was to be achieved through the contact, and the quality of feeling conveyed to court clients. Of more than incidental interest, too, were the methods used in this particular court to solve the legal problems created by a social procedure.

The original plan was to report only on the judges as a group, just as this study seeks to discuss probation officers as a group. However, examination disclosed major variations in outlook and considerable differences in conduct of court sessions. There were, too, apparent failures to follow court rules. Thus, while the study is not concerned with individual judges per se—for their probable approaches to the assignment are known or can be known upon appointment—it had to be concerned with understanding the several approaches, illustrating them, and clarifying which ones best advance the goals of a juvenile court. The insights and premises of the mental hygiene movement and of those who created and developed the children's court idea provide the vantage point for the observations which follow.[1]

JUDGES IN ACTION. As a case begins, the attendant ushers all parties concerned into the courtroom. The children involved in a delinquency petition stand before the judge; their parents sit or stand behind them. Other witnesses or people connected with the case are directed to seats about the courtroom. The petitioner takes the witness chair. Children in neglect cases are not in the room unless summoned by the judge. Court rules are sufficiently flexible to permit a wide range of procedural diversity at the point of an

---

[1] What follows is based on: courtroom observation; case reading; discussions with some of the judges, representatives of community agencies who frequently appear in court, and court staff; and the independent observations of a large group of professional and lay members of the Citizens' Committee on Children of New York City, Inc., who visited the courts in another connection.

initial case hearing in both delinquency and neglect cases, and such differences are regularly observed.

Most judges begin by ascertaining the identity of all those before them. Some use the opportunity to ask children their names and addresses and thus begin personal contact. The first step in the formal procedure is to review the allegations, and have the petitioner verify his signature and swear to the truth of the allegations. There is at this point considerable variation in the degree to which judges explain the allegations and proceedings to those involved, or inform them of their rights to "a reasonable adjournment for counsel or the production of witnesses or for other good cause." [2] Some judges are quite careful to review allegations and to emphasize the client's right to counsel; others fail to do so. With regard to the latter, there is no doubt that the manner in which the judge refers to the right to counsel—if he mentions it at all—is one of the determinants in the client's decision about obtaining legal help, although financial considerations are usually controlling. Most Children's Court cases are heard without counsel, and many with experience in the Children's Court agree that lawyers, as currently prepared, ordinarily contribute very little to such proceedings, particularly where no question exists about the truth of the allegations. Far too many lawyers bring with them to the courtroom their traditional emphasis on technicality and orientation of contentiousness;[3] yet counsels do seem at times to safeguard rights of their clients, which may well be overlooked in a context where the judge has both judicial and administrative functions. This whole area is one in need of considerable clarification, as revealed by the following case situation:

A 14-year-old girl contended that two boys had forced her to go with them to a neighborhood roof during a school recess, by telling

---

[2] New York City Domestic Relations Court, *Rules of Practice,* Rule 7 (c).

[3] Abbott states that the facts are not in dispute in 90 percent of delinquency cases and that the key question is what the court can and should do for the child. Abbott, *The Child and the State,* II, 335-336. It has also been said that "since the child is not on trial, neither the prosecuting attorney nor defense attorney are needed." *Report on Juvenile Court Laws,* which is Report 3 of National Conference on Prevention and Control of Juvenile Delinquency, p. 6; see also Tappan, *Delinquent Girls in Court,* p. 192.

her that they had a gun in their possession. There they were joined by other boys, and several had intercourse with her. The lawyer representing two of the boys was able to establish in his cross-examination that the girl had ample opportunity to ask for help en route but failed to do so. His presence assured a fuller questioning of the boys than was characteristic of the judge presiding, and introduced some questions as to the girl's prior conduct. The judge, on the other hand, pointed out that one did not have to prove that the girl had been compelled to submit to intercourse in determining whether the boys' conduct was delinquent. Once the boys were adjudicated as delinquents, the lawyer could only ask for "leniency," a relatively meaningless request in a court without punitive intent. By contrast, the Probation Department liaison representative in the courtroom was able to provide the judge with social studies of the boys prepared at Youth House, which made a major contribution to disposition plans.

In sum, the lawyer's presence led to a repetition of detail, subjection of a disturbed girl to sharp cross-examination, and a "criminal" approach to disposition. Yet it also assured more careful questioning of witnesses and review of the facts than is common. Other situations too reveal this as the chief contribution of counsel in the small minority of cases which employ legal help. Of course, in those few cases where certain complicated legal problems arise involving institutional transfers, jurisdictional rights, or possible appeals, lawyers are indispensable.

The right of adjournment for "the production of witnesses or for other good cause" is not often exercised. While most judges explain the right to counsel, few clients are given to understand that they have a right to sufficient time to discuss a situation with a child, to bring witnesses, or to decide what they wish to do about the problem confronting them. Particularly in the case of delinquency petitions inaugurated by police on the day of an arrest or the following morning, a parent may find himself at a hearing at which the child is adjudicated delinquent, without prior opportunity to discuss or consider developments. There may be similarly rapid adjudication in some neglect situations which do not come through the Bureau of Adjustment.

All of this is readily understandable in historical perspective. At one time children in this city, as elsewhere, were often detained in unsuitable shelters for long periods of time and without legal authority. To remedy this abuse, the law specified that the child, if detained, be brought to a court "with all convenient speed" as soon as the court was in session, and consequently, today, hearings are held with dispatch. While a hearing at the earliest possible moment is desirable for purposes of determining whether a child needs to be detained or assured temporary shelter, it hardly follows that a final decision as to whether a child is actually delinquent or neglected must be made at the same time. The law intends that parents be given ample opportunity to consider and prepare their "case," yet this important right is seldom explained in sufficient detail, if mentioned at all. In effect, the right to proper "notice," an intrinsic part of "due process," is all but lost to clients under these circumstances.

After the preliminary steps, the judge's responsibility is to "hear and determine the facts, rendering a decision thereon." He is to seek the facts as indicated by the "preponderance of evidence" rather than apply the criminal court standard of proof "beyond a reasonable doubt."[4] There are some judges who carefully differentiate fact from hearsay and allow parents and children to question witnesses. They call on all involved and form a complete picture before adjudication. Where evidence is not conclusive and a further hearing is necessary, decision is reserved. Other judges begin the proceeding with the testimony of the petitioner and tend to follow leads developed in this testimony or suggested by the responses of the children and parents. They turn from person to person, asking questions relevant to the moment, trying to clarify what occurred and, perhaps, why. They may end the proceeding without hearing some of the parents or witnesses.[5]

[4] *Rules of Practice,* Rule 7 (d), is quoted for reference to rules of evidence. See *People* v. *Lewis,* Court of Appeals (1932), 260 N.Y.S. 171.

[5] The treatment of witnesses in the Court combines peculiarly Children's Court philosophy with vestiges of criminal court procedure. Yet the need to safeguard individual rights makes the task of suggesting specific modifications in traditional procedure complex indeed, and this report merely records some of the issues.

In a large proportion of cases, as noted, there is no question about the allegations involved. The child has told his story, and the witness has identified

Most judges do not take either of these two extreme approaches. They modify procedure somewhat in the interest of following leads and extend to everyone concerned some opportunity to be heard. One judge often gets a complete picture even prior to the testimony of the petitioner by asking the children what they did. Since he sometimes sees the children in the courtroom in sequence rather than together, this is quite effective in clarifying what occurred. Some of the judges differentiate sharply between the point at which adjudication is made from that at which the propriety of parole or remand, as well as the various alternate long-range plans, is considered. Others seem to regard these as parallel, or at least not separable, phases of procedure.

When jurisdiction has been established, the judge must decide whether to parole a child to his parents or to arrange for shelter or temporary detention. He must also assign the case, when necessary, for Probation Department investigation and for physical and psychiatric study. There are marked differences in the degree of responsibility assumed by judges at this point. Some discuss interim plans with clients, preparing them for immediate and subsequent steps, whereas others merely announce their decision, leaving a confused parent and a frightened or resentful child to be ushered out of the courtroom, perhaps to the detention room, by an attendant who must hurry back for another case. Judges' actions differ just as widely when, after investigation, children and parents reappear for long-range dispositions.

---

the child or his property. Nevertheless, many individuals, whether they come as witnesses to substantiate the evidence or as petitioners, spend long hours in the waiting rooms before appearing in the courtroom. Once in the courtroom, they have little function. Sometimes, if several children, some of them under sixteen and some over, have been involved in an offense, the witness must spend time in two courts. It is difficult to change this, however, since witnesses should obviously be available for questioning during a hearing in those cases where some of the facts are in dispute—and this cannot, without infringing on individual rights, be determined in advance. For the present, one can merely accept the situation as inevitable and state that witnesses are in this manner fulfilling their functions as citizens. Because the Court's atmosphere and methods are also at stake, however, it might be possible to reconsider procedure in use of witnesses after some experience with a Bureau of Applications (Chapter XI).

Under the New York Children's Court plan, the judge thus serves as an adjudicator during the initial phase of the first hearing, concerning himself with the evidence occasioning the Court's intervention in a case, and then as the leader of a "treatment team" who must plan temporary and long-range dispositions. The assignment is obviously an extremely difficult one, requiring legal and judicial competence, on the one hand, and, on the other, knowledge and skill in human relations, as well as knowledge of community resources. Despite its complexity, several judges do successfully demonstrate the integration of these attributes.

The many aspects of the assignment and the vast opportunity inherent in it are best grasped by a composite action picture of two judges who demonstrate well-integrated use of legal and social tools. Only a handful of the eighteen judges who serve the Children's Court approximate such performance:

Judge H. says and knows that the offense for which the child is brought to court is no more than a symptom. In his questioning of a child, after establishing that an offense occurred, he seems to be seeking for motivation. Before disposition hearings, he carefully studies case folders. Whenever possible at the disposition phase, he manages to discuss complex case situations with probation officers and agency representatives in advance. His attitudes toward probation officers and clients have a major effect on the courtroom atmosphere; everybody seems to be oriented to understanding and planning helping measures. Showing considerable awareness of heavy case loads, Judge H. tries not to add a case to the probation case load unless it is really necessary. Good use seems to be made of referrals to private agencies. Since this approach offers high standards, it helps to suggest new skills to be sought. Since adequate measures are sought for each child, the availability or lack of community resources becomes accentuated.

Judge H. is one of the few judges who writes his thinking into his notes on the petition, enabling him to follow through when the case returns and to begin at the point at which the initial hearing ended. Several other judges keep informal notes for their own use.

Two case illustrations suggest the creative possibilities of an approach such as this:

In discharging a boy after favorable probation Judge H. talked in a friendly way to the boy and his mother. He examined the folder carefully, first saw them together, then separately, and then together again. His concern went beyond whether there was further trouble or not, the usual criterion for ending probation. He asked about the other children in the family and explored the economic difficulties and health problems. He seemed eager to see that everything possible had been done with and for this family in the course of the probation contact and that whatever help could be given by other agencies in the community had been initiated. In this case, as in others, there was a warm, interested discussion with the boy and an expression of confidence in his ability to get along without court contact in the future.

Whenever observed, this judge revealed sensitivity as to who should be present in the courtroom with whom and under what circumstances. Although the heavy calendar imposed some limitations, in every instance in which it was crucially important to do so, child or parent was kept out of the courtroom while the other was questioned. Thus, in one disturbed family situation in which the father abused wife, children, and a niece, but which actually got to the Court because of a delinquency petition against the boy, the judge was careful to get the boy to the detention room before questioning the parents. There was a detailed review of the entire case record and of all petitions, old and new. The probation officer wanted to dismiss the case because the boy was not the real offender in the stealing, and had merely been "going along." Judge H. raised the question of why there was not a neglect petition in light of the total view of the family which had evolved in the course of the investigation. Thus, in contrast to a probation officer who saw only the minor offense, the judge stressed the needs of the entire family. After full discussion with the probation officer, the judge questioned father and mother and brought out the abusive conduct of the father and the aspects of considerable neglect in the situation, establishing a basis for neglect action if found desirable. Since questioning the boy was necessary, the judge made it as easy for him as possible by asking him only for confirmation of what the mother and father had both said. In the course of the testimony, the picture developed of an extremely infantile father who competed with his children for candy, took advantage of their physical weakness, and read comics in bed when not working. The father's need for psychiatric examination was interpreted skillfully, and he was prepared by the judge for the experience. Before the hearing was over it was quite clear that the father was the basic problem in this situation. The boy was paroled under supervision, and a plan was made to follow through.

In responding to judges with high standards and attempting to serve clients in the manner they expect, probation officers find that each case requires far more intensive study and follow-up work than is the rule and far more than the total case load generally allows. Most probation officers seem happy at the opportunity to work with such judges and do some of their best work on cases reported to them; but the size of their total work load and the pressure of other responsibilities limit the number of cases they add to the calendar when these judges are sitting in the disposition Part of the Court.

The majority of judges define their roles in ways which in some respects do not seem to be consistent with the intent of the law and in others fail to implement it successfully. It is not uncommon for a judge to emphasize the offense and to grapple very little with its significance or with clues which might suggest the best ways to help. Several judges, extremely careful about procedure up to the adjudication phase, do nothing to prepare clients for subsequent phases or to help inaugurate long-range corrective measures effectively. Nor do they seem to take into consideration the fact that many of the parents who come to court are poorly educated or foreign born and cannot understand at all what it means or can mean when the judge says, "I find these children to be delinquent," or, "I find these children neglected." Even the better educated parent needs more than a technical pronouncement in the midst of a new and traumatic experience.

While most of the judges refer to the Court as an agency for the protection and help of children, their stated intent is negated by their apparent inability to understand human behavior and their failure to make full use of available aids to such understanding; for, without being psychologist or psychiatrist, the judge must approach the child before him with the recognition that behavior is meaningful and can be understood. Because most judges lack preparation for this approach, plans are often based on momentary impulse, on personal patterns of work, or on superficial devices.

Courtroom routine, for certain judges, is a continual round of lectures to parents and children about public relief, church attendance, and human conduct, with assurance that following the judge's advice along these lines would resolve the difficulty. While relatively normal individuals might respond, under proper circumstances, to admonition or advice in a courtroom, this is hardly so for the many more upset or disturbed individuals known to the Court. For individuals caught by strong forces or great stress, advice and threats are superficial approaches at best. As the community's spokesman, the judge is expected to state community disapproval of certain conduct. In the course of his discussion with child and family and questioning of witnesses he must of necessity convey the community's disapproval of disturbing or harmful behavior. These attitudes toward particular conduct (not toward individual children or parents) are best communicated indirectly, as implicit in the entire process, rather than deliberately as a specified step in procedure, i.e, a "lecture." Only then can the Court's expression of disapproval be seen as an aspect of the desire to help rather than as its dominant theme.

One judge, who has a standard lecture for children about their parents, handled a fairly common type of case in this manner:

A chubby boy of about 15 came into court with his very well-dressed mother, a widow. At 5 A.M. one Monday morning he and his friend passed a tavern which had been broken into. Since the door was open, they entered and emptied the vending machines. At 7 A.M., they were apprehended walking down the street with the loot and quite intoxicated. The boy had been sent to the hospital to recuperate. At first he would not talk to the police at all. In reply to questions from the judge, the mother told of problems she had with her son, including late hours and delinquency. Without knowing the slightest detail about the family and the mother, the judge lectured the boy about how good his mother was, about all she did for him, and about how ungrateful the boy was. Since there was no space in Youth House, the boy was paroled home pending investigation.

Surely the Court cannot achieve a helping relationship with a child unless he feels that he and his family situation are understood. A judge who, without exploring the facts, assumes that the mother is a "good" mother may for all time label the Court, in the boy's mind, as an agency which does not seek to know or understand what has occurred. An even more incongruous situation was created when another judge lectured a child at length before the probation officer could inform him that the woman before him was not the child's own mother but a foster mother, who had but recently met the child.

Some judges "order" children to promise improved behavior or to write reviews of selected books. It would appear obvious that a judge who is seeing a child for the first time, or who has seen him briefly once before, can hardly have a relationship with him strong enough to justify the request for a significant promise. Moreover, even should the adult be able, occasionally, to evoke a response on which a sincere promise can be based, there is need to know the child well enough to be sure that the promise does not represent a goal which, because it cannot be achieved, will inevitably add to the feelings of failure.

Particularly ineffective "lecturing" by judges or "ordering" of new conduct patterns is observed in the regular attempts of several judges to improve behavior by enforcing religious participation of children who come under court jurisdiction. The Domestic Relations Court Act of the City of New York directs that a child remanded or committed to an agency or institution which is not public should be placed with people of the same religion "when practicable." Similar instructions are recorded with regard to choice of foster parents and appointment of guardians, and such provisions are also included in the Standard Juvenile Court Act.[6] Also "when practicable," a child is to be assigned to a probation officer of the same faith; this is common practice in case investigation, and very strictly adhered to in supervision. These legal requisites create, of necessity, a considerable degree of court alertness to a child's re-

---

[6] Sec. 88 and Sec. 25 of DRC Law. The "Religious Protection Clause" first appeared in a New York State law in 1875 (Ch. 173) in relation to institutional commitments. It was dropped in 1876, reinstated in 1878, and has remained in the law since that time. Welfare Council of New York City, "Report of Conference on Better Services to Children," p. 10. The Standard Act provision is in Sec. 19.

ligion, an alertness increased by recognition on the part of judges and probation officers that under certain circumstances children can receive significant help from their religious groups and that religious participation may have an influence on the total personality and on the solution to the child's problems.[7] However, in capitalizing on such alertness to order or emphasize religious observance without consultation as to the parents' wishes in regard to religious upbringing and without much concern as to whether there is readiness to use religious help or any relation between the problem and religion in the particular case, certain judges are acting outside a court's authority and are also engaging in practices as inefficient as other types of "lectures" to children, already described.

One judge frequently inquires of probation officers during hearings whether children "have broken the moral code," know the Ten Commandments, and go to church regularly. Another judge, whose pattern of raising religious questions is similar, has on occasion insisted that a child on probation write the Ten Commandments a given number of times and submit them to him or to the probation officer. Some probation officers follow up on such courtroom discussions by checking regularly as to a child's church attendance, insisting on religious participation as a condition of probation, and requiring registration for the theoretically voluntary "released time" from public school for religious instruction.

The most extreme pattern is that of the judge who has a fixed routine which follows adjudication: he asks the children their religion, tests them as to their knowledge of the Ten Commandments, and lectures them about commandments they may have broken. This discussion usually takes up the bulk of the time which remains after adjudication, and the manner in which the child responds is often a major determinant of next steps. Thus:

In one instance two children knew the Ten Commandments while

[7] The view that religious resources can be of great personal help to some children in trouble, if called on for appropriate cases at proper times, is not contradicted by the fact that available research shows that, in the general population, religious observance and contacts do not of themselves decrease delinquency. The studies are summarized by Teeters and Reinemann. *The Challenge of Delinquency*, pp. 158 ff.

the third did not. The judge asked the first two if they knew they had sinned and received affirmative replies. He told the third boy he did not even raise the question with him because he could not possibly know the difference between right and wrong without knowing the Ten Commandments; when the judge repeated this to the child's mother, she began to cry. Later, when referrals to a guidance clinic were suggested by the reporting officer, the judge referred only the boy who did not know the commandments, stating that the other two obviously knew right from wrong.

In one case, three boys involved in purse snatching were tested carefully by the judge as to their knowledge of the Ten Commandments and of their religion. He then told them about the importance of confession and the requirement under confession that they make restitution. The statute does not require that restitution be made. Since their religion would require it, he said, they might as well make such arrangements at once; discussing their allowances, he explored the weekly amount each could pay to the woman from whom the purse was snatched, urging their parents not to give them extra money to meet this obligation.

Another case involved two boys of the same faith, the mother of one of whom had changed her church affiliation. One boy knew the commandments and said he went to church regularly; the judge therefore talked to him about how much wrong he had done. The other proved to know nothing at all in this sphere. Since the mother said she went to a new church while her son was considered a member of his original faith, most of the hearing was concerned with arrangements for this boy to get religious instruction. The judge talked, too, about going to church on saints' days, and of the importance of taking advantage of "released time."

On occasion, between adjudication and final disposition, this judge orders a child to register for "released time" religious instruction, which is presumably optional. He has stated that his final plans about commitment or probation might depend on whether or not the child complied with this order.

There is little doubt that one cannot fully understand or help children without appreciation of the place of spiritual and moral values in their lives. Moreover, there is no question that religious leaders and sectarian agencies, representing sources of such values, can often be important allies to the judges and probation officers in their attempts to help some children or their families. Most judges try to use religious resources in this sense. The few who introduce the religious issue without considering its helpfulness or propriety in the given case or the wishes of the family are engaged in questionable coercion as they seek to "use secular institutions to force one or some religion on any person." [8] They are, moreover, ignoring all that is known about how one initiates effective help or promotes religious interest. The Presiding Justice has said:

There are some who refer to our work with children as that of reclamation. This is only half the story. You can reclaim pig iron from the dump heap. There is nothing useful in that. But if you melt down the iron and add an alloy, manganese, you make steel. Our purpose is not mere reclamation; we want to build character.

No real character is built without the alloy of religion. The mixing of this particular alloy in with human conduct so that it will be accepted and used, and not rejected, is one of the most delicate operations known to science—and it is a science, a science of love and understanding, as any clergyman will tell you.

However, the cold, tense atmosphere of the courtroom is not the place for this chemistry of the soul. You cannot make cold pig iron absorb manganese; and you cannot get a courtroom-cold boy to accept religious platitudes from the bench.

Religion cannot be forced down the throat. Authority and punishment sour it. Necessarily, the judge is associated with authority. He serves an essential purpose in bringing back to shore the boy or girl who is swimming out to sea in the face of a tempest. But, after the child is turned back and landed on shore, the job is only half done. That child must be convinced of the danger he incurs, and the task of doing this is exceedingly difficult for one who had to use force, so to speak, to rescue him against his will from the waves.

A judge is suspect to this child who hates the adult world. He represents the ultimate in authority and punishment to which most of our children are case-hardened by the time they reach us.

It is just common sense that advice and leadership are accepted only from those whom you respect and love. Probation officers, in time, are able to establish that rapport with the sick child which makes it possible for them to talk helpfully about character and spiritual values. But it is very rare indeed, if ever, that a judge in the few

[8] Opinion by Justice Douglas in *Zorach* v. *Clauson*, 343 U.S. 306.

moments of his contact with the child can bridge the abyss of hatred
that has been built up over months and years.

A sensible judge, I think, is one of the most suppressed and frustrated persons in the world. He wants to talk to the child out of
the fullness of his experience, about a decent life and about things
spiritual. But the wise judge knows that the courtroom, yes and
he himself, are associated in the mind of a child with the punishment
mechanisms of society. A thoughtful judge, moreover, knows that at
this time, when the child is resentful and disturbed, it may be a
distinct disservice to religion and its potential future usefulness to
the child to moralize on the subject of things spiritual. Religion
should not be associated with punishment. So this judge will not
attempt to mix in the alloy of religion at this inopportune moment.
He will leave this important task to the future when the child will
be receptive to words of wisdom imparted by someone whom the child
has learned to respect and accept.[9]

Insensitivity on the part of judges is a major handicap in any
court which seeks to be considerate of those who come before it.
Its seriousness is multiplied many times in a court which aims to
help. A judge particularly lacking in perceptiveness, who never
questions the soundness of his rapid evaluations of people nor the
wisdom of his decisions, is seen in action in the following case
situations, observed seriatim:

In one case, a neglectful father, with no visible means of support,
was told by the judge that he probably was a gambler. The judge so
convinced himself and became so angry that he sent the man out of
the courtroom and did all the planning with the wife.

In another case, the judge had previously seen the mother and
obtained from her the address of the putative father. With the father
and the uncle in the courtroom on his order, he had the child called
in and told him to shake hands with them. Without knowing what
it meant to the child, the judge described the many positive qualities
he was sure characterized the father and uncle and got the uncle's
agreement to have the child live with him (the father boards there).
He then had the child kiss uncle, father, and mother in sequence,
without the least idea of the significance of that brief experience or
of the long-range plan.

A young girl was brought to court on a shoplifting charge. Because

[9] John Warren Hill, an unpublished communication (March 4, 1952).

they failed to keep their appointment with the probation officer, with the result that the investigation was not completed, mother and child were called into court on a warrant. The judge interrogated the child about her spelling and the content of what she learned in school. He commented on her prettiness and he scolded the mother for her lack of interest. Then, in the midst of the proceedings, he announced that the girl looked unhealthy and that he wanted the clinic doctor to see her. In a "godfatherly" way, in the presence of the girl, he said that although she was 15 years old, she looked 11 or 12 and he asked her if she did not feel that he was interested in her and wanted to help her. The discomfort of parent and child at this insensitive treatment was apparent to all in the room.

A judge may combine superficial devices to demonstrate how much he "cares" for children and how well he "understands" them with what to the courtroom observer appears as aggression toward, or particularly inconsiderate handling of, parents. One judge, for example, regularly tells the parents that he does not care about them, but about the child. He frequently makes snap judgments without examining previously available data. While reiterating the principle that planning must be in terms of the child's welfare, he negates this by his own procedures. He seems to be arbitrary with, and sometimes cruel to, parents in the courtroom. To one mother, he read his notation on the petition about her immaturity; he told a father to "face the music" about his defective child. Another judge makes derogatory remarks to staff members and visitors about members of some ethnic groups.

These actions of a few judges illustrate some of the most insensitive work in the Court, but by no means constitute the only questionable kinds of performance. There is, for example, the judge who boasts about how well he knows children, but often enters long, whispered discussions with staff members or visitors while clients stand in fear before the bench for fifteen or twenty minutes. Another judge makes "assembly line" decisions after hearing probation officers' recommendations; occupied with writing his decisions on the petitions, he barely looks up as children are whisked in and out of the courtroom. Other judges do not act quite so hastily, but they too often fail to consider the meaning of the experience to those present or to seek to interpret court actions, decisions, and plans to those whose lives are so vitally affected.

Better equipped for some facets of the task than for others, most judges are uneven in their approaches. Some are "legalists" and procedure-minded, while others seek to be "counselors." Some are "audience-oriented," while others bring their best knowledge to bear as they seek to focus on the child. Each manifests an individual combination of concern with procedural safeguards, sensitivity, and knowledge of the elements of the helping process. Thus:

One judge has a stern appearance which at times he seems to use deliberately to frighten children, and to convince them that the Court takes their conduct seriously. On the other hand, not infrequently on hearing a new delinquency case and paroling a boy in the care of his father, he notes indications that the father plans to beat his son, and says in a kindly way that the child realizes his wrongdoing, that certain supervisory obligations exist for parents but that beating will not solve the problem. On occasion, he has reacted with extreme anger to certain offenses and has made immediate decisions to commit children. In other kinds of case situations, he plans carefully, as in the following:

Two boys were arrested after wrecking a stolen 1950 automobile. As the story developed, they had been riding in a 1951 car, which one of them had stolen a week previously; upon finding themselves out of gas, they stole another car. The judge noted the previous petition and probation record of one of the boys, obtained the complete report from the probation officer, and decided on commitment to the New York State Training School. Although it had seemed as though the second boy had taken the lead in the incident, he was helped to retell his story: he had been shielding the first boy out of loyalty, although he himself was unquestionably involved. This boy was paroled home, and the case was to be investigated by the Probation Department. Both children were sent out of the room at times so their parents could speak freely; this procedure gave a far more complete picture than had otherwise been available.

Often, even when good intent and kindliness are apparent, a judge lacks skill in questioning, interviewing, or utilizing courtroom observation. The child's manner in the courtroom inevitably sets a process in motion in which fixed speeches are made and predictable actions taken. Tears, defiance, withdrawal on the part of a child, invariably have foreseeable effects on certain judges; a parent's decision to argue, agree with the judge, cry, ask for "another chance," call an attorney, and so forth, all lead to equally patterned responses. The Court's official record contains evidence of how such stimuli, rather than more profound review of case detail, determine next steps.

Judges are prone to a major occupational hazard—the feeling that they can readily appraise a situation and regularly make wise decisions not subject to question. A court in which there are few attorneys, no representatives of the press, and practically no reviews by higher courts, yet in which judges are called upon daily to make many decisions of major consequence, lends itself particularly to such hazards. A number of Children's Court judges have succumbed to them to a disabling degree:

One judge, for example, embarrasses some children by testing their reading ability but seems to be kind to other children and gets appreciative letters from them. Since he directs them to an "audience" rather than to the child, the value of his comments to the child is a matter of chance. He is convinced that, after very brief discussion, he can evaluate a case adequately and seems quick and alert—but these hasty impressions are often as not unsound; he sometimes writes notes on the petitions or dictates statements into the record which describe adults and/or children as disturbed, immature, amoral, reacting to inferiority complexes, and so on.

While there are no universally accepted criteria for the performance of judges at the initial case hearings, and while there is as yet some controversy about the extent to which traditional courtroom procedure may be modified to the purposes of the Children's Court, many of the current practices are hardly defensible. The law clearly intends that the judge determine whether the preponderance of facts justifies assuming jurisdiction and that he then attain such understanding of the forces which are operative as is essential to plan for the necessary "aid, encouragement and guidance" of the child. Hence, while the judge must concern himself with the offense, he must not stop at the offense. Furthermore, in inaugurating helping measures, a good judge will try to make people comprehend and participate in the process which is meant to aid them; he knows that clients must be understood and feel understood and that disturbed people and those under stress are not "reformed" by lectures, admonitions, or the exacting of promises. Only a small minority of the judges act in the light of such knowledge and seem to be concerned with the need to preserve due process while simultaneously exercising skill in human relations; seem to be able to express the community's dissatisfaction with particular modes of conduct while they themselves remain concerned with the meaning of the behavior of the child or parent.

DISPOSITIONS. Following the receipt of probation case studies made in the weeks after the first court hearings, the judge must arrive at a disposition plan for each case. In most instances, the case comes for disposition planning before the judge who conducted the original hearing, but the court rotation scheme does not always allow this. The same wide range of attitudes, orientations, and skills governing initial hearings is necessarily reflected at the disposition phase. Indeed, as an observer passes from judge to judge, he finds a children's court whose many sections seem to be at very different stages of evolution from their criminal court origins:

One judge makes dispositions after an attempt to weigh what are characterized as "strengths" and "weaknesses" in a child and family, but his plans tend to reflect neither his own skillful appraisal nor the use of appraisals made available by consultants, so much as trial and error. Institutionalization may be suggested because probation has failed, without considering whether what is known about a child might explain the probation failure or indicate the prognosis in the institution. Occasionally, however, his dispositions reveal careful review of available material and quite full appraisal of a child.

Another judge is obviously eager to help children but sometimes seems overwhelmed by routine. He wishes to evaluate cases carefully and to exercise independent judgment. His questioning is clumsy, constantly betraying his own point of view and prejudices and often missing what the probation officers mean. He concentrates during hearings on making proper entries in the petition but also stops to read relevant documents carefully. Quite often when children are before him he asks them with real interest what they have done, and seems to obtain candid answers. When these selfsame children return for disposition, he is faced by the community's lack of resources. Comparing the State Training School with "a good private boarding school" he will state, a short time later, that "after all, it will be good for him to go somewhere where he can't have his way and will be made to learn what was wrong with what he did." On occasion he has approved commitment plans without having the child in the courtroom.

A third Children's Court judge feels, when receiving probation officer reports as part of long-range disposition planning, that it is not in his province to question their work. He therefore relies completely on clinical and probation recommendations. In effect, most reports are not reviewed, and recommendations, if at all feasible, are accepted uncritically. Children and parents are whisked in and out of the courtroom while the probation officer states his recommendation and the judge enters it on the petition as a disposition. Unless a question of fact arises, parents and children are usually not even spoken to. The judge takes no responsibility at all for interpreting to them what has been decided. Calendars are completed with dispatch, but the law's intent that cases be carefully considered is violated.

A fourth judge distrusts psychiatrists and hence usually refuses to entertain a probation officer's recommendations for psychiatric study. Where study has been made and a report is available, he frequently chooses a so-called "alternate" common-sense plan. In one case, a probation officer, with his supervisor's agreement, worked for several months until parent and child were ready to attend the Court Treatment Clinic. When the case came before this judge, he convinced the mother that the plan was unnecessary and gave parent and child some "advice."

There are judges who decide to send one child to a state school and place another on probation, depending on the severity of the offense, thereby acting as do most criminal courts and denying the whole purpose of creating a court which would remove problems of children from criminal court procedures and modes of disposition. There are others who really do attempt to discern which plan will best help the child, and they arrive at dispositions accordingly. There are judges who carefully study all relevant reports and records, while there are those who ask a few questions and forthwith make a decision, ignoring completely the intent of the Domestic

Relations Court Act in providing for probation case studies and psychiatric examinations.

There are a few judges who see themselves as the coordinating members of a case disposition team. They assemble the reports of the field workers (probation officers), diagnostic experts (doctors, psychologists, psychiatrists), and various community representatives and decide on a disposition only after consultation and discussion. They do not, however, fail to assume full responsibility for final action and for preparing the child for the disposition. There are, too, judges who go so far as to accept recommendations of psychiatrists and social agencies automatically and uncritically. On the other hand, there are those who have little regard for probation officers, psychiatrists, or school officials, who do not think that their own planning requires discussion, and who merely announce a decision, often without examining records and reports:

One of the last group is the object of many complaints that he does not understand the court staff situation and is therefore unreasonable in his criticism of probation officers. Also, it is noted that he too often subpoenas representatives of social agencies when their presence is hardly necessary. Furthermore, in his emphasis on a child's religion, he is unwilling to understand the circumstances which may make it necessary to assign a case for investigation to a probation officer of another faith, and he conducts the hearing as though such an officer were incapable of understanding the family. In his refusal to look at psychiatric reports in most probation or supervision cases, he often undermines the relationship of the probation officer with the family.

A few judges have specifically instructed probation officers not to prepare a child for placement as a possible or probable court disposition, even when the probation officer's experience indicates that such disposition is highly likely. They believe that in such preparation the probation officer is infringing on the judge's prerogatives. Most judges, however, have not limited probation officers in this manner and seem to consider such rules contrary to the interests of the children concerned.

The majority of the judges are not characterized by the "pure" form of either approach; for they sometimes read and appraise the significance of reports, often read and accept realistic psychiatric recommendations, occasionally consult, sometimes take responsibility for interpreting proceedings and plans to clients—but too often do none of these things and announce decisions based on momentary impressions, habit, impulse, and prejudice. The combination of heavy calendars and judges' conceptions of the assignment thus seems regularly to turn the disposition Part of the Children's Court into an "assembly line," which some judges conduct by rapid decision-making and others by relying completely on the probation officer's recommendations. Only a few stop to give careful consideration to all cases, particularly during those phases of case action where crucial decisions are involved.

There is great strain at each monthly rotation when probation officers must make the change from the work patterns and expectations of judges like Judge H., for example, to those of other judges—or when they must make the change in the other direction. At stake are the seriousness with which their reports are to be read, the extent to which their opinions will be asked and respected, the sensitivity with which clients will be interviewed, whether or not certain institutions or clinics will be considered as possible treatment resources, the concept of how to help people, and so forth. In short, because of the differences between judges and due to the rotation calendar, the beginning of a month may in effect mark for probation officers the commencement of a virtually different job in an almost different court.

Noting how the most skilled of judges are frustrated by the lack of proper resources, there are those who would explain questionable patterns largely in terms of such lacks—but examination of practice discloses that an individual's skill and his view of the task he faces are reflected in his use of resources, as in all else. It is nonetheless important to record (as detailed in Chapter IX) that serious problems arise regularly as judges find themselves unable to make interim dispositions to detention facilities or shelters because of lack of space. Nor are detention facilities and shelters the only resource problem which handicaps judges in their planning. Many of the needs are best described after the discussion of probation services, but at this point it should be noted that the Court must constantly contend with long delays when it wishes to schedule psychiatric and psychological examinations for children in various public and private facilities or at the court clinic. At the time of this writing, a six-week wait for appointments in the court clinic proper and a three-week wait at Youth House was routine. Unless special emergency arrangements prove possible, the Court must in some cases arrive at case dispositions without the benefit of reports it considers important. There are often far longer delays facing the Court as it makes referrals for treatment and guidance to mental hygiene and child guidance clinics and agencies. Even more distressing delays and more critical inadequacies exist in the field of long-term placement facilities both for neglected and for delinquent children. Many children are placed in settings with which judges are far from satisfied, and others must be returned to the community against the better judgment of all concerned.

The pressure of the calendar is often cited as another explanation of inadequate courtroom practice. During the year 1951, for example, the following hearings (cases on the calendar) were listed for each borough:

Manhattan	20,101
Brooklyn	16,844
Bronx	5,862
Queens	5,042
Richmond	827

While many of the calendar listings involve very little courtroom activity or only routine procedures (see Table 3 for the number of new cases actually heard), calendar pressure does tend to be considerable from late fall to early spring in the two largest boroughs, Manhattan and Brooklyn. At such times, the sheer number of situations to be attended to creates acute strain which makes relaxed discussion and careful consideration difficult. Moreover, a "culture" has developed around the judge's job, so that the pace set in the large boroughs in the busiest months and the pattern of work developed under pressure continue to dominate the scene in all boroughs, even when the calendar is not crowded. For the most part, judges spend less time in the courtroom, when the calendars are light, rather than use the opportunity for more careful consideration of each case. It is this observation, and the fact that the differences between judges obtain whether or not a given judge has a light or a heavy calendar in a given month, which make it obvious that qualifications and conceptions of the assignment rather than calendar size are the basic determinants.

The above descriptions by no means include all the skillful and considerate activity of judges in the courtroom. Nor do the sketches convey the fact that during such hearings judges make many important and helpful decisions necessary to protecting large numbers of children, arranging placements, obtaining medical and psychiatric evaluations, or inaugurating corrective measures. Unfortunately, it must nonetheless be recognized that while these services are planned in the courtroom or agreed to by the judge following the receipt of reports and recommendations, their validity and/or effectiveness are adversely affected in serious measure by many of the work patterns and attitudes described.

The diverse and apparently contradictory patterns of work are understandable because there is thus far only limited verified knowledge as to the consequences of the various patterns and also because of the relationship of the community to the Court. It must be recognized, in the latter connection, that each of the patterns of work and concepts of the Court may have some backing in the community and may reflect what some portion of the public wishes to find in the Children's Court. Or, if not based on substantial public support, patterns and concepts have been perpetuated by public indifference, inertia, or sheer lack of information. Yet, even allowing for a wide variety in patterns of operation as part of an experimental process to assure growth or permit dissent, it cannot be held that all the approaches are equally acceptable for all time; for many are inconsistent with each other and not a few are clearly harmful to children and contrary to the intent of the Domestic Relations Court Law. Any effort to improve the Court must involve choices from among the prevailing patterns, based on available knowledge: those which advance the

Court's purpose must be identified, specified, and strengthened; the others must gradually be modified or discontinued. Ways must be sought of selecting judges who are capable of acting in terms of the best knowledge and skill—and prepared to lend their talents to further definition and refinement of the judge's role.

THE JUDGES IN THE COMMUNITY. Judges in the Children's Court are in a strategic position to note gaps or inadequacies in the community's pattern of institutions and social services and to call the public's attention to major needs. While not equipped for systematic long-range research to measure needs statistically, the Court has conducted several short-range surveys and has also cooperated in important efforts such as the study of temporary shelter undertaken by the Commission for the Foster Care of Children.[10] In addition, a number of the judges and the Presiding Justice (who is a member both of the Commission for the Foster Care of Children and of the New York City Youth Board) have spoken out clearly and forcefully on important occasions on behalf of children's services.

Particularly over the past decade, the improvement of several important facilities can be credited to the efforts of some judges. The small, experimental Treatment Clinic of the Children's Court, eventually incorporated as a permanent service along with the Diagnostic Clinic, was a product of the work of the Presiding Justice and several others convinced of an urgent need. It was, too, the readiness of a presiding justice to use the Court's subpoena powers at a critical time in 1944 which made it possible to investigate the S.P.C.C. and to expose its abuses in a report prepared by three justices of the Domestic Relations Court. As a result of the report, the substandard shelters were soon closed and the way was paved for a far better program at Youth House.

It was judges of this court, acting with responsibility for the children they commit, who prepared an extremely valuable and influential report on the state training schools. Moreover, several judges have played roles in the attempt to provide unsegregated and equal facilities for Negro children, long the victims of dis-

[10] Beck, *Simple Arithmetic about Complex Children*.

crimination by many different kinds of agencies. Nor should the influence of treatment plans urged by judges and by the Court's Treatment Clinic be underestimated, for these have significantly affected voluntary agencies' programs for children.

Most recently, during the long public debate about a proposal to confer upon the Court the right to fine parents up to twenty-five dollars for acts of vandalism committed by their children, the Board of Justices voted 10-2 to express the opinion that such action was in conflict with the purposes of the Children's Court. Their enlightened statement of the Court's philosophy contributed in important measure to clarification of the issue for the public and to the defeat of the proposal in the Board of Estimate.

While it is difficult to know when a judge is acting in the capacity of citizen, as a member of a public group, or as a member of the Court, the important consideration is that positive advances are being made in the field of children's services because of awareness of the implications of what comes to the courtroom, as well as the initiative or cooperation of several judges of this court and of the Presiding Justice.

SCHOOL PART OF CHILDREN'S COURT. Truancy cases are served in a specially designated Part of the Children's Court. Habitual truants are considered under the law as delinquents, and parents who keep their children from school unlawfully may be charged with neglect. The Children's Court enters into such situations since it has had sole jurisdiction over all violations of the state's Compulsory Education Law since 1932, and several hundred children and parents have appeared in the Children's Court annually on petitions related to truancy since that time.[11]

Prior to 1944, informal agreement between the Court and the Bureau of Attendance controlled the flow of truancy cases into the Children's Court. Case "quotas" so established were limited by the pressure on the Court of "more serious" cases and were inadequate. Children's Court judges, all of whom heard these

[11] Kahn, Lash, *et al., Children Absent from School,* Table 16, p. 66.

cases at one time or another, showed no uniformity in their approach to attendance problems. Judges complained about the poor preparation of attendance officers, who in turn insisted they had information which the judges failed to elicit.[12] As a result of this situation, a special Children's Court judge was appointed and assigned in 1944 to a newly created "School Part" of the Children's Court to serve the entire city, with occasional part-time help of other judges.

The original School Part blueprint provided a rather elaborate plan for case screening through the services of an assistant corporation counsel, psychiatric social workers from the Bureau of Child Guidance, attendance officers, and Juvenile Aid Bureau policemen. More formal legal steps were to be taken only where screening indicated them as necessary. The plan was never fully carried out, was gradually "simplified," and finally largely abandoned. The School Part began to operate like the rest of the Children's Court, except that it concentrated on attendance cases, lacked probation services, used the Bureau of Attendance staff for case study and "attendance probation," and did not have any rotation of judges.

Several appraisals of the School Part indicated that "Court action did not seem to accomplish the purposes for which it was established."[13] A child's attendance usually improved while his case was before the Court, but proceedings in nonattendance cases clearly did not improve subsequent attendance or scholastic and social adjustment. Parents were sometimes fined, to no avail.

The feeling grew that perhaps the major weakness of the School Part was its symptom-orientation. As administered, it was concentrating on the number of days a child was absent from school, seeing as its main task getting a child back to school, without fully considering the causes of his absence or whether improved attendance could be maintained. Many of the actions involved criminal or quasi-criminal procedures against parents under the

---

[12] For more detail and documentation see: *ibid.*, Chap. VIII; Goldberg, *Child Offenders*; Landry, *The Prosecution of School Non-attendants.*
[13] Landry, *op. cit.*, p. 260.

Compulsory Education Law (C.E.L.). In addition to obstacles and problems shared with the rest of the Court, the School Part was frequently handicapped by inadequate preparation of cases on the part of attendance officers, who more often than not were unclear about their assignments, differently conceived by judge, attendance supervisor, and the schools which they served.

In January, 1950, the Presiding Justice inaugurated a series of changes, making the School Part an assignment on the Children's Court regular rotation schedule, with the result that some of the judges deeply interested in cooperation with the schools on behalf of children were assigned. The change in judges was accompanied by certain basic changes in School Part philosophy and practice, and a skilled Bureau of Attendance supervisor and an outstanding Probation Bureau representative were made available.

Since then, the Court has been increasingly able to help attendance officers learn to screen cases adequately and use court procedures appropriately. Whereas School Part petitions were at one time largely C.E.L. and delinquency petitions (see "Adult Proceedings" statistics in Table 3.), deeper understanding on the part of staff has practically eliminated the former and substantially increased the number of neglect and delinquency actions. (School Part heard 757 new cases in 1951 and 991 in 1952; these cases are included in the court totals reported in Table 3.) In contrast with earlier practice, the C.E.L. petitions are no longer used in relation to mentally defective or mentally ill children; where parents do not cooperate in arranging treatment, neglect petitions are filed. Stress has been placed on efforts to adjust problems through school action prior to court procedure.

The attendance officers are now encouraged to come to court with maximum background data about a child. With the emphasis on the problem behind the truancy, there is far less readiness to close a case upon temporary improvement in attendance, while other problems requiring the Court's power and resources remain. Dispositions are based on more complete case study; and institutionalization, where necessary, is more often than formerly designed to meet a child's specific needs.

This new orientation, the recognition that children before the School Part are really the same children, with the same problems, known to the remainder of the Children's Court and that the investigations by attendance officers are often inadequate, has resulted increasingly in case referral to the Probation Bureau for full investigation. In such instances, the procedure is identical with that for other types of cases in the Court, except that the schools and the Bureau of Attendance are almost always involved in disposition plans. During the 1950 calendar year, a total of 374 cases was referred by the School Part for Probation Bureau investigation in the various boroughs.

Since Children's Court procedure and resources are now used in more constructive ways than formerly, developments in the School Part represent an important advance. They have not, however, taken place without cost. The judges who have developed the new School Part plans have not, of course, been able to serve in the regular Children's Court at the same time. An already overburdened Probation Bureau has been asked to take on a certain number of added investigations. Those who preferred the older "law enforcement" approach, as narrowly defined, have resisted the changes.

If improving the School Part means making it similar to the best of the Children's Court and using probation services, the question arises: Has the time not arrived to abolish the School Part and have attendance officers bring their cases to the regular court? Judges who currently serve the School Part could then share in the regular work in the more overburdened boroughs. This would be a dramatic way of stressing that it is not the symptom—in this case, truancy—which is the important aspect of a child's case, but rather the problem behind it.

Those who would retain the School Part have strong reasons on their side. They point out that the separate approach is rather new and deserves time for further development. Also, a judge in the School Part, who deals with attendance officers for several months, is in a particularly strategic position to assist the Bureau of Attendance in attempts to raise staff standards and modernize practice; this opportunity would be lost if school cases came before many judges in a given month. The school system is so complex that it would be inefficient to have more than a few judges strive to know it well and work with it closely. The existence of a special School Part, which deals only with attendance cases and meets in each borough at specified times, makes it relatively easier for attendance officers to plan their work week. Also, the attendance supervisor and probation representative, who move with the School Part from borough to borough and who have made major contributions to the improvements here described, would hardly be able to service attendance officers in all boroughs as they presented cases to the regular parts of the Children's Court. In addition, there are those who see as decisive the fact that (whatever the exact wording of the petition and its legal classification) parents seem to consider a School Part hearing less stigmatizing and as signifying a lesser degree of failure than a hearing elsewhere in the Children's Court. This factor, in turn, seems to affect their readiness to exercise initiative and to take help.

As the Children's Court as a whole is improved and as it comes to be regarded by the community less as a stigmatizing experience and more as the helping agency originally conceived, such considerations will no longer be crucial. The logic of good planning may suggest abolition of the School Part and full integration of school cases into the regular Children's Court program at such a time. For the present and for the immediate future, the value of the School Part remains considerable; efforts must, therefore, be directed to full consolidation of School Part gains. Since it uses probation services for certain cases, probation staff must be expanded in line with School Part demands.[14]

[14] This was to some extent recognized with the addition of six probation positions to the 1951 budget at the urging of the Presiding Justice. Secondary problems facing the School Part have not been touched here: the need to devise a method for reports to the Court by attendance officers on children who have been placed under their supervision; the question of which reports in the probation folder are to be shared with attendance officers, etc. For a fuller statement of the current plan and philosophy, see Memorandum of June 7, 1950, from John Warren Hill, Presiding Justice, to Dr. William Jansen, Superintendent of Schools, and the accompanying report based on four months of work in the School Part by Justice Justine Wise Polier.

PETITIONS AND LABELS. A philosophy which leads to the need to integrate the School Part into the rest of the Children's Court also has consequences for petition-writing procedure and for the use of the labels "delinquency" and "neglect."

PETITIONS. Recognizing that the child rather than an offense is its prime concern and finding it administratively sound, the Court has made a practice of permitting the judge to "discharge" one petition to another (making appropriate cross reference) in those instances in which a child, active in court on one petition, appears on another. However, petition-writing procedure has not completely kept up with the philosophy of the Domestic Relations Court Act. If a child is apprehended and either admits to, or is discovered to have been involved in, several delinquent acts, the police often swear to a series of petitions; this results in several hearings in sequence in which the child, sometimes in company with different companions and in the presence of a series of different witnesses, appears before the judge.

Currently, all the children involved in a given event appear on the same petition. Since the issue in a children's court is whether a *child* has so acted or is living under such circumstances as to require court intervention, it is reasonable to inquire whether all information about a given child could not be placed on one petition, and whether a separate petition could not be prepared for each child alleged to have part in an incident. Only in this way would a *child*, rather than an *event*, truly become the basis of petition writing. The judge would then have before him at the hearing one petition for each child involved. That resulting petition would be a complete statement of all allegations about a child, even though they arise from several incidents, and would contain a more coherent record of the Court's treatment; provision could thus be made for a cumulative record of a child. While the present allegation-based petition can trace its roots to criminal court tradition, there is no legal obstacle in the way of making the child the unit for petition writing, and other juvenile courts have already taken this step.

THE USE OF LABELS. As the needs of the child rather than the nature of the offense become the center of the Court's concern, the use of labels becomes increasingly undesirable. It has been noted that the Standard Juvenile Court Act recommends that, rather than label a child as delinquent, neglected, or dependent, the court merely describe in its findings the conditions which justify its assumption of jurisdiction. The New York State Citizens' Committee of One Hundred for Children and Youth affirmed that the stigma attached to the words "delinquent" and "neglected" could not be "helpful to the child nor to the court in dealing with the child." [15]

An important group of experts do, nonetheless, prefer the labels and the definitions attached to them in a juvenile court act. Some authorities, believing that the court intervenes in too many types of situations, favor retention of the labels and limitation of jurisdiction to conduct specified in detail. Others, who have seen the ultimate desirability of dropping the tags in order to stress the court's noncriminal nature and intent to help, are of the opinion that until courts are better provided with personnel and facilities, the tags will protect so-called "dependent" and "neglected" children.[16]

Those who wish to end labeling point out, in response, that the categories "delinquent child" and "neglected child" were formulated and defined in an era when far less was known about human behavior. It is known, too, that some courts term "delinquency" what others describe as "neglect." As long as the categories are used, people will think there is a fundamental difference between them; thus, a "delinquent child" is thought of as one who is involved in intentional and deliberate misconduct, in contrast with a "neglected child." These labels create handicaps

---

[15] National Probation and Parole Association, A *Standard Juvenile Court Act*, comment following Sec. 7, and *The Four Million*, Report of the New York State Citizens' Committee of One Hundred for Children and Youth, p. 140.
[16] Rubin, "The Legal Character of Juvenile Delinquency," *The Annals*, American Academy of Political and Social Science, CCLXI (January, 1949), pp. 1-8.

in arriving at dispositions, since certain institutions are designated for one group of children and others for another group. There are also different public subsidy policies in regard to per capita grants for each group. Labeling involves, in effect, reacting to the circumstances by virtue of which a child is identified as requiring help rather than to the nature of the need, while there is, in fact, no real difference between the range of needs of the children in these categories.[17]

Many cases appearing in the New York Children's Court have been labeled "neglected" and then at a later date "delinquent," and some have been labeled "delinquent" and then "neglected." There are some delinquency cases which do not, on probation study, reveal family disorganization and pathology, but they are few. There are some neglect cases in which no delinquent patterns are apparent—but one does not know what the picture will be like in a few years. These are closely related groups of children, and the overlapping is considerable. Recognizing this, certain judges have tended to adjudicate, where the neglect was obvious and on the surface, "delinquency due to neglect." Others have freely accepted new petitions which would "make" a delinquent child into a neglected one or vice versa, where this would help get around the obstacles to a treatment plan, or the lack of placement facilities, created by a label.

If the intent of the juvenile court is carried to its logical conclusion, the labels would seem to serve no purpose, for the treatment plan should be based on the needs of the child, not on labels. The strongest case for the preservation of labels may be made on the basis of the need to protect the child, since a statute may specify in detail when a label may apply and the labeling process thus assure that there is a preponderance of fact justifying the court's assumption of jurisdiction, but more detailed review of this latter argument (Chapter X) will suggest that one can adequately protect a child against improper intervention by a court without using this unsatisfactory device. The time has

[17] Greene, "Probation—Philosophy, Function and Fact."

clearly arrived for legislative action to discard the outmoded and unnecessary labels "delinquency" and "neglect."

THE COURT REPORTING OFFICER. Close liaison is needed between judges and probation staff during the initial case hearing so that dates on which investigations are to be completed may be set, probation officers assigned, and instructions issued by the judge relayed. Since, except for the few instances of appeal or other special circumstances, the court stenographer's notes are not typed, it is necessary also to convey to the probation officer a picture of particularly significant courtroom developments in a case. It is an experienced probation officer, known as a court reporting officer, who has gradually become the chief liaison person between the courtroom and both the Probation Department and various community agencies and who therefore is one of the key people in the Court. In Manhattan and Brooklyn this is a full-time responsibility; but in the Bronx, the reporting officer carries a small probation case load in addition. In Queens, the court reporting officer also conducts the Bureau of Adjustment, while because of the Court's size, there is no need for a reporting officer in Richmond.

The position of court reporting officer was originally established to provide a probation officer who would report to the judge for all probation officers on so-called "no appearance" cases (those requiring routine action rather than a full hearing), request calendar changes, and convey the judge's instructions. Within a short time the daily needs of the Court imparted other emphases to the position. Probation officers must, for the most part, make their own courtroom appearances, although a supervisor or the reporting officer may on occasion substitute. The reporting officer now performs the following functions:

1. Maintains a roster of all probation officers, their religions, their districts, and the number of new cases assigned them during a month. At the time a judge refers a case for probation investigation, the reporting officer indicates who the probation officer

will be and the day on which it would be appropriate for the report to be presented, since all probation officers are in the field on certain days. When it appears that a case will require investigation and the probation officer to whom it will be assigned is in the building, the court reporting officer calls him to the courtroom so that he may hear the testimony and have his first contact with the child. If the officer is not present, the reporting officer makes brief notes about the proceedings which are subsequently forwarded to the probation officer.

2. Makes referrals for tests, examinations, and observation on the judge's order, if a case has not been assigned for study by a probation officer, and sends appropriate reports from the Court in connection with such referrals. Hence, as liaison officer, he is expected to be informed about the various community resources, their facilities and waiting lists, and to answer inquiries of the judges about these matters, as well as offer suggestions for available and appropriate services.

3. Prepares child or parent for the services of a public or private social agency or for the separation involved in commitment, when court dispositions are made on cases not assigned to probation officers.

4. Obtains the detailed data which must be telephoned to the Placement Division of the Department of Welfare when short-term placement is necessary for neglected children on cases not already under supervision.

5. Maintains contact with client and agency and reports to the judges at the time indicated in those cases in which the judge wished to see "how things will work out" or whether another agency could be helpful—while leaving court action open.

6. Helps with the clerical routine following the judge's decision on a case, when the work load permits.

Although these assignments are quite specific, the court reporting officer's assignment is actually flexibly defined and, to a degree, reflects the person in the job. An experienced and respected officer is able to provide extremely valuable service in the manner in which he suggests and initiates referrals, bridges the gap between probation officer and client, finds placements, calls the judge's attention to relevant reports, and conveys a warm feeling for people. Several of the officers handle the assignment satisfactorily, and at least one of them serves the Court in outstanding fashion. It is highly likely that the latter is able to overcome, to a large extent, the obstacles created by the court atmosphere and patterns of procedure.

THE COURT MUST PROGRESS. Review of the work of judges and others in the courtroom, while revealing important and helpful service, points up issues and problems requiring serious consideration and responsible action. In summary:

Physical setting and all other factors which determine court atmosphere.—Much can and must be done to assure the kind of court setting which will contribute to the achievement of court goals. Poor physical facilities and adult court trappings condition far too much of the climate. Attendants must be oriented to the purposes of the Court. Ways must be sought to add to the informality of the courtroom and to decrease the number of persons present at all times.

Resources.—Much must be done to develop the proper liaison machinery and provide the Court with needed placement resources and clinical consultation. While most of the problems of resources can be solved only as part of a broader community effort, the Court can accelerate the process by use of its strategic position to identify and report on needs. (Some of the specific resource problems are detailed in Chapter IX.)

The labels.—Because they serve no treatment purpose and are recognized as outmoded, the arbitrary labels of "delinquent" and "neglected" must be dropped by the Court.

Individual rights.—There is great need to consider how individual rights can be guarded while justice is individualized through informal procedure. To a considerable degree, the Children's Court serves poor and uneducated people; what is more, its procedures hardly encourage appeal to the higher courts, and thus leave great authority in the hands of the judges.[18] Because some judges obtain a superficial picture of the facts or of the case

[18] Polier, "The Role of a Juvenile Court in 1948."

background at the first hearing and, ignoring reports, little more at the second hearing, the extent to which individual rights are protected and sound decisions made during adjudication and disposition comes into question. For, while some judges relate well to the children, study their cases, and make careful findings and dispositions, others have brief, superficial, and transitory contacts, either leaving the crucial work to the Probation Department or interfering with such work by improper decisions and orders.

Suggestions made for the future direction of the Court must seek both to strengthen "due process" safeguards in the procedure and protect individuals by assuring careful review of their problems. At the same time, in the light of the Court's purposes, an effort must be made to substitute child-centered for offense-centered petitions.

Religion in the Court.—Religion, as a source of enrichment to human living, contributes most effectively to the well-being of children in trouble when called upon in voluntary fashion, at appropriate times, and only in carefully selected cases. Major responsibility and rights in this realm must be left to parents and churches. A few members of the court staff have adopted the particularly ineffective and questionable practices whch have been described; the community must insist on their immediate elimination.

Relations of judges and probation officers.—A children's court cannot achieve its objectives while there are grossly contradictory views about the relation of judges to probation officers. Some judges see themselves as meeting with probation officers and arriving at plans together with them; as team members they clarify and record their thinking. Others act independently and leave so few notes on the petition that their thinking cannot be reconstructed. Fearful of how certain judges will dispose of cases, many probation officers, where possible, select dates on which judges considered more sympathetic to their own concepts of their assignments are sitting. Others, under pressure of heavy work loads, do not seek out the judges with the highest standards for serving cases. Surely this situation requires reexamination and some broad consensus about roles while at the same time leaving adequate leeway for individuality and flexibility.

Patterns of judges' activity.—In short, the many different interpretations of the judge's role cannot all be considered as reflecting the Court's intent. It is necessary to consider how the disposition and adjudication phases of the assignment can be developed and what would be required to implement a program most in keeping with the Court's goals.

It is widely held in the juvenile court movement that adjudication is a legal function but disposition a function of clinical knowledge, yet this study has shown major failures in the courtroom in the conduct of proceedings (see above) as well as in case evaluation or in the use of outside clinical resources by judges. For many children the potential damage is fortunately modified by the fact that, even when reports are not read or their rationale grasped or accepted, judges are usually willing to accept clearly formulated psychiatric recommendations. (As will be shown, because successful implementation requires more than routine acceptance—even when resources are available—this by no means assures good service to children.)

Perhaps the key question to be explored is whether judges should be expected both to adjudicate and to arrive at dispositions. Once there is some agreement about the answer, it becomes possible to examine the implications for court procedure and auxiliary services. Then, in the light of a concept of the proper role of a judge (Chapter XI), it becomes necessary to ask whether new methods of selection would assure—or be more likely to result in—judges capable of more skillful performance. Clearly, many of the judges are now unable to provide leadership in the type of undertaking envisaged by the law.

These matters require fuller elaboration, but only in the context of discussion of the remainder of the Court. Their implications will become clearer after review of case study, treatment, and auxiliary services.

VI. THE CASE STUDY IN THE
PROBATION DEPARTMENT

It is widely agreed that without a competent probation department there cannot be a successful juvenile court. Achievement of the court's basic objectives requires individualized appraisal of, and planful work with and for, children, rather than routine processing—and the effective operations of the probation department are a necessary condition of such service.

While the means a society chooses to deal with offenders reflects the prevailing concept of individual worth, it is also, ultimately, the method considered most likely to prevent other offenses. It is therefore not surprising that in the course of developing its special role, probation has reflected utilitarian as well as humanitarian considerations. The general recognition that for many individuals the fear of punishment is not an effective deterrent has been as important a component in its history as has the impulse to help or the desire not to hurt individuals who are themselves the victims of their life circumstances.[1]

THE GROWTH OF PROBATION. The direct precursors of probation in England and the United States were such judicial expedients for conditional suspension of judgment or application

[1] For elaboration, see particularly United Nations, Department of Social Affairs, *Probation and Related Measures.* Chap. I, "The Meaning of Probation," and Appendix D, a special report on "Probation in the United States of America," are valuable sources. There are also helpful discussions in:

of harsh laws as benefit of clergy, release on one's own recognizance, release on bond, or provisional filing of a case.[2] Probation cannot be said to have existed, however, until conditional suspension of judgment, on the basis of reasonable expectation that the offender would not repeat, was combined with procedures for the selection of those to be placed on probation and for "provision of actual assistance to the probationer in the form of personal supervision and guidance."[3]

There is agreement that it was John Augustus who, in 1841, added supervision to the prior concepts of suspended sentence and release on recognizance. And although the probation idea was born in adult courts, it was the juvenile court movement which provided the impetus necessary to expand it from a program in a few states to a method of rehabilitation used throughout the country.

Probation has been recognized by the higher courts as a lawful way of disposing of adult cases, based on a court's right to suspend sentence.[4] In children's courts, however, probation is recognized and interpreted essentially as a necessary instrument of protection: delinquent children are not considered guilty of crimes but rather as manifesting in their conduct the need for such protection, and the parents of neglected children are to be supervised in the interest of the welfare of their children. Whether for children or adults, "Probation is not to be interpreted as leniency or mercy allowed because the court has been swayed emotionally. It is a form of treatment consciously chosen."[5]

Massachusetts passed a law in 1878 formally establishing the first probation system; other states slowly followed.[6] Since 1900 progress has been nationwide, and a national association to promote probation standards was created in 1907. Much of the interest

---

Tappan, *Juvenile Delinquency;* Teeters and Reinemann, *The Challenge of Delinquency;* and Timasheff, *One Hundred Years of Probation, 1841-1941.*

[2] This is elaborated in *Probation and Related Measures,* pp. 15 ff.

[3] *Ibid.,* p. 4.

[4] Pigeon, *Probation and Parole in Theory and Practice,* p. 82.

[5] *Ibid.,* pp. 82-83.

[6] Detail in Appendix to Timasheff, *op. cit.*

of this group, the National Probation and Parole Association, has been in work with young people.

Some states have placed probation systems under direct court control while others, emphasizing the special skills required, have preferred to vest such control in an administrative agency. In some instances, probation responsibilities are included among the general child welfare services of states and counties.[7] New York State, which had made early use of it, formalized suspended sentence in a statute in 1893 and passed its first probation law in 1901; children were included in the coverage of the law of 1903. A State Probation Commission, established in 1907, had only administrative responsibilities originally but became an advisory body in 1928 and is now known as the Division of Probation, Department of Correction.[8] The New York City probation program in the Children's Court began with the assignment of eighteen probation officers in 1912.

PROBATION AS SOCIAL WORK. Although there are those who do not agree, the view most commonly expressed in professional probation literature is that probation is a form of social work; that it is, in fact, casework and occasionally makes use of group work.[9] It is generally held that

The best of the probation officers . . . are modern trained social workers of high character, skilled in casework and capable of using social resources and giving intensive supervision in cooperation with psychiatrists and psychologists. . . . Probation thus practiced is not leniency but extra-mural treatment in harmony with a demanding program.[10]

[7] Pigeon, *op. cit.*, pp. 90-92.

[8] Details in New York State Department of Correction, Division of Probation, *Manual for Probation Officers,* Chap. I; also Timasheff, *op. cit.*, pp. 51 ff.

[9] Some writers hold that the probation field has not received adequate attention from social work and that, currently, probation skills can be taught either in sociology departments or in schools of social work. See, for example, Reckless, "Training Probation and Parole Personnel," *Focus,* XXVII (March, 1948), 44-48. All those in the probation field recognize that important contributions have been made and will be made by sociology, psychology, etc., although the general position is that social work training is now basic.

[10] Van Waters, "Adult Offenders," in *Social Work Year Book,* 1951, pp. 39-40.

In instances where separation of child from parent is considered neither necessary nor desirable, and where immediate discharge of the case would be unwise, a form of "supportive supervision" may be chosen by the court as an alternative. In probation, social work has developed a way of evaluating cases prior to disposition and of giving treatment content to subsequent supervision.[11]

Intake, case study, and supervision are casework only if undertaken by individuals who have the professional knowledge and skill to understand parent and child, and to contribute to adjustment by helping with environmental and/or internal or relationship problems. In addition, group work and community organization skills, as defined in social work, may supplement these efforts.[12] In contrast, although sometimes labeled as "casework," checking up or policing in the narrowest sense of these terms does not involve this more basic approach.[13]

Increasingly, the trend in the correctional field is toward expansion and intensification of knowledge and use of the casework process. It is generally agreed that this does not mean that cases are not to be referred to other agencies for specified purposes. If probation officers are to be responsible for case study and supervision, as defined above, they must be "social workers, who for work in the courts are called probation officers or probation counsellors."[14] They need generic casework skills, including the ability to make referrals for service as well as to provide guidance within their own agency.

Expressed goals are often far ahead of actual practice, and probation has only occasionally achieved the highest casework standards. Inevitably, varied conclusions and policy implications

[11] Witmer, *Social Work*; Teeters and Reinemann, *op. cit.*, pp. 416 ff.; Grace Abbott, as quoted by Bruno, *Trends in Social Work*, p. 170; National Conference on Prevention and Control of Juvenile Delinquency, *Report on Juvenile Court Administration* (Report 4); Van Waters, *op. cit.*

[12] Dressler, *Probation and Parole*, pp. 7-8 and p. 193.

[13] Witmer, *op. cit.*, p. 409.

[14] *Report on Juvenile Court Administration*, p. 7. See, too, discussion by Hoey of casework as probation in "Social Work: Its Base, Skills, and Relation to Other Fields," *Social Casework*, XXXI (December, 1950), 406, as well as the most recent statement of standards by the National Probation and Parole Association, which describes probation and parole as "part of the general field of public social work."

have been drawn from this fact. Some would be satisfied with otherwise unprepared college graduates who are subsequently given in-service training to orient them as "investigators" or as "big brothers." Others see psychology, sociology, or public administration as suitable preparation for the assignment. Still others recognize probation's relation to casework, but can visualize no way to overcome practical obstacles and recruit trained staff; they would be satisfied with "probation aides." And, finally, there are communities and departments in which major differences of opinion prevail as to future policy because it is not universally recognized that the language, procedures, and structure of a casework service have been adopted, but skilled leadership and staff able to implement a casework program have not been made available. Here, in a sense, casework has done the probation field a serious disservice: a structure has been provided which is valid only given understanding and competence, but the full import of this has not been effectively conveyed to administrators or to the public. Superficial borrowing of terminology and procedures has been facilitated, and desired personnel have not been available when sought.

Despite obstacles, partial successes, and setbacks, juvenile courts can cite probation departments which meet standards for good casework service and can point to successful and highly impressive accomplishments. Through its national organization, the probation movement itself has formally agreed that while many difficulties exist, the soundest basis for development is casework. Thus:

Probation shall mean casework services during a continuance of the case. Probation shall not be ordered or administered as a punishment, but as a measure for the protection, guidance and well-being of the child and his family. Probation methods shall be directed to the discovery and correction of the basic causes of maladjustment and to the development of the child's personality and character, with the aid of the social resources of the community.[15]

[15] National Probation and Parole Association, A *Standard Juvenile Court Act*, Sec. 18.1.

Social work in a court faces some problems very different from those known to the more traditional treatment agencies. For instance: How can law enforcement functions be combined with casework? What are the characteristics of the treatment relationship in an authoritarian setting? How is the staff for such a setting to be trained? Since these and related problems are far from finally solved, an experimental orientation is most necessary. However, even now, certain well-established casework elements have been accepted as basic to any setting and will in all likelihood remain part of any future development.

The Division of Probation in New York State has for some time regarded probation as a casework assignment and in its manual so describes it.[16] Similarly, the New York City Children's Court leadership has held that while probation is a maturing profession, the Court must meet the best casework standards developed to date. Hence, probation practice in the New York City Children's Court may be evaluated on this basis; and this study undertook a casework review of the probation functions with full recognition that there are those who would not consider such standards realistic. The ready availability of casework literature and consensus in the profession make it unnecessary to summarize criteria for good casework at this point.[17] Rather, criteria will be specified in the course of appraising the investigation, case evaluation, referral, planning, and supervisory activities of probation officers.

PROBATION DEPARTMENT PROCEDURE. Two distinct assignments, the study of the case before the judge arrives at a plan and the guidance of children placed on probation by the judge, are charged to the same personnel in the New York City

---

[16] *Manual for Probation Officers*, pp. 232-234. The Acting Chief Probation Officer of the New York City Domestic Relations Court makes a strong case for probation as casework in Leeds, "Probation Work Requires Special Training," *Federal Probation*, XV (June, 1951), 25-28.

[17] The study follows the generally accepted "diagnostic" school of practice in social work rather than the so-called "functional" orientation. The basic concepts and skills referred to are elaborated in the revision of Hamilton, *Theory and Practice of Social Case Work*. The "functional" view about probation is stated by Pray, *Social Work in a Revolutionary Age*.

Children's Court. The probation officer-in-charge in each borough is responsible for case assignment after the judge orders an investigation. In practice, it is the reporting officer in the larger boroughs who maintains a monthly tally sheet and who either calls the appropriate probation officer to the courtroom or forwards to the officer a copy of the petition, on which have been noted significant developments during the hearing and special instructions from the judge.

At the beginning of the month, cases are assigned for investigation strictly in accord with the client's religion and sex. Later in the month, exceptions are frequently made to equalize investigation case loads. This means, in effect, that probation officers conduct investigations of all kinds of cases in all parts of the boroughs to which they are assigned.

When, following investigation (case study), the disposition is probation (in delinquency cases) or parole and supervision (in neglect cases), it is the probation officer-in-charge who makes the assignment. Here, because the contact will be over a longer period of time, deviation from assignment by religion is not permitted except in unusual circumstances or where, as in the smaller boroughs, the staff is small and assignment by religion is not always possible. In Manhattan and Brooklyn an attempt is made to consider geographical allotment of territory as well, but often without success. In other boroughs the need to match the religion of child and officer, as well as the sex—except for younger boys—results in supervision case loads covering the entire borough and requires that officers of different religions make visits in the same neighborhod, often at the same time.

When the officer receives a case for investigation, he is also given a "return date," which is usually about two to four weeks later. The date for the hearing is set by the judge, in consultation with the reporting officer, who, as noted, is responsible for knowing the "court days" of each probation officer. Details of clerical and administrative procedure vary from borough to borough, both as to order of subsequent steps and responsibility assumed by the probation clerk.[18]

Whenever possible, some of the probation officers interview parents and children in cases assigned for investigation immediately after the first court hearing. Some conduct full interviews, others fill out the face sheets, while still others merely make future appointments for home or office interviews. Probation officers are expected to make at least one home visit in the course of an investigation; but not infrequently, because of heavy work loads, case studies are completed on the basis of office interviews alone, supplemented by review of previous court data and reports requested from agencies. More typically, an investigation consists of a brief office contact with parent and child on the day of the first court hearing, a home interview with the parent and child and, quite frequently, school visits and collateral contacts with complainants, neighbors, or others in the community. Children are sometimes called to the office for their major interview.

The probation officer is expected to dictate his investigation report following a standard outline which is somewhat different for neglect cases than for delinquency cases. Because of an almost chronic shortage of clerical staff and consequent typing backlog and because they are often unable to complete investigations far enough in advance to dictate, a considerable number of officers sometimes type their own investigation reports and at other times appear at the court hearing with an oral report. A chronological record of contacts is also dictated in cases which have been assigned to the probation officer for supervision. Special forms are followed in recording court action on cases, whether following investigation or in the course of supervision. The case supervisors,

[18] In general, it is necessary to: fill out cards for the probation case file and for the supervisor's control file; complete a manila folder with the case name and a probation number; fill out the face sheet of a form entitled "Investigation Report"; send a report form to be filled out in the child's school; schedule physical, psychological, and psychiatric examinations ordered by the judge; request clearance from the Social Service Exchange and request from agencies reports listed on the clearance slip which the probation officer wishes.

technically senior probation officers, may examine case records prior to the probation officer's reporting the results of the investigation to the judge, at the time the case is assigned to a probation officer for supervision, or when special problems arise.[19]

The probation officer must thus divide his work week and, indeed, his work day, among case investigations, supervision of delinquent or neglected children, dictation, reporting in the courtroom, conferences with his supervisor and with agency representatives, clerical work, telephoning, and many other duties. Obviously, all these Probation Department (also referred to as the Probation Bureau in the Court and throughout this text) operations cannot be examined simultaneously. Consequently, this report considers the major activities of probation officers one at a time: first, the investigation (case study); then, in a subsequent chapter, the other activities of probation officers as they supervise children on probation, appear in the courtroom, work with their own supervisors, or seek placements for children.

INVESTIGATION (CASE STUDY). Most juvenile courts outside New York City provide for case investigation prior to adjudication.[20] In New York City, in the main, adjudication takes place prior to assignment of the case to the Probation Bureau—very frequently, in fact, on the day the petition is filed. On occasion, the judges exercise their right to adjudicate at a later hearing and order investigation at once. Where case study uncovers new facts, judges may nullify previous findings or order new petitions—as, for instance, a neglect petition against parents in a case which originally came to court because of a child's delinquency,

The term "investigation" is still preferred in the correctional field, although most authorities who stress the casework basis of probation now see the investigation as a "case study" undertaken by probation officers and urge adoption of that term since "case study more nearly expresses the comprehensive type of inquiry

[19] The supervisor's role is discussed in more detail in Chap. VII.

[20] Sussman, *Law of Juvenile Delinquency*, pp. 29-30; also Teeters and Reinemann, *op. cit.*, p. 263.

now considered essential as a basis for treatment."[21] Such study must concentrate on the child's social environment and personality, in an attempt to comprehend the significance of the current situation to him and to his family. Understanding of this kind derives from careful review of social history, current social setting, personality, and interpersonal relations. It makes possible, and should ultimately be formulated in, a case evaluation, "a diagnosis," and is prerequisite to the inauguration of helping measures. Whether these are wisely selected depends on: the ability of the probation officer to understand the child, to evaluate the case data assembled, and to make valid recommendations; the willingness of the judge to consider the probation officer's formulation carefully, without necessarily being bound by it; and the extent to which "disposition" is regarded as a treatment plan based on case study and courtroom observations. The formulation finally accepted may be that of judge, probation officer, psychiatrist, supervisor, or the product of a conference. It may utilize reports of social agencies, examinations, tests and observations by other groups, as well as the Court's own data. To achieve the Court's aims, all these aids to understanding must be employed in a unified strategy for rehabilitation.

Review of investigation records and observation of probation officers' interviews and of courtroom proceedings were undertaken to determine the extent to which case studies by probation officers provide a sound basis for planning in this sense. It was found that case records, however curtailed their dictation, could be used as basic data for study since they represented a fair sample of interview content and of the level of comprehension brought to analysis. A total of 152 probation records, representing recently completed cases in all except the Staten Island court, were carefully analyzed and appraised. The work of 76 different probation officers was involved in these investigations, a reflection of considerable staff turnover, since the average number of probation officers in the field at the time of the study was 60. Several officers later assigned to the Bureau of Adjustment were represented in this sample.

[21] Pigeon, *op. cit.*, p. 249.

The cases reviewed represent a wide range of situations: 87 percent came to the Court initially on delinquency petitions; 71 percent were cases in which the judge made his findings of delinquency or neglect at the first hearing; and the remainder were cases in which the judge made his findings later or decided to dismiss the petition. All religious, age, and ethnic groups in the court population were represented in these cases. Allegations were substantially admitted to the judges or probation officers in 80 percent of the cases and denied in 14 percent, while in the remainder of the cases admission of allegations was not relevant (institutional transfers, etc.). Many of the "admissions" were, of course, accompanied by "explanation" of the circumstances leading to the "offense."[22]

Following investigation and sometimes after several temporary remands and/or adjournments to await necessary reports or examinations, the judge's initial disposition was probation in 58 percent of the cases. This includes neglect cases placed under court "supervision," cases seen in the Court's clinic or other clinics for treatment as part of the probation plan, and cases in which major treatment responsibility was assumed by voluntary social agencies. In 25 percent of the cases, the judge's disposition was placement or commitment for foster home care or institutionalization; or commitment to a mental hospital followed a court remand to a psychiatric hospital for observation. The remaining 17 percent of the cases were dismissed, discharged, suspended by the judge, or received some other initial disposition plan. At times, such disposition was accompanied by referral to another agency.

These data for the case sample vary somewhat from city-wide data in the 1951 Domestic Relations Court *Annual Report*, which

---

[22] In connection with these statistics it should be noted:

1. The proportion of neglect cases in the Court is far higher when one is concerned with petitions than when one examines probation cases alone. Even considering this, the study's case record sample of probation and supervision cases is overweighted with delinquency cases. This overweighting did not characterize the observations of probation officers at work, at which time many interviews on neglect cases were witnessed. There is every evidence, too, that the quality of an officer's work with neglect cases is consistent with that in delinquency situations.

2. Many of the cases not adjudicated at the first hearing are those in which not all parties concerned were available. In effect, then, the cases were adjudicated at the first hearing at which all parties were available.

states that 61 percent of cases investigated in that year were placed on probation, 15 percent were committed, and 23 percent discharged. However, the *Annual Report* lists cases sent by the Court to Kings County Hospital or Bellevue Hospital on remand and later committed from these institutions as discharges, while they are here tabulated as commitments. When this difference is considered, the data are actually quite similar and the sample is found to be sufficiently representative of court dispositions for purposes of evaluation.

APPRAISING THE CASE STUDIES. In most of the investigation reports heard in court or analyzed in the case sample—between 300 and 400 cases—it was apparent that the probation officers tend to fill out the headings in the outline mechanically, avoid recommendations, or make plans which do not clearly follow from analysis of investigation data or from an understanding of what would help one ultimately to emerge as an adjusted individual or, if necessary, be assured of continued community protection. These failings are characteristic of partially trained workers who have mastered devices superficially. Probation officers too often use a case study outline routinely, displaying a lack of dynamic analysis similar to that of the early professional social workers of whom Mary Richmond wrote in 1917: "Case records often show a well made investigation and a plan formulated and carried out, but with no discoverable connection between them." [23]

The need to learn the use of a case study as a dynamic tool rather than as a gesture is recognized as a proper part of the investigator's task in the *Manual for Probation Officers* which emphasizes that:

Investigations and interviews are of no value in themselves. They are only the means to an end. The material contained in an investigation or the facts elicited from an interview must be made to work for the benefit of the treatment processes. "Not only must the facts be assembled, but they must be related to each other logically and interpreted professionally, so that a picture of the individual and his setting emerges in a form ready for use." [24]

[23] Richmond, *Social Diagnosis*, p. 348.
[24] *Manual for Probation Officers*, p. 239, quoting Pigeon, *op. cit.*, pp. 267-268.

One cannot ask less than this of interviews and case studies because less would mean that the selection of services and treatment plans for individual children would not be sound. In analyzing probation practice in detail, it is nonetheless necessary to stress at the outset that the Court cannot now, in the main, employ and retain personnel fully qualified to conduct case studies of such caliber—nor do many other public and private children's services.

The careful examination of probation investigations in the light of professional standards is thus, in a sense, unfair to present incumbents but, nevertheless, necessary to the ultimate aims of the Court. Details of qualifications, salaries, staff supervision, conditions of work, probation administration, which have in the past made it unrealistic to expect staff to manifest higher levels of competence, are elaborated at a later point (Chapter VII). Here it is necessary to stress that professional standards must be employed in looking at practice if the community is to be made aware of the consequences of current provisions in terms of services for children. And, the fact that the children who come to the Children's Court are particularly deprived and represent the failures of many other agencies in the community is only all the more argument for demanding adequate service in the Court. The cycle of failures must be broken.

In general, while the case studies are currently inadequate when judged in terms of the needs of children and the criteria of the *Manual*, this does not mean that useful service is not rendered by probation officers acting as "investigators" in the more traditional sense. Many of the neglect and delinquency cases reveal severe social and personal pathology requiring public intervention. In providing the factual data about the physical conditions under which some children are living, probation officers enable them to be removed from unhealthful and neglectful homes. Officers assemble data about abusive conduct of mentally ill parents, equipping the Court to act. Data about economic problems, school adjustment, or relatives and family life are summarized to provide the necessary factual basis for planning, although such facts are usually not competently appraised, nor placed in logical juxtaposition to one another and evaluated in relation to a plan. These traditional investigation services must be recognized as having value in relation to the Court's role as protector and promoter of child welfare. It seems highly likely, too, that the probation officer as investigator of "facts" and as a kind of "big brother" (Chapter VII) is the model envisaged by those who continue to support current qualifications and to resist completely professional standards and salaries for probation officers.

HOW CASES ARE ANALYZED. The probation officer presents the basic identifying case data on the face sheet of the "Investigation Report" form and is expected to complete a social study, following a standard mimeographed "Outline for Investigation Report." Exact tabulations have been made of the types of data reported in three of the major categories, since these are crucial to planning and reflect most clearly the competence achieved in the social study ("Child's Version and Attitude," "Parental Version and Attitude," "Summary and Recommendations"). The other headings are reviewed more briefly.[25]

Nature of Petition.—The probation officer is instructed to copy the body of the petition verbatim and to record who appeared in court with the child. Following this, he must "note in capital

[25] Thus the Probation Department's own instructions to staff are the starting point for this evaluation. The major headings, to be discussed in sequence, follow:

Nature of Petition	Leisure-time Activities and
Previous Court Record	Special Interests
Bureau of Adjustment Record	Mental and Physical Condition
Family History	Child's Version and Attitude
Home and Neighborhood	Parental Version and Attitude
School	Summary and Recommendations
Religious Affiliation	

The heading "Petitioner's Statement" is not discussed since it is usually omitted, the petitioner's statement being summarized under "Nature of Petition." The heading "Social Agency Record" is not discussed, since all that is usually involved is a listing of agencies reported on the Social Service Exchange clearance slip. Reports, when they are requested, usually arrive after the investigation report is typed and are summarized in the chronological record. In some instances the case reader questioned the probation officer's failure to request certain reports; but, with the many considerations involved, it was difficult to establish objective criteria and determine how often important reports were not requested.

letters the disposition of the Court and any notations the Court may make on the petition." [26] In delinquency cases, corespondents must be listed by name, address, and record number. In neglect cases, since his presence is optional, mention must be made of whether the child was actually in the courtroom.

The outline, as indeed the rest of the record, makes no provision for a picture of the child, family, and family interrelationships as obtained at the first court hearing. Occasionally such data are presented under "Child's Version" or "Parental Version" or the judge's notations give some impressions and are transcribed. In most cases, valuable leads obtained by the judge, reporting officer, or probation officer, if present at the first hearing, are not included in the case history or considered in the total analysis.

Previous Court Record.—The probation officer is instructed to summarize briefly the previous court record of the child involved (delinquency cases) or of any other members of the family (neglect cases). The emphasis is on place, docket number, nature of petition, and disposition.

Quite often, useful leads in previous records are incorporated in the new report, in any of the relevant sections of the case study summary. The probation case folder contains reports of case study and treatment in connection with previous petitions; these too may be requested and examined by the judge during the hearing. At best, this represents valuable continuity in case analysis; but, not infrequently, superficial evaluations are thus uncritically perpetuated.

Bureau of Adjustment Record.—A brief summary of the Bureau of Adjustment contact is to be dictated under this heading.

The probation officer usually draws only on the brief statement of allegations dictated in the Bureau for the use of the petition clerk and often forwarded to the probation officer with a copy of the petition. In more than half of the instances examined, the Bureau of Adjustment record contained important leads about

[26] This and subsequent quotations in this section are from the "Outline for Investigation Report" for delinquency and neglect cases. Each outline is a two-page statement mimeographed by the Court.

family problems and the personalities of parents and child which were not noted by the probation officer either under this heading or elsewhere in the Investigation Report. In some instances, differences between the evaluation by the Bureau of Adjustment worker and that of the probation officer were resolved by ignoring the Bureau of Adjustment record.

Family History.—The outline emphasizes facts about family members: age, birthplace, education, citizenship, length of residence in the city, place of marriage, places of employment, income, data about other children. There is also a request for information about "moral and ethical standards of the home" and the "reactions of various members of the family toward each other." Records of institutionalization of family members are also to be described.

Most of the probation reports summarize facts under family history with varying degrees of completeness. Some have full data about the mother's employment from the time she left school; others give exact details about the marriage of the parents and the school attendance of other children in the family, and so forth. There is little selectivity from the point of view of what would be needed for either analysis of the situation bringing the family to court or the planning in any ultimate court disposition.

Only a minority of the records include under this heading the requested information about relationships in the family, although probation officers occasionally present such data in later sections of the report, either on the basis of their own views or repeating evaluations of the relationships as recorded in reports from other agencies or clinics. In the vast majority of the records there is no evidence of study or understanding of "reactions of various members of the family toward each other," however vital these might be considered in diagnosis or planning dispositions.

Home and Neighborhood.—Instructions call for a description of the size of the home, rental, sleeping arrangements, "and probation officer's observations of conditions in the home." The neighborhood is to be discussed from the point of view of housing, congestion, resources, and delinquency rates.

The data requested are usually well recorded and seem necessary to the planning in many cases. The probation officer's observations about home conditions are often decisive in cases involving neglect petitions and represent the factual basis for many court decisions to remove children from their homes. As one reads many records, however, particularly in connection with delinquency petitions, there emerges the distinct picture of data gathered only because the outline requires it. Thus, almost all records state whether or not there are recreation centers or playgrounds in a child's immediate neighborhood, whether it is a high-delinquency area, whether the neighborhood is congested—but they do not relate these facts to what occurred to, or might be done for, the child. Later, in the summary, these items are listed at random as possible explanations or as helpful to planning, but their significance for the particular child under study is seldom weighed.

School.—For neglect cases, the outline specifies only that the "official school record" is to be included; for delinquents, it asks particularly for attendance and conduct data for a year, including the current term, by months. In addition, the probation officer is to report on the "Child's Attitude towards School." In practice, probation officers supply the maximum data for both groups.

The basic source is a special form sent by the Court to the school; most probation officers dictate the response on the form into the record verbatim. This gives factual data about grades, attendance, and conduct, their worth depending, of course, on the different standards used by teachers. Most of the reports also give valuable data in response to questions about subject disabilities, physical defects, and psychological tests taken by the child. The question about causes of absence is seldom answered well, since it is not clear what is expected and teachers have only limited data. Teachers do, however, mention "truancy," and thus provide important information. Some supply helpful observational material in answer to a question as to whether a child appears "neglected," speaking particularly about a child's clothing and cleanliness or an appearance of poor health and undernourishment. In some instances, however, probation officers seem to interpret the lay use of the term "neglect" in its more technical sense and regard a teacher's reply to this question as confirmation of the need, or lack of need, for legal action against parents. Useful data are generally presented in answer to a question about a child's behavior problems in school.

All of this establishes the child's attitude toward school only by indirection. Only in a minority of the cases are probation officers able to visit the school as part of the investigation, although school contacts are made more often while children are on probation. In some instances, the more skilled probation officers are able to develop, as part of case study, a much fuller understanding of the child's attitude toward school, his relationships to teachers and others, and his problems in getting along in a school, as they reflect and relate to his total personal problems. More often, the discussion of attitudes toward school is limited to a repetition of what a child says about school, particularly about why he truants.

Religious Affiliation.—The outline calls for data about the religion of the children and their parents, the names of churches attended, the regularity of attendance, and the degree of compliance with religious obligations. Facts about baptism are to be obtained and verified where possible. The probation officer is also asked about the "practical meaning of religion" and its "application to everyday experience" by the child.

Probation officers are particularly careful to complete this section of the case study. The facts of a child's religion, baptism, and so on, are necessary because of the legal requirement that cases be assigned to officers of the same religion as the child and that, except where public institutions are used, commitments be made to institutions operated by members of the child's religion, when practicable. The care in completing this section probably also reflects the emphasis placed on religious observance by several of the judges and by the Court as a whole. For instance, the form sent to schools for periodic reports of children already on probation contains the following question: "Has Child Been Registered for Released Time for Religious Instruction?"

It is clear that in a social study a careful appraisal of what religion means in the life of a child or family, as one factor in a total configuration, may well serve as an important index of family stability and ability to cope with a problem, although this will vary considerably among the different religious and ethnic groups in the population and between individual families in the same group. Some of the case histories seek to view religious observance in such a way, but these are in the minority. Most include a routine compilation of the required facts.

Leisure-time Activities and Special Interests.—This topic appears only in the outline for delinquency investigations. Emphasis is on "interests, hobbies, affiliations with organized groups, group adjustment, character of companions, places of recreation."

The reports usually state whether or not a child participates in group and other leisure-time pursuits and list the activities in which he takes part: sports, going to movies, reading comics or books, and so on. To the extent that these data help one see the child as a real individual, they are useful. Often as not, however, this section of the report becomes the mere answering of questions about what a child does or does not like to do in his leisure time, and thus the record again becomes a compilation of unappraised facts. The studies are particularly weak in analyzing a child's "group adjustment" or the "character of his companions," and thus miss potentially helpful clues to his total pattern of interpersonal relationships and his personality.

Mental and Physical Condition.—This section of the outline is apparently meant to combine data about a child's medical and developmental history with a picture of his mental, emotional, and physical condition at the time of the study. The probation officer is instructed to record his own observations and the statements of parents if "no mental or physical report is available."

Probation officers usually record such items of developmental and medical history as early conduct or habit disorders in a child's life and summarize whatever medical, psychiatric, or psychological reports are available at the time. Since many reports are not received until a later date—and, indeed, many of the examinations are not ordered until the court hearing—most of the important data of this kind have to be summarized and filed in the probation folder later.

The medical and developmental data, as recorded, are useful in answering inquiries by the Department of Welfare and other agencies concerned with placement or study of children. Only rarely, however, do probation officers assemble the kind of developmental history implied in the outline and potentially of great value as an index of the child's emotional status and of possible sources of disturbance.

THE LEVEL OF CASE APPRAISAL. Analytic thinking rather than a factual account alone is clearly called for in the instructions for the remaining three sections of the investigation report: "Child's Version and Attitude," "Parental Version and Attitude," and "Summary and Recommendations." Detailed illustration and statistical analysis of these portions of case records therefore provide a more complete and objective basis for judging the quality of probation officers' case studies.

For purposes of this evaluation, four categories of judgment were employed: *Good* analyses were those on a level necessary to sound disposition planning in the sense described above; they showed use of the level of skill and understanding available to competent graduate social workers. *Acceptable* analyses were those which sought to serve the objectives of a social study in presenting material analytically, but they displayed incomplete understanding or mastery of concepts and were successful to a limited extent; they were the kinds of studies which, in many agencies, are characteristic of partially trained personnel who are, nonetheless, soundly oriented as to goals. *Poor* analyses were those which made some gestures toward an approach to case study but failed at even partially analytic presentation; and *completely unsatisfactory* analyses gave nothing but routine, limited, arbitrarily selected and unanalyzed data. These categories are based on available criteria for competent case study as carried on in qualified agencies and institutions, public and private. They represent standards of evaluation clearly implied in the Court's own instructions to probation leaders and in the *Manual*. However they rate in these regards and however incomplete such data may be for truly effective planning, the bulk of the probation case investigations, as already stated, do present useful factual and descriptive data necessary to the Court's day-by-day case decisions.

Questions may well be raised (and have been raised) about (a) the legitimacy of using categories like "unsatisfactory," "acceptable," and so on, and (b) the formulation of conclusions in statistical terms. It would, of course, be preferable to report groupings in terms of service to children and families or only in terms of degree of helpfulness and to say, for instance: "This category includes all cases in which the worker was helpful; the second category represents maximum service," and so on. However, this is not feasible in a study in which, by both necessity and choice (see Appendix), court process and procedures are evaluated but results are not followed up. Moreover, even in a follow-up study, one could perhaps seek to characterize full case studies as "helpful," but this could hardly be attempted for each segment of a case study. The segments are here the units for evaluation because their very examination clarifies in some detail the nature of the current probation work and what it is that better qualified staff will bring.

The percentages are, of course, derivatives of the criteria developed and the methods of analysis (see Appendix). They are to be viewed merely as convenient ways of graphically representing and summarizing the evaluations made and not as having calculating-machine precision in characterizing the work.

Child's Version and Attitude.—The outline asks that for all cases the probation officer indicate the time and place of the interview and the child's "manner and appearance." Beyond this, the delinquency case outline is more detailed than that for neglect cases. In the latter instance, the probation officer is to describe whether the child shows respect and affection for his parents, whether there is more attachment to one parent, the child's complaints, the extent of his desire to remain at home, and his "reaction to situation." In delinquency cases, the probation officer is asked to report particularly on the attitudes of the child toward parents, siblings, others, and toward his family situation. The officer is also to appraise the child's "outstanding characteristics, tractability, response to suggestions and discipline" and to summarize the child's version of the offense.

The entire probation investigation report was reviewed, and statements relevant to the "Child's Version and Attitude," whether or not presented under this particular heading, were considered part of the officer's total appraisal of the child. The headings "Family History" and "Mental and Physical," for example, often yielded such material. Data selected from reports received on the case and incorporated into the case study were also considered part of the probation officer's thinking.[27]

The analysis of the statements of the "Child's Version and Attitude" disclosed that, in terms of the standards described, the distribution of the case sample was as follows:

	Percent
Good	0
Acceptable	7
Poor	44
Completely unsatisfactory	39
Not rated	10
Total	100

A study was considered "completely unsatisfactory" if nowhere in the study the probation officer did more than repeat the allegations and/or give the child's version of the situation or the incident. The addition of detail about the incident or facts about the place of the interview was not considered as improving the report, except under circumstances discussed below. Fully 39 percent of the 152 records analyzed were rated "completely unsatisfactory" in the study of this crucial area. For example:

A 15-year-old boy was brought to court by a detective and adjudicated delinquent because he and two others were accused of beating a 13-year-old boy. One of the group, not this boy, was said to have stabbed the victim, so that hospitalization was necessary. After recording minimal factual detail about the boy's parents, home, neighborhood, religion, recreation, and medical history, the probation officer dis-

[27] A similar procedure was followed in the analysis of the probation officer's reports of the "Parental Version" and of the "Summary and Recommendations," which are described later in the chapter.

cussed the "Child's Version" by limiting himself completely to the "alibi" of the boy and his story of an incident in which he separated several others in a fight. Nothing in the investigation represented an attempt to understand the boy, explain the incident, or clarify the help he needed. When this boy was later placed on probation, the recommendation did not grow out of any conception of how probation could help; and the officer served only as a policeman who checked up, rather than as either caseworker or "big brother."

A 14-year-old boy was brought to court with several friends by a policeman. There were two simultaneous petitions involving purse snatching and mugging. The early section of the case history, as prepared by the officer, contained a good deal of factual data. In the section here under discussion, the officer recorded the boy's version of the incident and his denials. The officer stressed the worthy objective of getting the boy to bring his whole gang in so that "an attempt at redirection might be made." There was, however, no evidence in the record of any real attempt to understand the boy as an individual or his problem. The officer was, therefore, not prepared for a similar petition a few days later. Nor was it possible to understand from the case study why, on the first day he was to report on probation, the boy disclosed that he no longer wished to stay at home.

Many of the reports (44 percent) were rated as containing "poor" analyses in the light of the Court's objectives and—always— the needs of the children involved. As repeatedly indicated, it is felt that little more can be expected of most probation officers in the Children's Court as presently qualified. These were the cases in which the probation officer went a little beyond the mere repetition of allegations or of the child's version of an incident, making a very weak attempt at presenting a personality picture of the child, or a description of his appearance, manner, attitude. In some instances, it was evident that the probation officers felt the obligation to picture the child more clearly but lacked professional skills to do so. There were also instances in which the subsequently received and incorporated reports from the clinic, psychiatrists, or a social agency added an "acceptable" summary of the "Child's Version" to a case study otherwise "poor." By the same criteria, all probation officers who were observed during home or office interviews discussing these matters with parents were rated "poor" or "unsatis-factory."

The discussion of the "Child's Version" in the case of a ten-year-old boy typifies the "poor" group:

The boy, his 13-year-old brother, and a companion broke into a shop and took $100 worth of property, which they sold. After completing the earlier sections of the investigation report in routine fashion, the officer filled the section in question by stating that he found the boy withdrawn and difficult to talk to and that the boy admitted this offense as well as a previous one. Clearly, this description of the officer's impressions of the boy and his behavior in the interview is more useful than a mere discussion of the child's version of the incident. It does not, however, fully serve the objectives of a case study.

The achievement of the Court's objectives would assume, on the part of the probation officers conducting investigations, an ability to obtain and organize data representing an adequate statement about a child's personality, his relation to parents, brothers and sisters, about his situation and the possible meaning in his life experience of the events which brought him to court. In some cases this may require several interviews and collateral contacts—yet less than this cannot be justified in the light of current concepts of diagnosis and disposition planning. Only 7 percent of the records reviewed met standards outlined above as "acceptable." This level of work, considered a reasonable goal in the Court and in other agencies employing partially prepared personnel, is routinely the minimum for passing for students at the halfway mark in graduate social work training after a year of course and field work. (Court staff, it will be recalled, are required to have a year of experience prior to appointment.) Included in the "acceptable" group were several records where a full formulation was not attempted, but was not deemed essential, since there was serious question as to the child's involvement in the incident and the need for court intervention. In limiting himself to the child's version of the incident and his own opinion of the facts, the officer was probably doing all that was called for by the case situation.

One of the most comprehensive analyses in the entire group of cases was made in the case of a 13-year-old boy who was one of five who had broken into a food store and taken $100 in cash, most of which was not recovered. After a far more detailed discussion than is usual of the total family situation and the school status, and routine completion of other sections of the outline, the probation officer began the "Child's Version" by stating that the boy spoke openly of his part in the burglary. Summarizing the details of the incident, the probation officer went on to describe the boy as confused and immature. He saw this reflected in his school difficulty and his inability to adjust to groups. The current and the previous stealing were interpreted as the boy's effort to gain group status. Because he was attached to the mother, he might, it was felt, avoid trouble in the future if permitted to go home. The attempt was made to evaluate a child's personality and relate his difficulty to that evaluation, an approach found only in a small minority of the records.

The "good" category was meant to represent the type of skill fully qualified staff should be able to bring to such an assignment, but none of the cases could be so characterized; as will be seen, the Probation Bureau is not generally able to attract and hold personnel who are qualified to render such service.

Fifteen records (10 percent) were not rated at all, since the case circumstances made the outline inapplicable or the data unavailable. Among them were neglect cases in which the child was not interviewed and some cases where circumstances were such that the probation officer was of the opinion that his function was to "investigate" facts. In the latter connection, it is questionable to assign cases to the Probation Bureau if the offense is deemed casual or if police study is necessary to gather evidence. Once an assignment has been made for case study, however, superficial review of allegations does not seem justifiable, and more complete evaluation is called for.

Parental Version and Attitude.—Following the "Child's Version," the case study turns to the "Parental Version." In addition to describing the place and time of the interview and the manner and appearance of the parents, the probation officer is to discuss their view of the situation (neglect cases) or of the allegations (delinquency cases). The guide then lists the following topics:

"attitude of parents toward each other and toward parenthood; emotional relationship with children, including favoritism, rejection, coddling and disinterestedness. Are parents very lax or over-strict in their discipline and supervision? Plans for future."

The framework for the kind of analysis which most experts in the child welfare field would consider sound, in any attempt to understand a child and to develop disposition plans, is thus provided. Most probation officers, however, seem unable to utilize the opportunity offered by these topics. Their work relative to "Parental Version" could be rated only slightly better than was that for the preceding section:

	Percent
Good	1
Acceptable	13
Poor	44
Completely unsatisfactory	36
Not rated	6
Total	100

In 36 percent of the 152 records analyzed, the probation officer limited himself to the "completely unsatisfactory" procedure of recording the parent's, or both parents', version of the situation, sometimes adding a statement as to the time and place of the interview, often reporting what the parent wanted the judge to do but never what the experience seemed to mean to the parent. For example:

A girl who was soon to be 16 was brought to court by a detective for stealing $125 in cash and several hundred dollars' worth of jewelry from an apartment in which she was living while her parents and police sought her. She had told her boy friend she was leaving home, and he pretended to his mother that she had married him so that she would have shelter while he was in the Army. It was from his home that she disappeared with the money and jewelry.

The probation officer recorded the girl's mother's statement during the interview that all was well until a quarrel about her daughter's friends. The child then disappeared, and the police were notified. There were weekly phone calls from the girl until she returned and told of the stealing. The case study ended without any further picture of the parents, although one would assume that they were very much involved in the girl's decision to leave. It was the Youth House social worker who later described the mother's rigid attitudes about relations of boys and girls and the problems thus created between mother and daughter.

The S.P.C.C. accused a father, reported to be alcoholic and unemployed, of neglect of his daughter, aged 3, and son, aged one. The mother worked to support the family. The S.P.C.C. officer reported a noontime home visit when the father was in bed, the home filthy, the children dirty, and the baby lying on paper covered with urine. Wine and beer bottles were all around. The S.P.C.C. alleged that friends often made late evening visits to play cards, drink, and smoke in the presence of the children. The entire discussion of the parents in the probation officer's case study was limited to the mother's explanation of her working because of her husband's unemployment, her assurance that the children were not left alone, and her statement that her husband was upset at his failure to find work, but was not alcoholic. The father, when seen, convinced the officer he was seeking work. Both parents agreed that the home atmosphere "needs correcting." The probation officer did not go beyond surface statements in his appraisal and saw these people as "responsible individuals." The family's complete breakup and collapse a few months later, requiring placement of the children, suggests the possibility that more accurate appraisal might have led to more immediate and systematic efforts to help.

In 44 percent of these cases, the probation officers went beyond the parental version of allegations and what they wished to do, adding something of how the parents saw the child, their roles in the home, and/or their attitudes toward, and their strictness or laxity with, their children. Selected aspects were covered well in different cases, but no one case wove them all into a full appraisal. In the light of the objectives of the Court, this is considered "poor" work, although it is recognized that it has long been the pattern expected by many in the Court and community and that probation officers as currently qualified cannot generally prepare more complete and adequate analyses.

In the case of a 15-year-old girl, whose mother initiated the Court's delinquency case when she became pregnant, the probation officer recorded in great detail the mother's version of her relationship with her daughter and of her changing attitudes toward the girl's wish to marry an 18-year-old boy. Despite detail about the mother's thinking, there was no independent appraisal by the officer of the mother's views and no attempt to relate them to the problem faced by the Court in arriving at a disposition.

Slightly more case records (13 percent) made "acceptable" presentations of the parents' version than of the child's version of the situation, perhaps reflecting the generally broader experience of social work in looking analytically at adults. These records showed an awareness of the nature of the parent-child relationship and how it might be associated with the problem brought to court, or might be regarded as an avenue for coping with it. Though lacking this awareness, the records of some cases in the group contained sufficient information about the relationship between the parents to convey the feeling tone to which the child was exposed in the family. Cases were classified as "acceptable" as long as the officer wrote a reasonable and plausible analysis or adapted such analysis from an agency report, whether or not the case reader fully agreed with the formulation. In a few instances, the discussion was limited to opinions in the family or the family version of an incident, but the case circumstances were such that this appeared sufficient:

In one case, in which the S.P.C.C. filed a neglect petition, the probation officer followed both the leads in the petition and the judge's comments at the first hearing. He drew a picture of how the mother's disturbed conduct and lack of understanding of the needs of the children led to an unwholesome relationship and the unreasonable behavior stated in the petition.

In another neglect case, in which a father requested court intervention because the mother could not care for the children properly, the officer gave a detailed picture of the parents' marital difficulties over the years, the attitude of each to the court contact, the strengths and weaknesses he believed each might bring to a solution, and the kind of help necessary.

There was only one case characterized by the kind of skilled appraisal of the parent which the Court's own outline implies (classified "good," but an outstanding achievement considering the obstacles).

Summary and Recommendations.—In this crucial section of the case report, data from the entire outline must be selectively summarized, and the probation officer is instructed to give his "own appraisal of the case," to "evaluate the moral and material assets and liabilities and make a definite plan." Where commitment or remand is recommended, the availability of space for the child is to be determined if possible.

This section of the case studies reflects, of course, the characteristics of previous sections. In a large number of cases, the officer fails to make recommendations or suggests plans which can hardly be considered adequate. In several instances, however, good selective use is made of data from psychological, psychiatric, and social work reports from other agencies, and hence the summary is superior to the remainder of the case study.

Under current procedures, only the judge can order psychiatric and psychological examinations. Therefore, when case study indicates the need for such examination, the probation officer must bring his request to the courtroom on the next reporting date. He must make a similar request for psychological and psychiatric study if he wishes to secure placement in any of a large number of institutions. The result is that probation officers very frequently submit case studies with no recommendations except that for psychiatric examination—the recommendation in more than one third of the cases analyzed. Judges adopted the probation officer's recommendations in three quarters of the cases where they were made; but these statistics do not tell whether this action reflected agreement on the basis of careful analysis, confidence in the probation officer, the fact that the usual recommendation called for probation—the most frequent disposition—or the willingness and ability of the officer to "fit the recommendations to the judge."

Appraisal of the "Summary and Recommendations" section in the case sample yielded the following results:

	Percent
Good	3.0
Acceptable	16.0
Poor	37.5
Completely unsatisfactory	37.5
Not rated	6.0
Total	100.0

In case summaries rated as "completely unsatisfactory," the probation officer often merely listed once again some of the facts in the case history, postponed a recommendation pending receipt of certain requested reports, or, more often, suggested the need for psychiatric guidance without specifying the reasons for it. To an unknown extent, the omission of recommendations by probation officers probably reflects the failure of some judges to read case studies and recommendations, or even to discuss the officer's opinion. In this court, as in many others, there are judges who do not wish specific recommendations from probation officers or who are particularly opposed to certain plans (i.e., psychiatric study). In other instances, the judges have not questioned the failure to present recommendations, so the officers omit them. Under such circumstances, probation officers tend to make no effort to present coherent analyses even of the data they themselves have assembled and which, supposedly, justify requesting psychiatric study or waiting for certain reports prior to making plans.

There are, of course, cases which are so complex that a recommendation should not be made prior to discussion with the judge, but the "Summary" should properly present the probation officer's view of why this is so. There are other cases in which there is particular need for psychological and psychiatric study and, since the judge must authorize this, the summary must contain such a recommendation and can go no further. Here too, since the need to use expensive and limited resources is at stake, the considerations must be reviewed. Over a period of time, given a larger and better qualified staff, ways might be found to enable the probation officer to take initiative in scheduling such examinations, when the parties concerned agree. He could then more readily take responsibility for making recommendations on the basis of completed studies. There is substantial evidence that using the recommendation for a psychiatric examination as a climax to a case study, rather than as a tool en route, is for the insecure, unskilled worker a means of circumventing what he cannot undertake, namely, appraisal of the case and recommendations. While this situation is understandable and perhaps even wise as long as staff is only partially qualified, it does not represent a sound arrangement for the future since it minimizes the potential role of an important part of the court team.

The chief characteristic of the records rated "completely unsatisfactory" for their final summaries was the tendency to miss important leads, to weigh "evidence" in relation to allegations, where more was obviously required, or to list facts, versions, opinions, without logically deriving a plan from them, although one might well be suggested. For example:

A 13-year-old boy and one over 16 were the subjects of a petition by another schoolboy who claimed that they had hit him over the head with a "zip" gun in a fight. In studying the background of the 13-year-old, the officer gave details about the father's life, schooling, work and home background. He described the family's apartment in a high-delinquency area and reported that they received free accommodations as superintendents. The school report described the boy as a "somewhat lazy" truant whose classroom work and conduct were "fair." Softball, movies, and radio were listed as his major leisuretime occupations, and note was made of the fact that his church attendance was irregular. Nothing special was said about his physical or mental background. The section of the study on "Child's Version" was restricted to the boy's story of the incident and of the time the police picked him up when he purchased a switch-blade knife for a man who offered him twenty-five cents for the service. The section of the report on "Parental Version" stated only that the boy caused no trouble at home and that his father wished him to have "another chance." The probation officer summarized the case by stating that this was a first offense and that the boy claimed to have been provoked. Without presenting any analytic basis for it and apparently acting intuitively or in terms of the offense, the probation officer suggested probation on the grounds that the boy would be a good subject for rehabilitation.

The father did not appear for the next hearing, and it had to be put off for two days; the judge issued a summons. At the hearing, the judge was angry at the father's excuse and agreed to probation on condition that the Big Brothers would help and that a referral would be made to a Y.M.C.A. A short time after probation began, there was a complaint about the boy loitering in the park and possessing a switch-blade knife and a "zip" gun. The probation officer kept the case from court on the promise of boy and father that there would be improvement—there having been nothing in his case study to indicate such improvement was not possible. It was not until this boy discharged a shotgun with intent to kill that case study by Youth House and Bellevue Hospital revealed the extent of his disturbance and the need for commitment—all evidence of which had been missed in the probation case study.

An equal number of records (37.5 percent) were rated "poor." The probation officer in these instances conceived of his assignment beyond that of listing data, but his efforts were weak. Either facts were not analytically appraised as a basis for a recommendation or attempts at appraisal were awkward and unsuccessful. In a few cases there was evidence that personal bias colored the presentation.

It must be stressed that, because of the limited range of possible dispositions and because psychiatric recommendations are often incorporated, an officer's inadequate summary may well be followed by the best possible recommendation. What is more, in situations of gross mistreatment of children or obvious need to arrange placement, the listing of relevant facts in a summary is all that is required to enable the judge to act. Hence, "poor" summaries may be followed by appropriate courtroom decisions. However, under such circumstances, planning and decision-making are left far too much to chance. Only some of the cases have the benefit of recommendations from a psychiatrist; in all others the kind of case appraisal is needed which will show whether the Court should act on the basis of facts about physical aspects of the home, conduct of the parents, and so forth, or whether other data contraindicate such action. It is necessary, too, to consider how possible plans will be regarded by the various family members and how plans may be introduced most effectively. In short, placement, probation, and psychiatric study must be employed on the basis of understanding and interpreted as treatment devices lest they become what, to children and parents, can seem only like punishment. It has long been recognized that a client's concept of a plan and its interpretation to him are as significant ultimately as its exact details.

The "poor" records are illustrated by the following:

A 14-year-old boy and his 12-year-old friend were adjudged delinquent for stealing a pocketbook from the home of a friend they were visiting. His grandmother had previously brought the 14-year-old to the Bureau of Adjustment because of his truancy, stealing, and remaining away without permission; a referral to a voluntary Big Brother group had been made. The probation officer to whom the case was assigned for investigation compiled a detailed social history. In his final summary, he reviewed the allegations, summarized the Bureau of Adjustment contact, told about the boy's background (the mother had been raped at 16) and why the grandparents raised the child. He concluded that since investigation showed a pattern of delinquency for more than a year and P.A.L. and Big Brothers had been unable to help, placement was necessary. Because the boy spoke of an interest in farm life, the probation officer suggested an institution with a farm. This type of empirical "trial-and-error" procedure in case disposition has long been common in the correctional field and is to be expected of probation officers who are only partially trained. It can hardly be defended, however, since it fails to utilize the best that is currently known about work with young offenders.

Although the case reader may not have agreed with some of the recommendations they embodied, the "Summary and Recommendations" sections of 16 percent of the 152 records were rated "acceptable." In most of these cases there was an attempt which was basically sound—if incomplete and not comprehensive—to relate the child's personality and background to the court situation, and the plan seemed to flow logically from such understanding. Agency and psychiatric reports were often well used. One of the best records in the "acceptable" group is presented as an illustration:

A girl almost 16 was brought to court by her father, who spoke of her as a willful and disobedient girl who kept late hours. During the previous month she had stayed away from home for three days. She admitted two sexual experiences. The probation officer assembled details of how the parents had been separated and how this girl, when chased out by her mother for late hours and rejected by her father, stayed with a stranger until a relative prevailed upon the father to take her in. A full picture was obtained of the conduct complaints by each parent, their attitudes toward their daughter, and what each family member felt should be done. In summarizing the case study, the probation officer pointed to the girl's unhappy existence, with the parents separated and each living in an out-of-wedlock relationship. Although the child wished to return to her mother, who would take her on a promise to improve, the probation officer, exercising independent judgment, weighed all the disturbing factors in the case and suggested placement, the exact type to be determined by psychiatric study.

Four cases in this group were handled in even more competent fashion—an outstanding achievement for the officers involved. In two of these very good use was made of diagnostic material in a guidance clinic report. Six percent of all cases could not be categorized because disposition was dictated by developments prior to the completion of the investigation, or because circumstances were such that a simple factual summary sufficed.

As one observes probation officers interviewing, in home or office, one encounters the various patterns of work reflected in the case studies. Many of the officers begin interviews with casual conversation, but move as rapidly as they can to the case history outline, asking routine questions until the projected report is ready. Their emphasis is on facts, but they do not seem to regard the client's feelings as among the key facts. Some probation officers, too sensitive to "brush off" the wish of a parent to express his feelings, listen carefully, sometimes ask helpful questions, but are then unable to convert the experience into a source of understanding or the beginning of a helping process. A few conduct more skilled interviews and are able, as the tabulations show, to translate their observations into analytic statements which are useful in sound planning.

The long tradition of the probation officer as investigator has left particularly telling marks on some staff members. Not only do they seek facts, they interrogate. They weigh evidence. They care excessively about the details of the offense. They confuse personnel in schools and elsewhere who meet, in different probation officers, significantly different interpretations of the assignment. Their patterns are long established, and their supervisors, while often dissatisfied, are unable to effect basic change.

Unless caseworkers are fully trained, it does not ordinarily occur to them that they must, in all professional contacts, seek to recognize and control their own subjective needs and reactions. It is, therefore, not surprising that the Court's probation officers, most of whom are partially trained or untrained, are often unusually controlling with clients and sometimes quite punishing.[28] Case study, representing considerable invasion of an individual's private feelings and experiences, can be a damaging tool in the hands of the untrained and the unsupervised; the observations which supplemented the case analyses in this study showed the daily misuse of casework tools by large numbers of probation officers—perhaps the majority.

Particularly lacking in the probation staff, as currently qualified, are the interviewing skills which have been developed to a great degree by several professions; interviewing children is a separate, more complex skill and a basic requirement in the Children's Court, yet skillful interviews with children are rarely seen and staff trained to conduct such interviews are generally not available to the Court.

SOME FINAL NOTES. These failures in case study have serious consequences in the form of inadequate planning for many children, questionable choice and initiation of dispositions, and unsuccessful trial-and-error procedures. While it is recognized that probation, as a relatively new professional field, must remain experimental and flexible, much is already known and tested about one of its aspects, case study. There is impressive evidence that case studies in this court do not meet standards of adequacy in the light of knowledge and skill available at the present time to qualified staff and assumed to be necessary by both the *Manual* and the outline for case study distributed in the Court.

Because of the failings of so many probation departments, it is sometimes contended that case studies of the caliber sought are never achieved with respect to so-called "delinquent" children. Yet, the kind of case study needed as the basis for treatment planning was regularly attained with some of these very same cases by social workers at Youth House or in a few particularly skilled social

---

[28] There were too few fully trained probation officers (see Chapter VII) to permit any attempt to correlate levels of achievement with training.

agencies. Such studies were often made at the Court's request, and at times in connection with prior court appearance; since summaries usually appear in the probation folders, comparison is possible. In the instance of Youth House, of course, the child is on remand, and the social worker is able to pull together the observations of a series of staff members so that a fuller case study than could be completed by the probation officer is achieved. The important consideration, however, is not the amount of detail but rather the approach to, and quality of, the study. Unlike those of probation officers, studies by Youth House and a small number of other agencies consistently seek to formulate a dynamic understanding of a child as prerequisite to planning treatment. The crucial differences can be accounted for by the levels of qualifications demanded of staff, salaries, patterns of staff supervision, and definitions of the caseworker's assignment.

Some in the Court have said that probation investigations are constantly improving and that recent in-service training efforts have had their effect, but they agree that a long road is yet to be traveled. There must be recognition that headings of the case study outline are not receptacles for the deposit of random facts, but rather suggestive categories of analysis, to be flexibly used. There must be emphasis, in case study as in treatment, on the fact that the feelings of parents and children have too often been overlooked; plans in which they have no part cannot be successful. A determined effort must be made to end the drift into disposition which is too often the substitute for a plan reflecting a child's needs and a community's best resources.

VII. PROBATION AS TREATMENT

The National Conference on Prevention and Control of Juvenile Delinquency expressed broad consensus in stating:

> Probation treatment . . . is essentially a task of re-orientation, re-education, a process of guidance and reconditioning in which the *relationship* between probation officer and child is the vital element which effects the changes or modifications in attitudes, habit, and environment needed to bring him into closer harmony with the requirements of society. [Italics added.] [1]

As the probation field has matured professionally, there has been increased understanding of the central place of that relationship between probation officer and child. Lectures and even concrete services have little effect without it; advice has meaning only in the context of a relationship in which it is given; and concrete services do not contribute to rehabilitation unless the probationer can "participate in the solution of his own problems. He becomes able to deal with difficulties constructively only by dealing with them, not by blindly following the advice of others." The probationer may need emotional support and help in expressing his fears, his likes and dislikes, at one point in the helping process, while he may require tangible and concrete services at another. [2]

Probation represents different things in different courts. It ranges

[1] National Conference on Prevention and Control of Juvenile Delinquency, *Report 4, Juvenile Court Administration*, p. 16.
[2] Flynn, "Probation and Individualized Service," *Federal Probation*, XIV (June, 1950), 70-76.

from relatively ineffective efforts to supervise or advise children to programs offering considerable help. It includes divers activities, from the unskilled assistance of enthusiastic volunteers to professional social casework, sometimes supplemented by psychiatric treatment. Experience has shown that each approach has value for some cases and that professional work is often profitably supplemented by the help of Big Brothers and other volunteers. There is wide agreement, however, that as knowledge, skill, and adequate staff become available, efforts must be made to render the most effective help by placing treatment responsibility in the hands of personnel who have been suitably prepared in the "application of modern, scientific casework to individuals outside institutions." Such probation workers must have the ability to develop, understand, and control personal relationships with the children they are trying to help.[3]

The professional task of the probation worker is complicated by the court's need to maintain some form of control, such as regular reporting, to assure compliance during the probation period. It has, in fact, been asked whether measures taken for community protection negate treatment endeavors; but analysis of the concept of authority has led to the view that probation authority is different in degree, not in kind, from all other social reality. In almost all casework there is the problem of helping a client deal with the demands and limitations of the social environment (reality), and the worker's ability in this sphere is an indispensable attribute.[4] There is, however, the added fact in probation that the client has, because of his conduct, been particularly singled out for compliance; this often makes the inception of treatment measures especially difficult.

[3] See the quotation from the report of the Wickersham Commission which appears in United Nations, Department of Social Affairs, *Probation and Related Measures*, p. 7. See also *ibid.*, pp. 243 ff.

[4] Dressler, *Probation and Parole*, discusses these matters in great detail. Some have held that his emphasis on policing activities results in a job definition in which the probation officer could not be the kind of caseworker he describes. The New York State *Manual for Probation Officers* states the official position on pp. 242 ff. The theoretical implications of authority in casework are reviewed in Crystal, "Family Casework in Probation," *Federal Probation*, XIII (December, 1949), 47-53.

Any evaluation of probation in practice must begin with the recognition that it grapples with problems of particularly troubled and disturbed people, often living in the midst of severe social pathology. The evaluation must take account, too, of the fact that probation will probably change with experience and refinement of its methods, and that it cannot narrowly apply traditional case-work practice. Nonetheless, in the light of what is known about how people in trouble are assisted, it is reasonable to ask: (a) whether treatment is based on a clearly formulated concept of the problem and of what might help, i.e., on a "diagnosis," in the broad sense of the term; (b) whether the probation officer draws competently on community resources and services as he seeks to help; and (c) whether he succeeds in developing a warm and friendly relationship which is the medium of treatment.

The answer to these questions with respect to the New York City Children's Court is largely negative. Since the same probation officers undertake both case study and treatment, this conclusion is not unexpected. An officer who is not qualified to develop the understanding prerequisite to treatment planning can hardly succeed in the even more difficult tasks involved in treatment itself. What is more, as will be seen, probation officers in the New York City Children's Court have so little time for interviewing children that, under the same circumstances, even well-qualified staff could do little.

THE NATURE OF PROBATION INTERVIEWS. The probation officer is assigned cases for "probation" or "supervision" by the probation officer-in-charge in his borough. Where possible, he receives cases in which he did the original investigation, but requirements relative to religion, sex, geography, and equitable balance of cases, and the preference that neglect cases be assigned to women probation officers, all converge to modify this practice. A substantial number of clients do not continue with the probation officer who originally investigated their cases or who saw them while the case was pending, awaiting completion of examinations and receipt of agency reports.

Court rules would not in themselves seem to be a handicap to the use of reporting as a flexible tool rather than as a rigid routine device. According to directives, delinquent children on probation are to be seen regularly, usually twice a month, in the office or at a so-called "reporting center"; although their parents are to be visited in the home monthly, this is not possible in a majority of cases. In neglect cases, the required monthly home visits with parents are more often observed; but the children are seen only occasionally during these visits. No particular length of time for probation is specified, and the treatment aspect is emphasized; most children on probation have contact with the Court over relatively extended periods.

TABLE 13. *Children Who Completed Probation in 1950-1952 Classified by Duration of Probation*[a]

Duration of Probation and Supervision	1950		1951		1952	
	Number	Percent	Number	Percent	Number	Percent
Under 6 months	595	22	650	18	819	22
Six months—one year	1,084	40	1,333	37	1,421	37
Over one year	1,049	38	1,617	45	1,556	41
Total terminated	2,728	100	3,600	100	3,796	100

[a] Based on data in New York City, Domestic Relations Court, annual reports, 1951-1952. Totals represent *children*, not cases. A given child may appear more than once during a year. Several children may be involved in one (neglect) case.

Home and office interviews.—Interviews conducted by probation officers observed both in the field and in the office illustrate the nature and characteristic problems of probation "treatment":

This was a first visit on a case recently transferred to Mr. A. for supervision. The mother had told the previous officer that her son was now behaving properly, but the school principal had reported to the Probation Department that the boy and his friend were doing "shakedowns" of other boys. The apartment proved to be an extremely disarranged railroad flat in a run-down tenement building. The family, consisting of mother and seven children, received public assistance.

The door was answered only after long knocking, and the "interview" consisted of a conversation conducted while standing, since there was no place to sit in the midst of considerable filth and disarray. In answer to the probation officer's questions, the mother stated that she had been to school to discuss the complaints with the principal. She doubted the charges because her son feared boys of his size. She agreed to go with him to the Reporting Center the following Monday, so that there could be further discussion of the complaint.

When the officer commented on the state of the apartment, the mother remarked that she agreed with the previous probation officer who also said that the place was in bad condition. They had been in the apartment ten years, and it was impossible to get repairs made. There were leaks; there was no heat. She hoped to obtain an apartment in public housing and had been asking for it a long time. Mr. A. asked permission to discuss housing with the Home Relief investigator. He indicated concern with the health of the children and the mother's management problems. The mother said that her 16-year-old son might seek work. She had been to court about the injury of one of the children and hoped to collect damages. She had also been called to court about a loan which had not been repaid when her husband died. In leaving, the probation officer urged that she discuss the matter of winter clothing with the Department of Welfare representative and ask for an extra food allowance for a thin, sickly son.

A visit to the principal at the school next door revealed that the deceased father had been superintendent of the apartment house and assistant custodian at the school; but since he drank constantly, the family required public assistance. The principal felt that the boy would "become a criminal" if something were not done. His reputation was so bad, teachers no longer tried to work with him. He had entered the school building illegally a number of times to do damage, truanted frequently, and did not learn. The probation officer agreed to see the boy weekly and to ask the judge to consider placing him in an institution. He urged the principal to give these details about the boy in court if the judge considered placement.

When observed in this and in other cases, the probation officer proceeded empirically, used available resources, listened attentively, and noted facts; however, his analysis of the problem and the plan he made were readily altered by the person last interviewed. Faced by a family which has been known to many social agencies, his plans reflected immediate pressure, and he was unable to use the interview to increase the understanding of the family's needs in significant measure or begin to develop a plan which, for once, might alter the situation.

Some of the probation work observed was on the level of "friendly visiting," adequate perhaps where only encouragement is needed but falling far short of what is required in more involved situations. Such contact is illustrated by the following:

While walking with a friend, the boy in this case accepted his suggestion that they break into a gas station. The father was epileptic and the boy himself had a heart condition, so that he was on the school suspense register. However, he was permitted to do light work and was quite successful in getting jobs. What usually happened was that the employer would learn his correct age, and he would be dropped because he was under 16. The probation officer told the observer that he believed that the boy was doing nicely; he had been on probation for six months, and this was a routine visit. In a short time, discharge could be expected. The probation officer did not believe he could do much for a youth with a rheumatic heart.

The family supported itself by taking care of a tenement house; at the time of the visit, the mother, the boy, and a sister were at home in an extremely dilapidated and crowded flat. The boy was just dressing and explained that he had again lost his job because his age was discovered. The mother gave very good reports of her son's health while he was working and of his help around the house. She spoke in some detail about the husband's recent epileptic seizures and her own difficulties with arthritis. However, they had continued with their job as superintendents to avoid asking Department of Welfare assistance. The probation officer's activity consisted largely of friendly conversation with the family members and general encouragement of the probationer to find a new job and to check on his health. He held out the possibility of an early discharge from probation. His approach failed to make real use of the opportunity of probation to help a handicapped boy develop long-range plans for employment and for other aspects of his life, despite evidence of need for assistance in this sphere.

In many delinquency cases, and typically in neglect cases, home visits are characterized by moralizing, advice-giving, and warning, although the probation officer has only superficial contact with the family:

On a monthly home visit in a case brought to court by the S.P.C.C.,
Mr. B. rang the bell at 9:30 A.M. and found the mother at home with
her several children. He looked about, asked the identities of the
children, and checked on the school record of the older girl. He then
asked about the whereabouts of the father of the youngest out-of-
wedlock child, with whom there had been severe quarreling. The
mother explained that he was back in the household, saying, "He
needs me and I need him." The probation officer dropped this topic
to remind her that she had promised to do something about getting
better furniture so that the older daughter, aged 15, could have guests.
The mother agreed to do what she could. The probation officer,
in the midst of a family situation characterized by financial need,
quarrels between the mother and the man with whom she lived, and
behavior problems in two of the children, devoted most of his time
to a lecture about how the girl must be able to entertain friends. He
asked further questions and before leaving reminded the mother of
what he called her "obligations."

Another visit by the observer indicated the superficiality of
many contacts with children as well as the obstacles inherent in
interviewing in the home. Important failings were revealed, but
ability to pick up some leads was noted in the case of a boy who
within a few months was to take part in a serious robbery:

The case originally came to court on the mother's complaint of
incorrigibility. The mother was out, but the father, who works evenings, was at home, an apartment in a very dilapidated two-story
building. The probation officer was visiting in response to the mother's
telephone call that the boy was in trouble at home and because he
had not reported to probation. As the interview began, the father
said that the mother had telephoned only to frighten their son, since
he had been doing some stealing at home, but this had not recurred.
The probation officer replied that he was happy to hear this and
asked to see the youngster, who was tall and in many ways effeminate.
The boy, when questioned in the presence of his father, was sullen.
He said he was getting along and explained that he did not report
to probation because he had not received a specific notification of
when to report. He liked to spend his leisure time at home. The probation officer encouraged him to join the P.A.L. and take part in
activities to "learn to get along with others." The boy seemed to
think the P.A.L. silly and said that he had tried such activities and

did not like them. Asked about his plans, he said he had applied to the High School of Music and Art to study art and voice.

Leaving the home, the probation officer indicated his awareness of this boy's effeminate characteristics and personal peculiarities and that he was considering a referral for clinical study. However, nothing in the contact in the home was directed toward further clarifying for himself the need for clinical study. It was, perhaps, the need to obtain the judge's agreement to referral which delayed preparation of child and parent for such a step. To the participants it could only seem as though the probation officer was "checking up" and giving some questionable advice.

A warm and trusting relationship between a probation officer and a child is occasionally observed, giving evidence that positive work can, indeed, be done and is done by some workers. There are a limited number of important probation successes on the part of some on the staff, but it was observed that these officers relate well to some children and not to others, much as does the layman. Whether they can offer useful service is a chance matter and depends on whether a child fits into their particular patterns of personal preferences and needs. Other officers—they are in the minority—have a broader range and are beginning to learn to use and control their relationships professionally, but most of them would require further help from supervisors and court training programs before they would be able to render consistently good service. Mr. C. is in this latter group and has, since this study, left the Court to complete his training:

Mr. C. begins each day by coming to the office to get messages and reports and to make telephone calls. He was ready to go out into the field at 9:50 A.M. when one of the boys on his case load was brought in on a new petition. He saw the boy and his mother, but had to ask about the nature of the petition. The boy had been picked up on suspicion of robbing children in the park, but told the probation officer that he was not the offender, and accounted for his time that afternoon. In fact, he had telephoned the probation officer two days previously to tell about the incident, but the probation officer had been out in the field. Four youths had held up a child, and this boy's name was given as one of those involved. His mother said that she wanted to believe her son "because he is so nice at home," but she knew he had truanted that day. The observer noted that this boy had confidence in his probation officer and knew that the latter would understand and believe him. There was a sense of trust and warmth. Mr. C. reminded him about their last talk a few days before and how serious it could be for him if he were truly involved. They would now have to go up to court. The mother was questioned about her other son, who was missing, and the boy said he did not know where his brother was. Mr. C. also talked to the boy alone and reminded him that he was helping him and wanted the truth. The boy kept to his story.

In reviewing the situation with the observer, Mr. C. revealed that he had thought considerably about the case. The previous probation officer had pointed out that this mother seemed to "need" a delinquent son, because of her own neurotic problems. Mr. C. said that the neighborhood was a bad one, and this boy was already known as having a poor reputation. The Park Department Recreation Center Director, who supervised the pool, tried to control the boys in the neighborhood and seemed to have this boy on his list as somebody causing trouble. This may explain how his name entered the case.

Mr. C. decided to delay going into the field in order to remain in court until the hearing took place. In discussing the neighborhood, he told the observer about four antisocial gangs. This boy was a member of one of the gangs which disbanded, but he had not seemed able to live down his reputation. He might be involved in more trouble but Mr. C. did not know. What is more, the mother seemed to say the right things and grant surface needs, but kept picking on her son and by no means understood what was going on beneath the surface.

The court hearing was brief since the detective wanted to return with a witness, and Mr. C. was then ready to go into the field.

In this, as in many cases involving delinquency petitions, the probation officer is faced with the problem of either weaning a child away from the group, so that he may develop new norms, or trying to redirect the group itself. Occasionally, a probation officer is able to take some initiative in relation to a total group, and there have been enough successes to suggest how important this aspect could be; but the pattern of probation work in New York City does not usually permit such attempts, and it is doubtful that a program of individualized services should. In this city, work with teen-age gangs is considered to be the province of the Juvenile Aid Bureau, P.A.L., the Youth Board, and, at one time, the Welfare Council.

"Reporting" to the probation officer.—To make it possible for overburdened staff members to see all the children assigned to them, the device of the reporting center was adopted, and it has developed chiefly in Manhattan. Usually one afternoon a week, but sometimes only twice a month, the probation officer has use of a room in a library, church, or community center, and a fixed portion of all "delinquent" children on probation to him arrive in a steady stream after school to report. The reporting center idea is currently not favored by most Probation Bureau supervisors, and where possible, reporting days are scheduled in the probation officer's own office.

Whether in the office or reporting center, probation work in no sense resembles the leisurely casework process of other agencies. There are no appointments, regular hour-long interviews, or fixed settings for work with a child. It was estimated by a Probation Bureau member a few years ago that probation interviews with boys in New York City consisted in most cases of semimonthly interviews, two to ten minutes long.[5] Even if the estimate is extreme and children are seen ten or twelve minutes each time—the estimate of this study—the contacts remain of negligible length. More than any other this one key fact reflects the essence of the probation problem in New York City. Court responsibilities cannot be fulfilled if most children are seen only five to twenty minutes a month, one to four hours a year, with many missing reporting dates altogether. It is little wonder that the more perceptive probation officers and supervisors view the task with a sense of frustration.

A more detailed description of probation "reporting" under present circumstances will underscore its limitations. The following is a brief summary of an afternoon—3:30 P.M. to 6:30 P.M.—spent at a reporting center with a young probation officer considered by his superiors as among the most competent. He is deeply inter-

[5] Brick, "A Study of Twenty Boys Who Were Committed to the New York State Training School for Boys through the Manhattan Children's Court," p. 86.

ested in the work and is eager for further professional training. Boys report to him twice a month in an attractive room in a public library, coming when they can, in no special order, and being seen in order of arrival. They wait in one room, or the corridor, and are seen in another.

Six boys were already present when Mr. D. arrived and many more arrived within a short time. At any given moment, a group of boys were waiting around, often running in the corridors and quarreling about who was next. Several presented reasons why they could not wait. Twenty-one different "interviews" took place in three hours, an average of nine minutes per contact, if no time is allowed for interruptions, of which there were several. Two or three interviews lasted fifteen or twenty minutes, cutting the time for the others.

On an average day, thirty boys are scheduled to see this probation officer at the reporting center, but only twenty appear. (Quite typically, many children on probation miss reporting days and require follow-up. Busy probation officers constantly have cases which they have not had time to follow.) The probation officer explained to the observer that, under the rules, the boys must show him their special school report cards each time. To avoid a too routine contact he tries not to begin an interview by referring to the card. When possible, he invites boys to the Boys Club where he is active, and refers many of them to a vocational guidance center. Occasionally, he gets several of the boys together to study rules of good conduct (see below) or to go to a ball game.

Characteristic interviews selected from the twenty-one conducted during the afternoon follow. The first lasted about ten minutes:

As soon as the 15-year-old boy had been greeted and sat down, he was asked: "What do you do for fun?" When the boy answered that he played football, he was asked where and with whom. He was then asked how his mother was and he replied that she still had a cold. The probation officer said that he had seen the father and was told that the boy was doing well. He wanted to know if the boy agreed, and received an affirmative answer. He was also told that things were all right in school. Then, in a rather formal fashion, the probation officer said: "We have noticed a great deal of improvement since you are on probation. I am happy about that and about your school record. If it continues, we can stop the probation. I guess that would break your heart." The boy replied: "No, sir."

The probation officer then said: "There are a few things we've tried to cover since you have been on probation. I want you to look over this and tell me what it means to you." The boy was given a chart which he studied. He then said that it meant that he should avoid bad habits. The probation officer reviewed with him, as though it were a lesson to be learned by rote, the value of good health, sports, and good food. He told the boy that they would go over one or two of the charts each week. He hoped that probation would give the boy better standards. He wanted the boy to see probation as "a kind of friendship" to help him.

Before the interview ended, the probation officer examined the school attendance card. The boy was notified of a group trip to a football game the following Sunday. He had planned a museum trip that day with some friends and was praised for it.

This probation officer, a conscientious, polite, soft-spoken young man, makes a good model for these boys; he conveys his warmth effectively. He realizes that the boys, who are members of an underprivileged minority, often lack standards of conduct to which they can turn; he feels that, as a member of their group, he should provide such standards. After the interview he showed the observer the charts dealing with health, loyalty, and good habits, which he had copied for use in the Court. Later, the officer said that these charts were not used with any other boys that day since there were so many to be seen.

The second interview took twenty minutes:

The boy was about 15 years old and large for his age. His interview began with a question about recreation. Learning that the probationer was a member of a team, the probation officer asked for details. When the boy was asked whether he wished to go to the football game, he said at first that he had to sing in the church choir that day, but then remembered that this was not a Sunday when the choir would perform. The probation officer showed him the report received from the school (forms are sent regularly) and told him that he was pleased with this good record. He asked whether the mother was working and then if the boy had discussed his being on probation with her. The boy said that his mother had made it clear that it was not proper for him, at his age, to have sex relations with girls. The probation officer tried to combine assurances that sexual impulses are natural with explanation of why the boy had to be careful. He apparently had discussed this with the youth at length and expected him to give proper answers to questions about venereal disease and about why young people should abstain from sexual relations. The boy could only talk about the danger of pregnancy. In response to a question, he said that his class in school had not yet had sex education courses. A woman had given lectures about "facts of life" at the Community Center club. The probation officer again discussed positive aspects of sex while listing limitations and dangers young people must consider, stressing that the boy was too young to assume responsibility for a family. He offered to bring him some literature which they could subsequently discuss.

After the probation officer checked the school record card, the boy wanted to know when probation would end. The probation officer replied that he hoped it could end as soon as the "basic information" was covered, that probation was not merely a matter of reporting but also an opportunity to talk over problems, and that would take time. "It is not punishment, but help," he said. He told the boy he especially wanted to help him because, with his father deceased, there was no man in the home. He asked the boy to explain that fact to his mother.

The boy then indicated that he was troubled because the girl with whom he was involved had told people in the neighborhood that he was the father of her baby. The probation officer assured him that the Court was on his side in denying it, "But I will be glad to go into your feelings, if you wish." The boy explained that occasionally he meets the girl's grandmother, who asks how his child is, embarrassing him. The probation officer said that of course he could not change that, but the record was clear. He would see what he could do about the boy's "attitude to the experience." In response to questions the boy said that his close friends knew it was not his baby, but that others teased him. Since he was on probation, he did not hit back. The probation officer encouraged him to "put the gloves on with them at the Boy's Club, if necessary," and not "hold it in."

It was clear that these two boys felt friendly to the probation officer and were sincere with him. The third boy, by contrast, was impatient with the whole procedure. All the boys present that day were accustomed to being dismissed rapidly and seemed to regard spontaneous discussion as out of place and prolonged questioning as tantamount to suspicion. Brief question-and-answer checking-up characterized many of the contacts:

Asked how he was doing, the third boy replied, "O.K." When asked what was on his mind, he made it clear that he was angry and wanted to go home. He said, in response to another question, that he felt "all right," and then said, "I know what you want to know. I am not in any trouble." He asked if the probation officer had seen his father, as planned at the last interview; when given a negative reply, he said that his mother could get a message to his father, who lived apart from the family. The probation officer did not explore the concern about the father at all, and merely indicated that the father had promised to come to the office. The boy repeated that there was no trouble.

This boy too was asked about his recreation, and he told about playing basketball. He was asked if he had anything to discuss, and replied, "No." He said that his mother was "all right." He was not interested in going to the football game. The boy asked the probation officer how he was "doing" (referring to the school report and using the officer's own characteristic phrasing), and the question was turned back to him. He thought he was doing better, but did not know what the teacher thought.

To many of the boys, this officer is somebody friendly who gives lectures and "checks up"; but in several cases he seems prepared to go further and make referrals for training or vocational guidance. While following his usual routine of inquiring about recreation, school, and family, he gives specific encouragement to a boy's apparent talent or interest, such as music. In one case, noting a teacher's comment that a boy seemed to be constantly fighting authority and required psychiatric study, the officer called the boy's attention to the many occasions when he seemed to be adjusting but then got into new trouble. He prepared him for psychiatric study by suggesting the need for an outsider to sit down with them and "figure out" why such trouble occurred.

The officer interviewed a number of boys who had been written to after missing previous appointments; in several instances, they had been in trouble since the last interview, and he discussed the new complaints with them. He told two of them that they had not followed his instructions, and the matter was now out of his hands; they were to report to court with their mothers to see the judge. Apparently not aware that he might have upset them by this news, he proceeded to invite them to join the group at the football game; they were not interested.

Three of the interviews included family members in addition to the child on probation: a disturbed boy of eleven, who was still truanting, was brought in by his sister who was told that a new court appearance would be necessary; a mother came in because the officer's plan to get working papers for her sixteen-year-old son seemed to threaten her relief grant; a father wished to discuss restitution for damage done by his son.

Although generally satisfied with his approach to work with children, this probation officer realizes that seeing the boys briefly twice a month is extremely superficial. To the extent that his schedule allows, he selects two or three cases for more frequent and intensive contacts, and his supervisor and the court psychiatrist give him special guidance for these cases. This supervision improves the specific service to a few children and contributes to the officer's own professional development.

When probation officers make use of their own offices instead of the reporting center, the details may vary, but the impact is the same. Some officers specify four days per month rather than two for children on probation to appear in the office, so that fewer children will come on any one day. To see all the children, an officer may work an hour or two after court closing time. In the larger boroughs, there are many children sitting on benches outside the offices or waiting in the corridors most afternoons of the week. In the other boroughs there is less crowding, but the group of children waiting is still considerable. At best, there are several children sitting and reading or talking quietly as they wait outside the office. At its not infrequent worst, there is a line of boys outside the officer's little cubbyhole—enclosed by a glass partition which does not reach the ceiling—constantly opening the door, asking to be seen. The contact is brief and semipublic, consisting of superficial checking up on a child to whom it is nothing but "reporting," in the narrowest sense.

Some officers arrange special office interviews with selected children, while others continue to do no more than look at the school report. A few may even say to the children, "If you do all right, we'll be real friends; if not, we'll be real enemies." [6]

As already noted, each child on probation carries a school report card on which the teacher is expected to fill in a daily grade and attendance report. The probation officer examines this card whenever a child reports and supplements this procedure by the request, every few months, that the teacher send a more extensive progress report. Examination of these reports is an important phase of most interviews in the office or elsewhere; since a very large number of probationers regularly lose their report cards, replacing cards become a routine activity.

PROBATION "TREATMENT" AS DESCRIBED IN CASE RECORDS. In order to follow a single case over a period of time and to test observational impressions against statistical tabulation, a representative group of probation "treatment" records was studied.[7] The case record analyses verified the conclusions drawn from the observations: probation "treatment" fails in most of its efforts and, in the main, is not an effective program for helping children who are brought to court.

Of the 152 records in this group analyzed in detail, 89 cases were placed on probation or under supervision by the judge, a ratio close to that in the entire court for 1951 (61 percent compared with 63 percent). The remaining cases in the group included 18 "pending" cases which had awaited final disposition action for considerable periods of time after initial case study. Of all the pending cases, these 18 in particular, by their description of efforts to secure placement facilities or to make alternate plans, were most revealing not only as to the resourcefulness and competence of the probation

---

[6] This self-same phrase, used by a few probation officers, was found in an earlier study (Kahn, *Police and Children*) to be popular with police officers in the Juvenile Aid Bureau.

[7] By checking records in cases which were observed, it was established that the dictated recording accurately reflects the content and quality of interviews.

officer, but also as to the lack of facilities on which the Court must depend.

While it had been expected that the probation cases could be classified into groups revealing varying degrees of competence and different approaches to probation treatment, this proved to be possible only in a limited sense. In the group of 89 there were 22 cases in which the period of probation was very brief prior to commitment or discharge, so that the worker's pattern of probation was not revealed, or in which major treatment responsibility while the child was on probation was carried by the court clinic or a voluntary agency and the probation status was only technical. In several other cases there was incomplete dictation of the officer's interviews and for this reason they could not be appraised. Many of the other cases (57) showed a pattern of probation supervision which could in no sense be characterized as treatment, guidance, rehabilitation, skilled referral, or, in most instances, even careful checking up. Ten of the records in the group of 89 reflected a somewhat more competent approach to supervision of cases, but only two of these could be said to demonstrate the kind of helping role a qualified probation officer should regularly fulfill—and one of these was a brief contact.[8]

In terms of the categories used in the previous chapter to characterize the case studies, the appraisal of probation treatment might be summarized as follows:

Good	2
Acceptable and poor	8
Completely unsatisfactory	57
Not rated	22
Total	89

[8] Probation reports, at the request of the Division of Probation in Albany, New York, classify terminated probation cases as "improved" or "unimproved," and two thirds of the cases tend to be classified as "improved." However, many probation officers classify cases as "improved" if there have been no reports of repeated offenses and no commitment, so that the Court can take the initiative in terminating supervision. Many cases so classified are in no sense improved and soon require new services of the Court or of other community agencies.

Although, to the extent they could be identified, effort has been made to describe different levels of skill, the findings were such that, inevitably, the main task is to report on the nature of uniformly inadequate service rendered to children and their families. In general, the records show that the officer's conception of his major duty is to "check up" on children and parents. He asks whether a child has been to school, what his favorite games are, whether he goes to church, whether he avoids his codelinquents, and whether he has stayed out of trouble. Beyond that, contacts usually consist of random advice-giving and warning about the consequences of further infractions of the law. Referrals for the services of other public and private agencies are decided without careful consideration of the total case and are often awkwardly initiated.

The details may vary, as may the consequences, but the following suggests the general trend:

A 14-year-old boy was brought to court by a Juvenile Aid Bureau officer after he had stabbed a 12-year-old child in the shoulder with a pocketknife. Seven prior minor offenses were known to the J.A.B. The boy admitted the stabbing but claimed it was an accident. He was remanded to Youth House during the period of probation investigation. The latter proved largely limited to matters of fact, giving background details such as the following: The family consisted of a widowed mother and five children, whose income depended on the salary of one son, social security, and insurance. All attended church regularly. There was a school record of truancy, bad conduct, and repeating grades. The boy attended a settlement house frequently, liked to read, and often got odd jobs. His physical condition seemed good. No appraisal of the boy was made by the probation officer, whose final summary merely stated that the 14-year-old had told him that the younger boy annoyed him and that the stabbing was an "accident." The mother was thought to be "protective," since she knew of his trouble in the neighborhood but considered him a model boy at home. The officer's final recommendation for probation followed a summary of such detail; he noted, too, that the boy spoke of a dislike for school, where he had been teased since having failed. The mother was said to be eager to help him adjust.

The case was assigned to another experienced member of the

probation staff for supervision. Youth House provided further details about the family, and the psychiatrist recommended a fresh start in a new school.

The complete case record entry made by the officer after the first contact reads: "Boy reported. P.O. feels good relationship is possible, boy promises cooperation. Will attend school and church regularly and avoid questionable associations."

The five subsequent contacts were on the same level, and a referral was made to a recreation center. Three months after the probation period began and after six contacts the officer reported: "P.O. takes every advantage to praise him for his effort and it gives him pleasure and feeling of security. Mother seen in home on ——, is a pleasant woman and promises cooperation . . . situation very hopeful."

A probation violation was reported a few days later: the boy and some friends broke into the recreation center and damaged some property; he stayed away from home several days. It was also contended that he was one of three boys who "molested" a girl. The judge considered commitment, and the institution accepted the case; but mother and son were convincing, and a referral was made to a guidance clinic. Within six weeks, the boy was involved in a burglary and several other offenses. His mother "threw up her hands," and he was committed.

Of particular note is not the new offense, since even highly competent probation officers have failures in a field in which much is yet to be learned, but the fact that a probation officer talks about a relationship while he merely has a child "report," in the literal sense, "checks up," and then adds a "pep talk." Neither probation officer in this case understood the child at all or had any meaningful relationship with him.

A 10-year-old boy came to court for a second time after having broken into a store with his older brother and a 13-year-old. They stole $100 worth of property, keeping some and giving some away. Judgment had been suspended on the previous petition when it was decided that his record was good and his role in a "shakedown," minor. The investigation yielded substantial factual data; the school reported behavior problems and agreed that a psychiatric study would help. No picture of relationships in the family was given by the probation officer who did the investigation, but the boy was described as "withdrawn and difficult to talk to." At the time of a remand in January after the first offense, the Youth House social worker noted particularly the boy's controlled aggression and fear of adults; psychiatric study had been urged. After the new remand in March, the Youth House social work report called attention to earlier Youth House and Court Clinic suggestions for referrals. They noted that he was a "mass of hostility" on arrival and was glad for the remand because if he had gone to school, "someone would have been killed." He was described as a boy greatly in need of emotional support, since he interpreted denial or frustration by adults as an attack. It was felt that he could eventually learn to relate if helped in a controlled but nonpunitive institution.

The probation officer's final summary was largely descriptive; he was convinced that the father was now alert to the problem and could control his younger son if the older brother were not there. However, since Youth House had suggested it, psychiatric study was now recommended by the probation officer. The judge placed the boy on probation and ordered a psychiatric examination in the Court Clinic. The Youth House warning about the need for a controlled environment was ignored.

Probation was ordered in April, and the boy was seen by the same probation officer in May. The older brother, also on probation, came in with him and there was a brief "checking up." There then occurred a transfer of officers; the boy was tested psychologically and examined psychiatrically in July but not seen by a probation officer. The Court Clinic made a diagnosis of "behavior disorder, schizoid trends" and suggested referral for remedial work in school subjects and "socially desirable value experiences," but the probation officer was not actually to see his probationer until October. Between July and the end of October his brother was seen three times, saying on each occasion that there had been no trouble of any kind. Two visits were made, but no one was at home. The father responded to notes by telephoning twice and giving favorable reports. Finally, since appointments were not being kept, the probation officer went to school to meet the boy and to get a report about "fights." After a brief discussion in November, the older brother, a mental defective in need of placement, was dropped from probation since it seemed of little use and since the father opposed placement. There was another checking-up session at school in December. Two January home visits (a year after the first contact) were unsuccessful and notes were ignored, but the school reported that things were "all right." The boy was finally seen in the office once in January and once in February to discuss the usual areas involved in checking up: school, recreation, church. He was asked, too, about his brother. The officer felt that his probationer was "getting along all right considering the environment" and planned to recommend discharge of the boy, except that nobody was found at home on a "final visit." Two weeks later there was a new petition and a new remand to Youth House, a little less than a year after the second petition. The boy had brought a bayonet to school concealed under his clothing, intending, he said, to kill another student. Interviews with school authorities and with the probationer indicated that he meant it and was relieved to be under control. This time the commitment recommendation was followed.

The bayonet makes this story more dramatic than most, but like many others it is a case in which many community services failed. The summary serves to accent characteristic court problems: changes of officers in midstream; periods of no contact; busy schedules of probation officers who cannot adequately determine why a child does not report; neglect of important leads in agency reports; extremely complex situations in which difficult decisions must be made; and, finally, the persistent motif of superficiality in contacts with children and their families.

Analysis of several other cases in the large group served poorly, or only partially, rounds out the picture and further clarifies some of the problems:

After a year and a half of probation, a girl, by then 17, was discharged because periodic inquiry revealed no new difficulty. Psychiatric recommendations and medical needs due to asthma were ignored. The mother became stricter, and the daughter's sexual delinquency was said to have ceased.

In the case of an 11-year-old boy adjudicated as delinquent, agency reports revealed need for specific medical service as well as follow-up on possible help with personality difficulties. As is often the situation, the probation officer who did the original investigation, received and recorded these reports, was not the one to whom the case was assigned for probation. In eight months of probation, the new officer helped the family with housing and obeyed the judge's directives by emphasizing religious instruction and getting the boy to participate in "released time." The rest was a matter of checking up, all other needs mentioned in the reports being ignored.

A year-long contact with a girl gang member diagnosed as "behavior disorder with trends of an anxiety neurosis" is typified in this quotation from a record entry by the probation officer: "P.O. cautioned the child against being impudent and getting into street fights. ———— said she would try to improve her behavior."

Most of the records in the ten cases that were somewhat better served still did not reflect levels of treatment which could be considered a good standard for future probation work in the Court. Here, probation officers went beyond narrowly conceived policing and checking up, although the law enforcement aspect remained an ever-present component of the job. There was more personal friendliness in these contacts; and referrals, while seldom handled with the skill which might prepare a client to use an agency's services and an agency to understand how best to serve, showed more understanding of specific needs. In a few cases, adequate emotional support was given to family members as placement plans were worked out:

In one of the best cases in the entire group, an obese girl, suffering from strabismus, misled by the wrong companions but fond of her family, found understanding support in two of her three successive probation officers. The officers apparently studied the psychiatrist's analysis and were able to follow the leads indicated. At the same time, the home situation improved in several important ways. Despite some setbacks, this girl clearly gained from her probation period.

A contrast in skills is found in a case seen by one probation officer for a year and then transferred to another for five months. The first officer interpreted her assignment as giving support and reassurance; but her methods consisted of formal reporting and questioning, and she never quite reached the 14-year-old girl, diagnosed as "behavior disorder with schizoid trends." There was a long period of no contact. The new probation officer, on the other hand, was sensitive to the child's feeling about being on probation and tried to get at that feeling. There was evidence that she had read and thought about the case record. She was considerate, observant, and more skilled in interviewing. However, contact ended a short time later because of factors outside the probation officer's control, and it was still too early to know whether the new worker had overcome the resistance generated by her predecessor.

In another case, one probation officer conducted the investigation while another was given responsibility for probation. The latter, carrying responsibility for a 14-year-old boy who had been involved in a homosexual act with an adult, showed no ability to carry through the major recommendations of the Clinic as to the proper pattern of relationship with the probationer. The following entry is characteristic: "P.O. encouraged boy to join Y.M.C.A. and become interested in boxing, basketball and swimming, ———— was advised to become a little more aggressive." The officer did, however, seem able to offer some emotional support to the boy.

Two of the pending cases reviewed, i.e., cases never placed on probation, revealed more sensitive patterns of work:

One probation officer gave considerable support in effective manner to a 10-year-old boy during a long period of delay while placement was being arranged. When the mother was suddenly called South by a death in the family, the probation officer went to Youth House to tell the boy about it.

Another probation officer made particularly good use of consultation at the Court Diagnostic Clinic in making placement plans in a complex case and in preparing the child for the experience.

In sum, all manner of analysis of office and reporting center activities as well as study of probation case records leads to an inescapable conclusion: the reporting and checking-up aspects of the assignment set the dominant note, while the treatment intent of probation is lost in the vast majority of cases. In a few cases, a favorable combination of probation officer and child leads to a warm relationship and supportive supervision. In even more cases, necessary referrals are made to welfare agencies, health agencies, or guidance clinics; but they are often poorly inaugurated, and hence do not necessarily lead to effective use of the services. In some situations, the presence of the probation officer or the threat of his action may introduce a temporary and limited deterrent effect. Very little of this, however, is the kind of treatment described in probation literature and needed by the disturbed and underprivileged children known to the Court.

To this picture, the questions must be posed: Why are the probation officers not better qualified? Have efforts been made to improve staff skills? What are the conditions of work and the facilities which determine how probation officers fulfill their assignments? Do they have competent leadership and are they backed by sound administration?

The New York City probation program is handicapped by many obstacles which have already been suggested and others yet to be reviewed. The study now turns to all of these, since their identification is the necessary first step in developing a program of improvement.

STAFF QUALIFICATIONS AND CONDITIONS OF WORK. An outstanding fact about the probation staff in the New York City Domestic Relations Court in recent years has been the high rate of turnover. Its causes are widely and probably correctly held to be the inadequacy of salary scales, the pressures of the assignment, and the lack of opportunity to do genuine professional work. The situation has at times been so difficult that the Presiding Justice found it necessary to accompany his 1947 budget request with this statement:

This Court was established by the legislature, with the considered approval of this City, on the certain knowledge that if properly staffed there would be social gains which would pay the community dividends in dollars and cents. . . . This Court has never been adequately staffed so as to render a full measure of service or so as to yield a maximum in intended dividends.[9]

[9] John Warren Hill, Presiding Justice, Domestic Relations Court, statement accompanying 1947 budget request. Many similar statements have been made by the Presiding Justice over the years.

One consultant told the Commissioner of Investigation in 1944: "Because of a shortage in man-power, the Court is not able to exercise an adequate supervisory control over children who are placed on probation in the community. Moreover, the Court has not been able to do so for some years past." Because of the pressure of current investigations, time required to find facilities for placement and treatment, and the need to carry clerical duties, probation officers had little time for probation supervision. Memorandum to William Herlands, January 11, 1944.

The Court's own supervisors, recognizing this situation and appealing for more staff in 1944, pointed out that "the amount of time being spent on supervision is alarmingly negligible" and urged a six-month cessation of probation. Minutes of Meeting of Children's Court probation supervisors, April 11, 1944.

Salary scales have been so low, the Presiding Justice added, that "the probation officers we are now getting to fill vacancies are with some few exceptions not qualified to render quality service."

At the time of this study, the total authorized Children's Court probation staff consisted of 86 positions. In addition to the 66 field workers in the Children's Court Probation Department, (6 of whom were authorized in 1951), there were 7 officers who devoted some time to Bureau of Adjustment, reporting officer, or other functions; 9 senior probation officers, known as case supervisors, who were the unit supervisors; 3 probation officers-in-charge, with borough-wide responsibility, and an assistant chief probation officer in charge of the Children's Court.

From 1922, shortly before the Children's Court was established as a separate entity, probation officers were selected by examinations open to all. By 1934, high school graduation was a prerequisite to taking the examination. No open competitive examinations were given for the positions of probation officers in Domestic Relations, Magistrates', or Special Sessions courts between 1936 and 1948, and the result was a staff which included a large number of provisional workers, many of them unqualified. Turnover was very high. Although four civil service grades for probation officers had been created as far back as 1938, it was not until 1948 that examinations provided the first opportunity to qualify competitively.

In effect, therefore, since no competitive examinations were given, Children's Court probation was hardly part of a civil service program between the years 1936 and 1948. Everybody in the department was technically a probation officer, but some were appointed as supervisors by the Presiding Justice; they could receive increases for "merit" but no mandatory increases, and most were paid according to probation officer classifications. The largely provisional staff of probation officers and the supervisors who were not so classified had no job security. Salary increments were too infrequent to keep pace with the cost of living. As a result, turnover was high, and unqualified or partially qualified personnel had to be retained.

The 1948 examination for probation officer required a baccalaureate degree plus thirty credits in social casework or allied courses before or after graduation, as well as a year of full-time, paid experience in a child-service or family-service agency. While this is not the equivalent of a master's degree in social work, advocated by some but considered unrealistic by others at this time, it establishes a higher level of qualifications for probation officers than that currently demanded for Department of Welfare social investigators, attendance officers, or Juvenile Air Bureau policemen.

Throughout the country, many jurisdictions do not have probation staff at all, some employ part-time officers, many do not use civil service selection procedures, and standards often are low. New York City, which more than meets the National Probation and Parole Association standards of a bachelor's degree plus a year of experience, compares very favorably, too, with New York State as a whole.[10] Despite this, the Court has consistently stated its desire to improve staff standards by providing educational leaves so that staff members might consider obtaining full graduate training. Several supervisors and one or two probation officers hold social work degrees. As this report went to press, a new probation officer examination was announced; candidates must have either a graduate social work degree or two years' experience.

In 1922 probation officers were paid $1,800-$2,400 a year. Although qualifications were raised in 1934, the salary minimum was lowered to $1,680 and not restored until 1944. A total of $300 was added to the maximum under the general 1945 civil service increase, and the range became $1,800-$2,700. A series of cost-of-living bonuses, some of which were later incorporated in the scale, eventually brought the basic probation officer scale, Grade 1, to $2,710-$3,720, the annual increment being $120. In 1951, a $250 cost-of-living adjustment was incorporated into the scale, and a beginning probation officer received $2,960. Senior probation officers, the so-called "case supervisors," received $3,780-$4,260. Supervising probation officers, the probation officer-in-charge in each

---

[10] Greene, "Probation—Philosophy, Function and Fact." For standards see: Teeters and Reinemann, *The Challenge of Delinquency*, pp. 405 ff.; Sussman, *Law of Juvenile Delinquency*, pp. 59-60.

borough, and the assistant chief probation officer were paid $4,320-$5,020.

At the end of 1952, after completion of this study, basic improvements in salary scales were authorized and, for the first time, created levels of compensation which would place the Court in a favorable position to attract fully trained social workers as probation officers and unit supervisors. Some dissatisfaction remained about increments, maximums, and compensation at the higher supervisory levels. The new scales, which were to be introduced in two stages, would assure that by July 1, 1953, the following salaries (including cost-of-living bonuses) would be paid:

Probation officers: $3,565-$4,625 (all increments automatic; seven at $120, one at $160, plus small cost-of-living additions).

Senior probation officers (the unit supervisors): $4,750-$5,255 (only the first two increments of $120 each to be mandatory; all supervisors will be at the lowest level of this new scale by July 1, 1953, and no increments are expected in the near future).

Supervising probation officers (probation officers-in-charge of boroughs and the assistant chief): $5,380-$6,115 (all increments are to be meritorious, and none is expected at the present time).

Chief probation officer: $6,380 minimum; no maximum specified.[11]

By the time examinations were announced in 1948 and civil service lists promulgated in 1949, salaries were so low and vacancies so many (over 70 in the entire Domestic Relations Court—more than half the field positions) that the original objectives of stabilizing the staff could not be achieved. Since the lists contained considerable overlapping between the Domestic Relations Court on the one hand and Special Sessions and Magistrates' courts on the other (110 people on both lists), and since many exercised the right of temporary refusal of appointment, not all vacancies could be filled from the lists. Nine provisional workers, some of whom had failed the examinations, were appointed or retained.

[11] Despite these increases authorized at the end of 1952, Children's Court probation salaries lagged behind those in General Sessions and in the county courts, which are not subject to the same budget procedure and which had slightly higher requirements for staff. (Chap. XI, footnote 2.)

From 1949 to 1953, the problems inherent in staff turnover and their consequences in the form of unserved case loads persisted. For instance, the Children's Court reported a 30 percent staff turnover in 1951. During 1950 there had been 40 changes of probation officers in the 67 positions, some of the positions being filled by several different individuals. In March, 1951, in a typical experience during this study's evaluation of probation, the Civil Service Commission certified 25 individuals for appointment in the Domestic Relations Court, but 22 declined, many because of the inadequate salary scale.[12] It has been generally recognized that many individuals have used probation jobs as a temporary way station en route to full social work training or to taking civil service examinations for better paying jobs in county courts.

Thus, although the 1949 list augured some improvement, particularly in the establishment of a relatively fixed group of supervisors appointed through competitive examinations, the court staff was not stabilized. Continued resignations, dropping of unsatisfactory provisional workers, and inability to recruit individuals of the required sex and specified religious groups have perpetuated staff instability and uncovered case loads. The consequent pressure has defeated attempts to establish regular patterns of supervision of staff and has contributed in important measure to many of the Court's professional problems.

While probation salary scales have shown gradual improvement over the years and are now for the first time comparable to voluntary agency rates for fully qualified social workers, there is wide-

[12] In a review in mid-September, 1951, covering developments for the period September 15, 1950—September 15, 1951, it was found that there had been 25 vacancies in the 60 probation field positions. Three of these vacancies had been in the same position. Some of the positions were filled in a month, some not for six months; a two-month vacancy for a position was typical. Twenty-one of the 25 positions had been filled by provisional workers during the course of the year. No permanent officers had been hired since April, 1951. As of September 15, 1951, 26 of 66 field staff positions were filled by provisional workers and 2 positions were not filled. As an indication of the local consequences of this situation, it might be noted, for example, that during August-September, 1951, there were 8 staff changes in 20 probation field positions in the Brooklyn office.

No borough office has enjoyed an extended period of staff stability, and the three large boroughs have continued to face major problems in this regard.

spread agreement that their inadequacy has in the past constituted an important element in the Court's inability to achieve staff stability. For more than a decade, court leadership, major community organizations, religious leaders, and the Welfare Council worked to improve the salary situation and the size of the probation staffs, but their successes were partial and stopgap in nature. The Probation Bureau continued to feel the consequences of the fact that staff found salary increments too slow and maximum rates inadequate in the light of job responsibilities, promotion possibilities, attitudes toward the Court, and the competitive market. Under the circumstances, individuals with considerable experience or those who had secured full social work graduate training could not, generally, be held.

It is thus a basic fact that the complex tasks of case study and probation treatment require fully qualified workers—and the Children's Court was until recently in no position to pay for those who had requisite qualifications as it recruited staff. It is nonetheless fair to add that salaries alone do not account for the weaknesses and professional problems of Children's Court probation. Also involved are: the conditions of the assignment; the varied conceptions of the job; the attitudes of certain judges; the poor physical facilities under which work is done; and the difficulty in finding adequate community resources for children. These elements are reflected in the performance of all probation officers, no matter how qualified, contribute considerably to staff turnover, and result in pressure for those who remain.

THE PROBATION OFFICER'S WEEK. It cannot be stressed too often that the probation officer's task has many aspects. He must organize his work week to allow time for:

Investigations of new cases, which must be completed and dictated by dates specified on the court calendar and which require reports in court on the officer's regular "court days"

Probation and supervision cases, including regular reporting by children, such as has been described, and home visits

Pending cases, which require written requests that children be considered for placement in institutions, conferences about such plans, arrangements for examinations and tests, etc.

Court appearances to report to the judges on new investigations, indicate progress and readiness for dispositions of cases on probation

Letters to agencies and clients, report forms to the schools, and occasionally—because of the heavy cylinder backlog in the typing department—shaving cylinders, so that dictation is possible, or typing reports

Transporting children occasionally to facilities for long-term care

Conferences with agency representatives, members of the court staff, and particularly with one's own supervisor

A steady stream of telephone calls to and from clients, agencies, court personnel, schools, institutions, etc.

Because the Probation Department has been continuously faced by the need to orient new workers and to ask those somewhat longer on the job to take care of "emergencies," case load totals (Table 14) do not give an adequate sense of the average probation officer's activities and responsibilities. On the other hand, it should be added that not all cases listed as assigned to an officer, and reflected in case load totals, are actively served during a given month.[13]

The New York City Welfare Council's special committee on probation services recommended in 1950 that a probation officer responsible only for "supervision" of cases be assigned no more than 60 cases, and that one responsible only for "investigations," 15 cases a month. Those who do both investigation and case supervision, as in the New York City Children's Court, "shall not be expected to supervise more than thirty cases while conducting seven or eight investigations per month." Similar standards have been proposed by other local and national groups. Given equitable

[13] The weaknesses of probation statistics and proposals to remedy them are described in Kahn, *Proposals for the Development of a Statistical and Research Service*. The reporting of numbers of cases seen in home and office interviews would greatly improve the data available; the Children's Court Probation Bureau recognizes this and is planning certain steps along this line.

TABLE 14. *Probation Bureau Case Loads, 1950-1951* [a]

| | 1950 | | | | | | 1951 | | | | | |
	City-wide	A	BOROUGH B	C	D	E	City-wide	A	BOROUGH B	C	D	E
Totals												
Investigations completed (children)	5,379	1,854	1,844	891	657	133	6,542	2,666	1,945	914	884	133
Probation completed (children)	2,728	954	958	393	347	76	3,600	1,522	1,023	549	409	97
Placed on probation (children)	3,399	1,114	1,238	555	402	90	4,021	1,720	1,249	540	428	84
On probation at year end (children)	3,762	1,304	1,306	685	381	86	4,183	1,502	1,532	676	400	73
Averages												
Average number of probation officers in field	59.5	19.8	19.6	10.4	7.6	2.0	59.0	20.2	19.5	9.0	8.3	2.0
Average number of case investigations completed per probation officer per month	7.5	7.8	7.8	7.1	7.2		9.2	11.0	8.3	8.5	8.9	
Average number of cases on probation at month's end in average month	41.0	41.4	44.4	39.1	38.1	28.3	48.2	48.6	50.8	56.1	37.9	26.2
Average number of cases pending at month's end in average month	13.3	16.2	16.6	8.5	6.3	5.0	19.0	25.7	17.1	17.2	11.6	7.6

[a] See note on page 203.

distribution of work on the basis of a stable staff, the investigation averages reported in Table 14 for 1950, the period the study began, would be considered reasonable. In four of the boroughs, however, officers were, during 1950, expected to supervise somewhat too many cases; even in this instance, however, the assignment did not preclude a good job since the totals included some cases which recurred in the course of a year. What made the load somewhat more arduous were the pending cases (ultimately tabulated as completed investigations), which often represent considerable activity: according to computations made in the course of this study, an average probation officer, during 1950, carried each month 13.3 such cases, i.e., cases on which investigation were complete but dispositions had been delayed while placements were being sought, examinations scheduled, or reports awaited. Despite these considerations, given staff stability, a relatively small increase in the number of field staff would have reduced case loads to reasonable size. However, the staff situation became even more difficult in 1951. Increases in all case load categories were substantial while staff turnover was constant.

Because of existing pressures, most probation officers tend to permit their workdays to organize themselves around priorities not of their own planned choice. Since reporting dates for new case investigations are set on the calendar, these represent priorities of

---

* City-wide and borough totals for investigations, cases placed on probation, cases in which probation is completed, and cases on probation at the end of the year are derived from City of New York, Domestic Relations Court, annual reports, 1950-1951. The computations of the average number of probation officers in the field are based on averaging the totals for field officers reported in the twelve separate monthly reports of the Probation Bureau in each borough. The Staten Island figure is "corrected" on the assumption, perhaps an overestimate, that the four officers devote no more than half time to Children's Court field work. The average number of monthly investigations per officer is obtained by dividing the investigations completed by the average number of officers in the field and that, in turn, by 12. The average number of cases on probation at the month's end is obtained by averaging for each borough, from the monthly Probation Bureau reports, the number of cases on probation at the end of each month and then dividing that average by the average number of field workers for the borough. The same procedure is followed for "pending" cases. No allowance is made for staff vacations or illness, with the result that the averages are minimal.

the highest order, superseded only by "emergencies" on the under-
care case load, such as a situation which leaves children without
care because something has happened to a parent, a new petition
in the case of a child on probation, which necessitates rapid disposition, or notification of the immediate availability of institutional
space for a child on the pending load. Certain of the cases on the
probation load are listed for specific reporting dates, so the officers
must be ready at those times to bring the judge up to date on the
situation. Other probation cases are not "dated," and it is the
officer who has responsibility for placing the case on the calendar
to suggest discharge or a new disposition by the Court.

In the three larger boroughs, where court is in session daily during the week, each probation officer is scheduled for two "court
days" a week. These are the days on which he is to report the results of investigations and the status of under-care or pending cases.
They are the days, too, on which the court reporting officer calls
probation officers to attend hearings involving new clients to be
assigned to them for investigation, or sends clients to their offices.
In one borough, half of the probation officers are expected to be in
the field on two days and the other half on two other days. These
days are known to all personnel so that court appearances can be
properly scheduled. The entire staff is in the office on the fifth day
for meetings, instructions, and so forth; but, since there is only
one judge sitting on this day, it is expected that much of the time
will be required for new cases and it is not intended that the major
court business of the officers on under-care cases be scheduled. In
another borough, where the Court is in session only twice a week,
officers are in the building on those days, except for emergencies,
and have two other days as field days.

Despite these plans for allocating time, on the basis of the courtroom schedule, many problems appear in practice. As a result, probation officers have too little field time to meet all their responsibilities and find it extremely difficult to organize the office day. In
two offices in particular, a tremendous amount of time is wasted
waiting around to be reached in the disposition Part of the Court.

To be more specific, home and community visiting by probation officers is constantly sacrificed to other priorities. Occasionally, because of special circumstances or heavy calendars, reports must be made in court on a pending or probation case on a probation officer's field day. Quite often, cases on probation are brought in on new petitions, and an officer may wait for the hearing even though it may technically be his field day. Finally, the need to dictate or type an investigation which is due may lead to a delay in getting into the field. The end result is a considerable curtailment of what little field time there is. When probation officers do get to the field they must concentrate on new investigations and other priorities at the expense of the presumed semimonthly home visits on neglect cases, monthly home visits on delinquency cases, and important collateral visits.

Since probation officers do not indicate in their monthly reports which parents and children have been seen and which not, it is not possible to convert these generalizations into statistical terms; but it can be pointed out, on the basis of record reading and observation, that it is a rare probation record which shows home visits and collateral contacts on a regular basis, and a rare probation officer who spends two full days each week in planned visiting. In fact, all probation officers must on occasion complete a case "investigation" in the office, for lack of time for the "mandatory" home visit.

The probation officer's day in the office is also to a great degree responsive to factors largely outside his control. First, as noted, he may be called at any time to listen in on the hearing of a new case to be assigned to him. This, however, is less of a problem than cases on the disposition or reporting calendar. Because of the heavy calendars and physical arrangements in the Manhattan office, attendants do not assume the responsibility of calling probation officers when their cases are reached. The probation officer must, therefore, take personal responsibility for checking in the waiting room to determine whether clients have come, checking in the courtroom as to whether their petitions have been brought up, and then placing case names on a list in the courtroom. It is this list which determines priorities in calling cases. The probation officer is held personally responsible for being present when his case is reached.

Since it is impossible to tell from a list of names whether one will be reached in fifteen minutes or in two hours, probation officers are always to be found waiting around in the courtroom in the Manhattan disposition Part. On days spent with probation officers, it was found that a two- or three-hour wait was not rare and a sixty- to ninety-minute wait, routine. The total of probation officer time wasted each month is, therefore, extremely high, and the tension created for the individual officer who must, on a given morning, manage to appear when needed in Part I, Part II, and the School Part is unbearable.

The situation in Brooklyn is not quite so difficult in this regard as in Manhattan since telephones are more accessible to the attendants who call probation officers. A certain amount of guesswork as to the judge's speed is still involved, and to avoid a lull while the calendar is heavy, attendants prefer to call probation officers well in advance. The smaller calendars and staffs and the physical relationship of courtroom to probation officers in the Bronx, Queens, and Staten Island make waiting far less of a problem—but these offices account for a small part of total probation personnel.

While trying to decide when to go to the courtroom, an officer carries out a number of other vital responsibilities. He may, for instance, interview a child or a parent about developments which will be discussed in court. Such interviews take place in detention rooms, waiting rooms, corridors, or in the probation officer's office. He must make or respond to many telephone calls; there is agency correspondence to be handled; children and clients must receive letters about new appointments; case reports must be dictated or typed; and plans or developments must be discussed with the supervisor.

Difficulties in controlling the course of the court day and poor physical facilities lend to the probation assignment a perpetually hectic aspect, lacking opportunity for planning, thinking, consultation, or even follow-through. This has by now been assumed to be part of the job and, because of prevailing habits, would probably represent an obstacle even if objective conditions were changed. It dominates the larger offices but is an element in all offices.

IN THE FIELD. Because children must be assigned for probation and supervision to probation officers of the same religious background, geography cannot be the major factor governing case allocation. Probation officers, particularly in the Bronx, Brooklyn, or Queens, may, therefore, have to cover far-flung territory on a given day. Despite precedent in other city departments, the Probation Bureau is not permitted to pay a mileage allowance to the few officers who have their own cars, nor are cars provided. Most of the officers in the field spend long hours during the workday on subways and buses.

Even some of the limited field time available is used unprofitably since, to assure an accurate picture of home and family, the probation officer is expected to arrive unannounced at the homes of clients. Almost half of these visits end with "no contact." While many of the probation officers modify this practice and make appointments for "investigation" interviews because their time is limited, most visits on under-care cases continue, in fact, unannounced. When nobody is at home, some probation officers leave notes and others do not; many of the clients respond by telephoning for office or home appointments. Both the time lost in this practice and the professional philosophy involved require careful review.

It must be added that the use made by some officers of already severely limited field time seems questionable:

In one case, three boys who had intercourse on a roof with a girl were adjudged delinquent. A detective had reported in court that a fourth boy involved fell from the roof and was killed when an adult chased the group. The probation officer to whom the case was assigned for study began with a visit to the police precinct to verify the boy's death. This was hardly his responsibility and was, as a matter of fact, already testified to in court by a detective. The officer then went to the Juvenile Aid Bureau to see if the boys were listed for other complaints—sometimes a necessary step for developing a personal relationship with the J.A.B., although in most cases a telephone call is sufficient.

It is generally not the recent appointees who stress the investigation aspects in this way, even where the facts are not questioned and what the Court needs are clues to a wise disposition plan. Pressure from petitioners for recovery of property seems to determine priorities for those officers who do, although basically that is a police rather than a probation responsibility.

In many families, adults who must be seen work during the day. Although the Court's personnel regulations do little to facilitate it, and although supper money, which can be paid twice a month if the probation officer does evening work in the office, is not paid when he makes home visits, probation officers sometimes schedule home visits evenings or Saturdays. Other probation officers see parents between 6:00 and 7:00 P.M. on reporting days when children are seen from 3:00 to 5:00 P.M. No equivalent time off is allowed for this extra duty; but because the task requires it, and out of a sense of concern and duty, probation officers are prepared to give extra time as needed. There are, indeed, several whose lives center completely around probation and who devote much of their "leisure time" to cases requiring special attention.

School visits are important to the probation assignment in many ways. While there are significant differences in the way various schools view the Court and work with probation officers, some officers have developed particularly fine patterns of cooperation. Although in the investigatory phase they must usually rely on written reports completed by teachers, once cases are assigned for supervision these officers make periodic school visits to discuss with principal, teacher, or counselor cases under care and, often, to achieve modification of a child's school program.

IN THE COURTROOM. The wide variation in ways in which judges use the reports of the probation officers and their knowledge of cases has been previously stressed. It has also been noted that these variations are of major influence on probation officer morale, status in the Court, and incentive for further professional training. The judge who carefully reads the report of an investigation, who discusses complex cases with officers in advance of formal hearings, whenever possible, not only serves the individual client better, but also contributes to a probation officer's concept of his job and gives him incentive to increase his skills. The judge who ignores probation reports and who sees himself not as a team member but as the Court is apt to plan less wisely and to demoralize the probation staff.

A considerable number of cases on the disposition Part calendar, i.e., those cases beyond the initial hearing stages, have to be adjourned periodically while the probation staff seeks placement facilities or while examination reports are awaited. Each time, the judge sets a new hearing date, usually in consultation with the probation officer, and the case comes up again on that date whether or not progress has been made.

Because of the rotation system, and because even when the judge who conducted the initial hearing is involved he cannot retain details on all cases, the probation officer may have to enter into lengthy discussion with the judge; and the client may have to come to court each time and wait to be seen. Some judges process such cases routinely, pass over them rapidly, and do not generally ask to see the clients. Others enter into lengthy discussion with the officer on peripheral issues and question clients, often without reviewing the full record. The sum total of these case situations accounts for a substantial portion of the time probation officers spend waiting in the disposition Part of the Court.

Other courts have handled the problems of periodic adjournment of cases, particularly where client appearance is not called for and no change in disposition plan is involved, by permitting some other staff member, often a supervisor, to report for the probation officer. It was initially expected that the court reporting officer would perform this function in the Children's Court, but his assignment, as has been described, developed somewhat differently. The probation officer's workday could be better organized and his load lightened if either his supervisor or the reporting officer (it would take several to assume this task) were permitted to make routine courtroom reports for him, and if he himself were allowed to make certain routine decisions relative to some aspects of reporting in conference with his supervisor. His supervisor, in turn, could settle other matters in conference with the judge.

Serious consideration should be given, too, to a proposal made by a Probation Bureau leader that only one day a week be scheduled as a "court day," the remainder of the week to be devoted to scheduled activity in the office and field. Observations also suggest the value of dividing the court day into early morning and late morning calendars—a proposal initiated in Chicago—as a means of making more predictable the time a given case will be reached.

OFFICES AND CLERICAL FACILITIES. Probation work is seriously handicapped, too, by generally inadequate auxiliary and office facilities:

In *Manhattan* the offices are two floors above the courtroom. They are small, poorly furnished, and badly maintained. Many probation officers share their offices. Other officers have "private" offices, but the adjacent office in some instances is separated by a low partition so that interviews, telephone conversations, and dictation are heard and concentration is difficult. Clients waiting for probation officers sit on benches in a wholly inadequate, long, narrow corridor. There is no receptionist service.

In *Brooklyn* the probation officers are in a loftlike arrangement, two floors above the courtroom and three floors above the street. Elaborate partitioning has not succeeded in converting dark, squalid, poorly roofed space into suitable offices. There are no private offices, except for those of two supervisors. A few of the supervisors and probation officers share their space with one other staff member. Some share office space with two or, occasionally, with three other officers. Efforts to schedule field days so that people assigned to the same "room" do not use it for interviewing at the same time can hardly be expected to be successful. The "rooms" are separated from one another by glass partitions which are not ceiling high, and there is neither privacy nor reasonable quiet. The central area which is surrounded by these "rooms" is subdivided into a waiting room for clients, file space, and a little office for the clerk. As he awaits his interview, a client views a

panorama of interviews, telephone calls, record reading, conferences, and dictaphone typists working in the far corner. On reporting days, large numbers of children mill around in this space.
In the middle of a morning, in one such glass-partitioned room
with four desks, one can observe two or three officers, one of whom
may be interviewing a client, another dictating a case investigation, and a third telephoning—all in the midst of the din from
the typing, telephoning, opening of files, and so on. Fortunately,
excellent facilities are expected in the new Brooklyn court building now in the early phases of construction.

The *Bronx* building is an attractive one, but was apparently
planned for a smaller probation staff. The offices are on two different floors; they are bright and attractive and have ceiling-high
partitions. The use of glass for these partitions hampers the feeling
of privacy in an interview and does not seem particularly suitable
for these offices. There is adequate waiting space for clients who
are to see probation officers, but the clerk's office is so located that
people who need to ask directions are as likely to turn to the probation officer-in-charge as to the clerk.

The *Queens* case load has outgrown the building; and, although
the need is not nearly so urgent as in Brooklyn or Manhattan,
improvements are necessary. Only one flight of stairs separates the
probation staff from the courtroom, so that attendants can readily
call staff members and clients can be directed up. However, since
a large part of the facilities has been turned over to the Family
Court staff, the Children's Court probation officers have a converted top floor which provides everybody with private space;
many of these spaces are separated by partitions which are not
ceiling high. Although the discomfort is not nearly that characteristic of Brooklyn, and the atmosphere is generally pleasant, telephone conversations are not private, dictation can be overheard,
as can interviews and conferences. This distracts other probation
officers and either amuses or upsets clients who must wait in a
small area surrounded by record files. The probation clerk, who
does not have an office, uses part of this area. The dictation problem has been partially relieved by the use, for more "intimate"

dictation, of a room designated at other hours for the psychologist.

The *Staten Island* staff is small. The office is comfortable and attractive. Although there are two desks in a room, staff schedules and availability of other space in the building provide sufficient privacy.

None of the court offices has sufficient clerical personnel, and at given times the situation has become acute. Vacancies due to death, resignation, temporary leave, are not filled promptly and only add to the difficulty. Frequent and prompt court requests for such personnel have been largely ignored by the budget-making authorities. The financial policy in the city involving an attempt at maximum "accruals" of salary from unfilled positions has made the situation critical.

Because of such inadequate clerical service, the probation officer-in-charge must devote substantial time to clerical routine in checking case loads and compiling monthly statistics. Dictation of letters and reports by the probation officer-in-charge or supervisor may be delayed because there is not enough secretarial help, or because the secretary is busy relieving a switchboard operator at lunch or an absent file clerk. The fact that typing positions are often unfilled, or even when filled are not sufficient in number, means that probation officers desert the dictaphones for their own typing of investigation reports. Frequently, during the year of this study, cylinders involving contacts on under-care cases were ignored completely in the typing room until a case was due to be reported on in court. The officer seldom had the benefit of an up-to-date record to consider as he saw clients for regular appointments. If he did, it was because his record entries were made in longhand or because he kept a system of independent records while awaiting the typing of dictaphone cylinders. For lack of adequate switchboard staff, court switchboards in all boroughs were poorly serviced, introducing inconvenience to clients and agencies as well as many inefficiencies.

SUPERVISING AND TRAINING THE PROBATION OFFICER. It is confusing to use the same term, "supervision," for a probation officer's activity in cases and for his superior's relationship to him, but there is no suitable substitute. Probation departments everywhere have sought to draw on the experience and theory of the social casework field relative to the educational, administrative, and personal guidance aspects of the supervisory process.[14] Whatever the differences of emphasis it is agreed that a supervisor, through case reading, review of reports, and observation, is in a position to appraise the performance of the staff members. Through informal contacts, as well as in regularly scheduled individual, and perhaps group, conferences, this understanding can be used to contribute to their further training and thus to their total competence.

Following promulgation of the 1949 civil service list, a group of unit supervisors (called "senior probation officers" by civil service and "case supervisors" in court) were assigned in the Court. The majority have made determined efforts to develop a pattern of professional supervision of the probation officers assigned to them; but, for the most part, the instability of the probation staff and the existence of uncovered case loads have defeated their efforts. These same situations make any appraisal of their performance potential impossible. They themselves emphasize that they need considerable consultation and professional leadership in fully defining the job and developing their skills.

Under current conditions, supervision is a "catch-as-catch-can" affair. In most offices, staff members are required to confer with their supervisors if they plan placement, discharge of a probation or supervision case, a court appearance in a case in which a child has "violated" probation, or if they wish to add a case to the court calendar for a special report to the judge. Cases also go over the supervisor's desk when formally assigned to a worker for

[14] See particularly the following articles: Levine, "Educational Components of Supervision in a Family Agency," *Social Casework*, XXXI (June, 1950), 245-250; Feldman, "The Teaching Aspect of Casework Supervision," *Social Casework*, XXXI (April, 1950), 156-161; Austin, "Basic Principles of Supervision," *Social Casework*, XXXIII (December, 1952), 411-419. An extreme position about the uniqueness of supervision in the functional casework field is elaborated in Virginia Robinson, *Dynamics of Supervision under Functional Controls*.

probation or for parole and supervision. Generally, such actions are handled in a routine and almost clerical way, in the spirit of "getting permission" from one's supervisor, rather than as the occasion for more extended supervisory conferences. Some supervisors try to do more in these brief unscheduled contacts, but circumstances make this difficult. Some have managed weekly conferences with individual probation officers for short periods of time, and a few supervisors have had conferences regularly for longer periods. Some have even attempted to follow a few special treatment cases intensively, as an educational endeavor, but staff instability has made it impossible to maintain and extend this kind of supervision. When a supervisor reviews a case record, he may use special pages attached to the inside of the case record folder to transmit instructions or suggestions. Examination reveals that these pages are used chiefly to call attention to omissions of fact or to regulations and policies; they give practically no evidence of serving as supervisory tools in the broader sense.

The task of developing an adequate plan of casework supervision has been complicated by differences of opinion as to the responsibilities of the so-called "case supervisors" and the probation officers-in-charge, as differentiated from what some would call "senior probation officers." [15] The Court's administrative leader-

[15] In 1951 the Presiding Justice faced a legal suit instituted by the supervisors, which called attention to these differences. When the first examinations for supervisors under the present system of civil service grades in probation were given in 1948, the same examination was taken by individuals currently serving as senior probation officers (case supervisors) and those serving as supervising probation officers (the probation officers-in-charge and the assistant chief probation officer in charge of the Children's Court). They were, in fact, all on one civil service list entitled "Promotion, Supervising Probation Officer, Domestic Relations Court." Those at the top of the list became the two assistant chief probation officers, those who followed became the probation officers-in-charge in the boroughs, and those below them became the case supervisors (senior probation officers). The members of this latter group were, however, classified and paid as senior probation officers, Grade 2, while the remainder were paid at a higher scale as supervising probation officers, Grade 3.

In asking for reclassification the case supervisors stated that a senior probation officer is a more skilled probation officer, such as a court reporting officer or a person who can work independently in the Bureau of Adjustment. In contrast, each of the case supervisors conducts a unit consisting of several

ship, the supervisors as a group, and the Mayor's Committee on Management Survey have held different views about the divisions of responsibility. Experience in many operating agencies would seem to point to the soundness of a definition of the unit supervisor's (case supervisor's) assignment which would stress that he be qualified (as the supervisors themselves phrase it) to:

Provide orientation of new staff to policy, procedures and standards of casework practice

Aid the individual probation officer, through supervisory conferences, record reading, and educational efforts, to increase his competence

Carry responsibility for seeing that standards of casework practice are attained and court orders carried out in individual cases and that clients are well served (concern with work organization of probation officers, level of case study, and treatment of cases, etc.)

Evaluate individual probation officers periodically

Report to, consult with, and cooperate with, the probation officer-in-charge in the borough.

Under such a plan, probation officers-in-charge, relieved of much of the current case detail and routine, could devote themselves to administration and supervision of the probation departments in each of the local courts, under the direction of the assistant chief probation officer in charge of the Children's Court.

---

probation officers and has full responsibility. Probation officers-in-charge provide higher level leadership and administer borough offices.

In replying to the claims of the case supervisors, the Presiding Justice held that the real supervisory control is in the hands of a supervising probation officer, the probation officer-in-charge, and that the case supervisors are completely under the latter's direction in every sense. The supervision "exercised by the 'case supervisor' is necessarily a lower-level, inferior, and restricted supervision and wholly incomparable to that of the supervising probation officer."

See Supreme Court of the State of New York, County of New York. "In the Matter of the Application of Elizabeth N. Corning [and 11 others], petitioners . . . against John Warren Hill, Presiding Justice of the Domestic Relations Court of the City of New York, et al. . . .," affidavit by John Warren Hill, June 28, 1951. The position of the supervisors in this action was not upheld.

They would be expected to provide professional leadership in all phases of the work. The term "senior probation officer," on the other hand, could be employed as the title for those who would undertake complex probation assignments in court intake or as reporting officers, but would not be used for supervisors.

Whether or not the assignments of the various levels of supervisors are defined in exactly these terms, it is clear that to attract and keep qualified staff, supervision must be strengthened. Suitable salary gradations within the range and between classifications will, of course, be necessary.

IN-SERVICE TRAINING AND FULL PROFESSIONAL TRAINING. In-service training programs have long been used in social agencies, and there has been much concern with them in the Court. Periodically, the Probation Bureau leadership has conducted such programs to orient new staff and raise levels of practice. A particularly difficult orientation task faced the Court shortly after the considerable staff changes resulting from appointments based on the 1949 civil service lists. At that time, major stress was placed on how investigations were to be conducted.

The first large scale in-service training course since the Second World War—and a very successful effort, as measured by almost unanimous staff opinion—was an introductory discussion series developed by the Probation Bureau with the active help of the court clinic. Attendance was compulsory, with the entire probation group participating in two sections on consecutive mornings. The eight lecture-discussions conducted by psychiatrists, psychologists, and a psychiatric social worker clarified the role of the psychiatric clinic in the Court, discussed concepts behind the major forms of psychopathology in some detail, and examined the relationship of the court clinic to the Probation Department.

It had been expected that immediately following the completion of this introductory series in December, 1950, there would be local follow-up in small discussion groups led by well-trained personnel from all parts of the Court. Staff instability at that time necessitated postponement of the plan, but it remains under consideration and promises to be a valuable training instrument.

Priority had to be given early in 1952 to a repetition of the basic lecture series for new staff members.

The Court has emphasized that:

Such [in-service] program is not designed, however, as a substitute for attendance at recognized schools of social work and attendance at such schools is recommended. Educational leaves will be granted, subject to the convenience of the Court, for requirements for the Certificate or Master's Degree in Social Work.[16]

At the time of this study, four Children's Court supervisors on various levels and two probation officers held graduate social work degrees and several others had completed a year of professional training. Many other probation staff members have taken individual extension courses at schools of social work in the evening but have not had the supervised field work.[17] The better trained staff members have found operational procedures, the personnel situation, and the philosophy of some in the Court, as well as salary scales, particularly frustrating. They feel, however, that an increase in the number of qualified probation workers would represent a significant step toward improvement.

Probation officers' general interest in further training was reflected in their excellent response to the possibility of New York City Youth Board sponsored scholarships for the academic year beginning September, 1951.[18] Because a full professional social work education is expensive and requires almost two years, it is not accessible to many staff members unless some financial assistance can be made available.

PROBATION LEADERSHIP. It is only proper to ask whether the poor morale in the Probation Bureau, reflected in staff turnover and the generally weak performance of staff, is traceable to

[16] Letter from Marion M. Brennan, Assistant Chief Probation Officer, to all members of the Children's Court Probation Bureau staffs, October 13, 1950.

[17] The reference here is to the "internship" under the school's supervision, not to the probation officer's daily assignment.

[18] This plan was rejected by budget authorities. A group of probation workers took part in the special institute on casework in authoritarian settings, conducted in the spring of 1951 at the New York School of Social Work.

inadequate leadership and to weak Domestic Relations Court administration in general. The study is unable to give any definite answer to the first of these questions: At one and the same time, the Court has had to cope with underpaid and unqualified provisional staff, judges who have varied concepts of the service to be rendered, and major problems of job definition and organization. For a good number of years prior to this study, the office of chief probation officer was filled only on a provisional basis, and no examination was given for the position. Shortly before and during the study, a new assistant chief probation officer in charge of the Children's Court sought to give much needed leadership but was partially blocked by the many obstacles mentioned and a job definition which allowed limited initiative. Since the completion of the study, a new provisional appointment has been made to the chief probation officer position, and the Presiding Justice has requested that the Civil Service Commission conduct an open competitive examination. The new chief has only begun to inaugurate a number of measures designed to strengthen the staff, and their success is not yet known.

At the same time that probation was handicapped in the manner described, the Court as a whole showed many evidences of administrative weakness. While administration per se was not examined in the course of this study, its quality was noted daily in numerous ways, of which the following are only illustrative: (a) Transcribing typists who type probation records are technically under the clerk of court. He has many other duties and, in most of the offices, is not located near the transcribing typists. Work was at a low level of efficiency in three of five offices at the very time that the Court was severely handicapped because records were not available on time. (b) Similarly, because the clerk of court had to assume custodial responsibilities, attendants and other clerks were generally unsupervised. (c) It was never clear who would supervise warrant officers serving court process. (d) There was no consistency from borough to borough as to who was to be permitted access to probation records or to dockets. (e) Many court directives were unknown to some staff members or were never implemented by any. A decision that probation officers were not to attend first hearings on cases was widely ignored. (f) Statistical reports were inaccurate. (g) Courts in the larger boroughs had highly inefficient switchboard service and poor arrangements for taking messages for field staff. In a sense, many administrative problems in the Court derive from the fact that the formal structure, which places major responsibility on a presiding justice, a director of administration, and a chief probation officer, assumes that there is a unified Domestic Relations Court whereas, in reality, the "unity" is largely a matter of judges who travel from court to court on the rotation schedules, some sharing of building space, the limited formal assignment of personnel with joint responsibility, and the single budget.

The long-range interests of the Children's Court require both strong administrative leadership in the total Domestic Relations Court structure and effective professional leadership for the Children's Court. One crucial decision to be taken is whether the plan for the future is to assume increased integration of both courts. If so, effective administrative leadership by a director of administration and a chief probation officer, both reporting to the presiding justice, are prerequisite to solving problems of plant and management, to raising the efficiency of secretarial, clerical, and court attendant services, and to leading the professional staff in essential reorganization of the probation job itself. Outstanding probation leadership could take major responsibility for creation of new probation standards, for helping define the place of the probation officer on the "team," for attracting and holding staff, and for interpreting the Court in the community. If it is found, however, that there can be no real integration or even unified professional policy between the Family Court and the Children's Court, there is some doubt as to whether the chief probation officer can have any but general administrative and policy responsibility. The respective assistant chiefs should, perhaps, then take major responsibility for professional leadership and staff development.

FROM "PROBATION OFFICER" TO "COUNSELOR."
Placing a child on probation or under supervision has little value
unless it represents a helpful counseling service. Current qualifications of personnel, in-service training, provisions for staff supervision, problems of job definition and procedure, and physical
facilities add up to the fact that, for the majority of children,
probation does not provide such a service. Moreover, case studies
as conducted by probation officers do not, for the same reasons,
assure the careful planning required by complex situations.

The failings disclosed in probation activity do not, for the most
part, result from inability of probation officers to fulfill assignments in the manner expected of them at the time of initial employment. The problem is rather that the Court has not been able
to command staff better prepared for the responsibilities assigned.
It is, therefore, particularly important to consider qualifications
to be sought in the future and the conditions under which the
Court might require such qualifications of staff.

In this connection it is encouraging to note the strong demand
within and without the Court for professional staff better able to
carry out their tasks. The standard of graduation from a school of
social work has been urged and encouraged. At the same time,
it has been recognized that it has not been, heretofore, possible to
fill staff vacancies in New York City, even at the current standard,
because of salary scales, job definitions, and working conditions.
Later chapters will, therefore, discuss the circumstances under
which the Court could recruit and hold more graduate social
workers and begin to require social work graduate training of
all new staff members, and what can be done through educational
leaves, supervision, and in-service training to raise the performance
of staff originally hired at lower standards.

Quite apart from details of qualifications, some attention has
been given by court leaders and others to choice of proper job
titles. Many writers in the field have held that the spirit of the
juvenile court movement and the conception of probation as
casework suggest the propriety of eliminating the term "probation

officer"; both "probation" and "officer" are terms with adult criminal connotations which have no place in work with children. Particularly in serving a neglected child, a "victim" whose safety has to be supervised, it is incongruous to turn responsibility over to someone called a *probation* officer. Many have suggested the term "counselor"; some, "guidance counselor." The standard Juvenile Court Act would have the term "chief probation officer" dropped in favor of "supervisor," "director," or "director of social work" as a more appropriate description of the staff member heading the Court's social casework program.

A formal effort was made in New York City in 1946 to substitute the term "counselor" for "probation officer" in the Domestic Relations Court Act and to speak of "supervision" of children in place of "probation." The brief backing the proposed change pointed out that current usage of the term "probation" "attaches to less blameworthy members of society much of the social disgrace that attaches to criminals." This effort was premature and failed despite support by the Board of Justices of the Domestic Relations Court. Considerable opposition was expressed by probation staff members who, later inquiry revealed, misunderstood the intent of the proposal.

Secondary to the concept of the probation assignment, but by no means of negligible importance to the immediate future and hence requiring early consideration, are proposals about the mechanics of probation work (for instance, that reporting centers be eliminated), about organization of the job (for instance, that officers not report in the courtroom on routine adjournments), or about courtroom procedure (for instance, that there be more carefully scheduled calendars, to permit the probation officer to plan his day better). Strong probation administration is necessary to give leadership in solving these day-by-day problems, in attracting new staff, and in preparing those currently on staff for new and better levels of performance.

A probation department determines, in large measure, the impact of the court on those who come before it. In the interest of sheer economy, a community cannot afford to spend considerable sums on court operations and then make it impossible to recruit and retain personnel qualified to render effective service to children. The improper institutionalization of children costs the city and state more in the course of a year than would adequate salaries for probation officers. Beyond considerations of economy and efficiency are the factors making for health and well being in a community; these too underscore the case for more adequate probation services.[19]

[19] Board of Corrections, State of California, Special Commission for Study of Adult Correction and Juvenile Justice, *Probation Services in California*, p. 43, re incarceration cost and also the estimate by Charlotte Carr, of Citizens' Committee on Children of New York City at Board of Estimate Hearing, 1951, concerning relative cost of detention as compared with probation. See also Board of Correction, State of California, *Final Report of the Special Crime Study Commission on Juvenile Justice*, pp. 28-29. An estimate at a meeting of the Advisory Council of Judges of the National Probation and Parole Associations in April, 1953, placed the cost of institutionalization as ten times that of satisfactory probation.

VIII. THE MENTAL HEALTH
SERVICES OF THE COURT

Throughout the years, the Bureau of Clinical Services has made major contributions to Children's Court operations. The psychiatric diagnostic and treatment services have, in particular, assured case evaluation and, for a limited number of clients, treatment where under other circumstances the Court could have done little. The approaches of other staff members to clients and to the Court's role have also shown clinic influences—although limited by factors previously discussed. Since the completion of this study the Court has launched, under clinic leadership and initiative, a research-demonstration project which, if successful and if translatable into regular court routine, may have major significance. While evaluation of the project must await research findings, it is highly important to understand what the clinics have done in the past and the new role which may be evolving. The latter might become the focal point for the basic improvements needed in all aspects of court services.

THE BUREAU OF CLINICAL SERVICES.[1] No attempt was made to review the operations of the Physiological Laboratory,

[1] Although the new name, Bureau of Mental Health Services, was adopted just as this report was being prepared for publication, this first section continues to use the title Bureau of Clinical Services, the name of the unit at the time of the study.

which examined 1,350 persons in 1951 and 1,421 in 1952, almost three quarters of whom were adults. Nor has the work of the Court's diagnostic and treatment clinics been studied in any detail. Impressions about the psychiatric, psychological, and physical examinations were derived from clinic reports as filed in the probation records, comparison of such reports with those of examinations in other clinics, and observation of their use by judges and probation officers. The quality of the work of the Treatment Clinic and its use by the Court were sampled through study of records of cases referred while on probation, examination of statistical reports, review of student theses written about the Clinic and the manuscript of a forthcoming study by its psychiatrist-director and its former social work supervisor, and conferences with court and clinic personnel.[2] Although such assembling of data was sufficient to clarify the clinics' contributions and to raise questions about them and their place in the Court, it does not permit a systematic appraisal similar to that made of the rest of the Court.

The Psychiatric Clinic in the New York City Children's Court developed in response to those needs which in 1909 led to the first court psychiatric clinic in the country, attached to Chicago's Cook County Juvenile Court. In the early days of the juvenile court movement, it was discovered that no judge alone could encompass all the knowledge and skills essential to serving all cases. The development of a treatment plan with a view to cure was gradually understood to require, at various times, the skills and auxiliary services available through medical doctors, psychologists, social workers, and psychiatrists. A clinic functioning in a court setting would enable such specialists to study delinquent children and suggest helping measures.[3]

The New York clinic was created in 1916 before there was a

[2] The study of the Children's Court Treatment Clinic by Dr. Harris Peck and Mrs. Virginia Bellsmith is tentatively called "Individual and Group Therapy in a Court Clinic" and is to be published by the Family Service Association of America.

[3] See Abbott, *The Child and the State*, II, p. 334; Addams *et al.*, *The Child, the Clinic and the Court*; Lowrey, ed., *Orthopsychiatry, 1923-1948*.

separate Children's Court. Initially located in a hospital, it devoted as much effort at its inception to frightening children into "telling the truth" as it did to case appraisal.[4] Its services were designed to be solely diagnostic, with emphasis on identifying mental defectives with a view to placement. After a period of joint financing by the city and the National Committee for Mental Hygiene, the Psychiatric Clinic was, in 1924, incorporated into the Court as a special service. While the concept of the Clinic's function expanded and the quality of its work changed with experience, under the influence of pioneering personnel and with the growth of the mental hygiene movement, there was to be little absolute change in its formal assignment or size for almost twenty years.[5] Until 1937 the Clinic remained diagnostic and provided reports on cases referred for study by judges at first hearings or later in contacts with children. At that time, the Treatment Clinic was established by the Domestic Relations Court for a number of compelling reasons: the scarcity of treatment facilities; the diagnostic indications that children and parents could be held together if treatment were available; the belief that children on probation requiring clinic treatment should not be seen simultaneously in two agencies, so that a treatment program closely aligned to probation was needed; recognition of the value of a treatment period which would enable psychiatrists to verify and eventually improve their diagnoses. The Treatment Clinic was planned by a justice of the Court and a professor of psychiatry at the New York School of Social Work, in cooperation with the Presiding Justice and the director of the Diagnostic Clinic; it was to be an experimental unit, using graduate social work students in field work. Initially, the city provided physical facilities, and its budget covered overhead expenses and salaries for a clinic director and psychologist. Foundation financing provided a half-time psychiatrist, a psychiatric social worker, and stenographic help. Eight students were assigned for training by the school.

[4] New York City, Domestic Relations Court, *Annual Report, 1938*, p. 20.
[5] The Clinic's history is elaborated in a special 1945 report by the Department of Investigations and a Welfare Council memorandum to the Russell Sage Foundation, April 1, 1942.

The treatment and diagnostic clinics, under one director, constitute the Bureau of Clinical Services, recently renamed the Bureau of Mental Health Services. The Treatment Clinic has had a history of financial crises as various sources of private funds became exhausted. In 1942 an extended effort was made to obtain full financing by the city and in that year, at the Presiding Justice's invitation, the New York Academy of Medicine appointed a committee to survey the Clinic. It reported appreciation of the work of the graduate social work students who carried almost all the treatment responsibility but urged that a nucleus of permanent psychiatric social workers be hired. It endorsed city financing as well as expansion of the Clinic, thereby supporting efforts which had been made by the Presiding Justice and other judges.

The first substantial new financial backing by the city, $16,000, came in 1946 after an active campaign by the Court and citizen groups. Major additional financial support was given by the New York City Youth Board during the 1950 and 1951 fiscal years to enlarge the Treatment Clinic on a temporary basis and the support was renewed in 1952 as part of the Youth Board's regular program.

As a result of various efforts, the permanent professional staff, as differentiated from students who remain for nine months, has increased somewhat, and paid staff in the Diagnostic Clinic at the time of this study was composed of: four psychiatrists (half-time); four psychologists, one of them the chief psychologist, who also served the Treatment Clinic (half-time); and four stenographers, including the office manager (full-time). The following additional personnel were at the same time employed in the Treatment Clinic: a senior psychiatrist who was consultant, conducted group therapy, and directed the Treatment Clinic (half-time); two other psychiatrists (half-time); a chief psychiatric social worker (full-time); three psychiatric social workers, one financed by the city and two financed by the New York City Youth Board, two of whom supervised students in addition to working with cases (one was designated as senior supervisor and assumed major responsibility for the student program, full-time); a remedial reading psychologist provided through Youth Board funds (full-time); and four stenographers (full-time).

Psychiatrists and psychologists devoted themselves largely to diagnostic studies but gave some treatment services, while the bulk of the actual casework with children and parents was and still is carried on by graduate students, under supervision of the Court's highly qualified senior supervisor and the staff caseworkers financed by the Youth Board. The senior psychiatrist, until recently in charge of the work of the Treatment Clinic and now director of the Bureau of Mental Health Services, has pioneered, with considerable success, in organizing group therapy for some of the children and their parents.

SERVICES. A judge's decision as to whether to request diagnostic study in the court clinic or elsewhere (given awareness of the need for such study) is conditioned by whether or not a remand is necessary, in which case Youth House does most of the studies; the length of the waiting list at the court clinic; the availability of Youth House space; and his opinions about reports from various sources.[6] Court and probation investigation records are reviewed at the Treatment Clinic when either judge or probation officer suggests that clinic treatment may be more appropriate than probation or some other disposition. A referral may not be made without the agreement of the judge; and the Clinic retains the right to review cases, accepting only those considered likely to respond to its methods. When a case is accepted for clinic treatment, it remains technically on the case load of a probation officer, but the Clinic takes major responsibility and regular visits by the probation officer are not required. The Probation Department is kept informed of the status of treatment. Reports must be made to the Court on

[6] Prior to inauguration of the Reception Unit project, the Clinic suggested that judges ask for diagnostic examinations following initial hearings only where the judge considered the child obviously defective or disturbed, or where the parent requested it on the basis of experience with the child. In other instances, it was considered sounder for the judge to await completion of probation case study. The Clinic had expressed the hope that it might eventually be possible for probation officers to consult with a psychiatrist before recommending diagnostic studies in the latter instances.

dates, if any, specified by the judge (although the initiative is generally left to the Clinic staff), and the probation officer and Clinic representative must appear before the Court when discharge or other disposition is to be recommended. The Clinic counselors, as the caseworkers are called, dictate brief summaries of their contacts into the regular probation records but maintain detailed records in their own files to facilitate more accurate diagnosis and treatment and, incidentally, to permit intensive supervision of the students by their supervisors. The latter are not considered official court records and are, by legal precedent, confidential.[7]

Both the Diagnostic and the Treatment Clinic, as currently staffed, are able to provide services only to a minority, albeit a substantial minority, of court cases: the Court Diagnostic Clinic sees about 20 percent of all new court cases; another 5 percent receive some kind of psychiatric evaluation elsewhere in the community. Few children's courts achieve even this rate of diagnostic evaluation. (Data about physical and diagnostic examinations given children and adults in the clinics in 1951 and 1952 are summarized in Table 15. Data pertaining to psychological tests are not summarized, since court tabulations list tests given rather than numbers of children tested.) Adults are examined if the Court's planning requires appraisal of their competence to care for their children or if clues to help needed are sought. Children are, for the most part, examined both physically and psychiatrically. The Treatment Clinic staff, which devotes a substantial amount of

TABLE 15. *Physical and Psychiatric Examinations in Court Clinics, 1951-1952* [a]

	EXAMINATIONS, 1951		EXAMINATIONS, 1952	
	Psychiatric	Physical	Psychiatric	Physical
Delinquent children	1,074	1,008	975	960
Neglected children	371	328	423	385
Adults	449	433	455	455
Totals	1,894	1,769	1,853	1,800

[a] Source: New York City, Domestic Relations Court, annual reports, 1951-1952. Family Court cases are included.

[7] The procedural changes under the Reception Unit demonstration plan are described below.

time to each case, was able to work with 250 children and 170 adults in 1950, 244 children and 145 adults in 1951, and 325 children and 165 adults in 1952. These latter totals are small as compared with the total court case load but not insignificant as one reviews the numbers of cases served by other clinics in the community.

THE ROLE OF THE CLINICS. Particularly in recent decades the clinics have been recognized as an important part of the Court. One of the judges who has witnessed its increasingly valuable service recently described the impact of the Diagnostic Clinic in this fashion:

As staff and court became accustomed to the work of the Diagnostic Clinic in New York City, fear and suspicion gradually yielded to appreciation and understanding. The obvious referrals of children clearly defective or mentally ill were extended so as to secure the help of a diagnostic report when the child presented difficult problems that did not yield to ordinary measures of probation. These diagnostic reports, including a physical examination, a psychometric report and a diagnostic interview were increasingly requested by a majority of the members of the court. Judges noted how frequently valuable help as to medical problems, intellectual capacity, educational deficiencies and deeper insights into the child's problems were thus made available. Probation officers baffled by problems requested the court in increasing number to refer children to the clinic for diagnostic studies.[8]

A generation which has come to expect the use of diagnostic facilities for a variety of purposes fails at times to remember that however logical such use may seem as a children's court development, it represents, in a sense, a major innovation in any court. Inevitably, when he was presented with the results of psychological tests and psychiatric study, a judge began to think about the child before him as a distinct person, with a particular history, specific problems, and identifiable needs. Where previously the seriousness of an offense had been his main concern, he could now consider which of several disposition plans would best meet a child's unique situation. A variety of environmental adjustments and special

[8] Polier, "Psychiatry and the Court Offender."

school programs could now be evaluated as possible dispositions. Equipped with clinical data and recommendations, the Court could also select institutions and agencies more appropriately and work with them in the interests of children.

While the Court itself has felt that not enough children are studied diagnostically and that those most in need of such appraisal are not always referred, the diagnostic studies have been carried out on a large scale and their impact has been considerable. Despite the limited ability of some judges to accept, understand fully, or utilize the materials (Chapter V), the consequent reorientation of others has been impressive. Despite the evidence of only partial success on the part of probation officers in interpreting or following through with the full consequences of diagnostic reports (Chapter VII), their objectives have been influenced and the case studies of some noticeably improved.

Thus, even without systematically appraising the quality of diagnostic studies, this report notes evidence of the Diagnostic Clinic's positive effects on many phases of court operations. It seems clear, too, that the Treatment Clinic, beyond serving limited numbers of children and parents, has also had educational value for the entire Court. Some members of the probation staff, in particular, have developed new conceptions of their treatment assignment and increased understanding of the treatment process, with the Clinic's help—but only on a limited scale.

In the Court and in the community at large there is agreement that the Treatment Clinic has proved itself sufficiently to merit adequate and regular public financing. Substantial expansion of diagnostic services has also been urged to meet court needs and end what is often a six- to ten-week wait for psychiatric consultation.

As indicated, the Clinic is dependent in considerable measure on social work students who serve clients directly but who must leave at the end of the academic year; the question is properly raised as to whether an enlarged permanent Treatment Clinic staff cannot be provided. The case problems known to the Treatment Clinic are so complex that more highly skilled and mature social workers, part of a permanent staff, should be available. Moreover, an enlarged permanent staff would decrease the number of times a case is transferred once a close relationship to a student-counselor is established; such a staff would also facilitate development of a consistent philosophy of treatment, expand research, and further the educational role of the Clinic in the Court.

There is no assurance that the children most in need of study in the Diagnostic Clinic are so referred. The senior psychiatrist has pointed out that the child's ultimate appearance in the Clinic is chiefly determined by "unorganized, random and fortuitous methods of selection." The Clinic's own studies have revealed that, over the years, a sizable group of critically disturbed individuals appear in court without referral for psychiatric evaluation, whereas a sizable proportion of the judges' referrals of diagnostic study are questionable.[9] Currently, the children who are referred for clinic study are selected on the basis of the impressions of judges in their often all-too-brief courtroom contacts with a child, their reactions to investigation reports, or the probation officers' recommendations. Since it is known that some cases requiring psychiatric evaluation are not identified in these ways and that judges vary in their ability to recognize disturbed children, as well as in their attitudes toward psychiatric help, the demonstration project described below should prove of real value.

There are those outside the Court who have objected, on professional grounds, to the development of a treatment program in the Court. They maintain that the court setting represents an obstacle to effective treatment and that a child who requires the assistance of a guidance clinic should be referred to services outside the Court.

[9] Peck, "Principles and Techniques in the Integration of Psychiatric Services in a Juvenile Court with a Community Youth Program," *American Journal of Orthopsychiatry*, XXII (April, 1952), 277-285. Also see Peck, "Relationship of a Court Clinic to Plans for the Mental Health Needs of Children in New York City," *Journal of Educational Sociology*, XXIV (May, 1951), 544-550. The Clinic estimated that 46 percent of the referrals made for diagnostic examinations in 1937 were justified, whereas 61 percent of the 1947 referrals were valid. There has been no more recent estimate, but the Clinic stresses that chance elements still enter into referrals in important measure.

Furthermore, it is contended, emphasis on developing the Treatment Clinic makes it possible to overlook the need to raise probation standards. It has also been held that it is poor community planning to locate treatment facilities in each agency when there are children requiring similar treatment (in this instance, treatment related to an authoritarian setting) known to a series of agencies. The result tends to be pressure for the development of parallel treatment units in several agencies.[10] Others maintain that with the present shortage of resources, the Treatment Clinic is surely needed, that a city as large as New York must have diversified resources, and that, in any case, a clinic *in* the Court is in a better position than outside clinics to serve specified court cases. The Clinic's relation to the Court, a source of authority, is seen as of distinct therapeutic value where cases are carefully chosen.[11]

This latter argument is a convincing one for the expansion and strengthening of the Clinic in coming years. It may, nonetheless, remain true that long-range planning of an integrated program of community mental health services for children will indicate a place for a clinic or clinics associated with authoritarian settings but available to all referral sources. At such time, the Court would continue to require a diagnostic clinic or, perhaps, the clinically staffed reception units being tested currently, to provide reports and recommendations essential to treatment, but might not require a treatment clinic per se. Given a fully qualified probation casework staff backed by psychiatric consultants, children who should properly be treated in court would be seen by probation counselors, while those who should not be so treated might then be referred to a clinic outside court.

THE COURT INTAKE PROJECT. Since the completion of the data-gathering and evaluation phases of this study of the Children's Court, the Court has launched a demonstration-research effort which may be highly significant in the Court's development and may be of interest to the remainder of the juvenile court move-

[10] Kahn, *Police and Children*, pp. 57-58.
[11] Peck and Bellsmith, *op. cit.*

ment. At the time of this writing, a demonstration year has been concluded and a period of evaluation and clarification of findings is to begin. There are not yet available the kinds of data essential even to preliminary weighing of what has been accomplished, nor has observation of the project been feasible. It is therefore possible only to describe the rationale of the project, its goals, and its operations as reported by those who are participating in it.

Convinced that the Court could identify clients most in need of some form of psychiatric evaluation or of treatment and could achieve integration with the total services of a community only as it carefully screened all cases appearing before it and prepared clients to understand and use court services, clinic leadership urged the demonstration initially to determine how such screening and explanation of the Court might operate, and to study the effects of screening on court dispositions. Financial backing was obtained from several philanthropic foundations, and responsibility was placed by the Presiding Justice in the hands of an advisory committee consisting of himself, another justice who had been associated with the launching of the Treatment Clinic, a psychiatrist involved in the Clinic's beginnings and known as a leader of the child guidance movement, a former president of the American Psychiatric Association, and the dean of a social work school (who was at one time a children's court judge). Operations were launched in Manhattan after the cooperation of a group of judges and of probation leadership was obtained. Following the hiring of personnel, criteria for screening were examined on the basis of periods of court observation and some pilot interviews by probation-clinic "couples" (a psychiatrist and a probation supervisor, a clinic counselor and a probation officer, etc.). At the same time, the Clinic experimented with devices for group testing and group intake interviews.[12]

Working with a limited group of clients in one borough, who participated voluntarily, and seeking to protect petitioners' and respondents' rights and to avoid interference with the evidence

[12] For the background of the demonstration see New York City, Domestic Relations Court, *Annual Report, 1952*, pp. 14, 24-27.

which must be weighed by a judge at the adjudication phase, the experimental Reception Unit conducted interviews, psychological tests, and perhaps a reading test before a child was called into the courtroom for the first hearing. By cooperation with the Probation Department, it was possible to do this without interference with the flow of work in the courtroom. It was reported—at the time this study went to press—that such interview and test data, supplemented where possible by Social Service Exchange clearance and necessary telephone calls to agencies to whom the family was known, were of considerable value to clients and court staff. Data gathered could be of help to the judge in interim disposition planning after adjudication; there seemed to be greater likelihood, too, of identifying children in need of intensive psychiatric study or even hospital observation before the second hearing and of clarifying which cases within court jurisdiction could best be treated under voluntary auspices.

The approach is best illustrated by a composite case, prepared by the Unit to indicate how it conceives of its assignment:

Billy's stomach felt queer. His face was drained of color and he might have almost fallen had the policeman not held his arm as they walked away from the petition desk. He was trembling with rage and fear.

"Policeman, officers, cops, dirty cops—just because I was fooling around with that girl. It was as much her fault as it was mine—if she hadn't yelled, I wouldn't have hit her. Now they are going to drag me and my old man into a courtroom before some crazy old judge. . . . Well, what is this, this is not a courtroom. What is that lady saying to my father?"

The "lady" was a receptionist talking to Mr. Rodriguez, Billy's father. "This," she was saying, "is a Children's Court Reception Service. We are a voluntary service here to help you and your boy understand what this court procedure is all about, and to help the judge know a little bit more about you and your difficulty when you come before him later in the day. It is not required by the court that you should see us and you may go directly before the judge if you prefer. If you wish, however, we will try to be helpful to you."

Mr. Rodriguez sighed, half in relief and half in apprehension. "I hope I don't have to see a doctor. Everything makes me so nervous," he said. He looked around and then added, "Well, maybe." There was again a silence and then in a rush of broken English, he said almost pleadingly, "Yes, please, I think I would like to talk to somebody. I have lots of trouble." Billy said nothing, but when the receptionist looked inquiringly in his direction he nodded assent in a half grudging, half suspicious fashion.

Within the next two hours Billy and his father were seen by a social worker and a psychologist who afterwards consulted with the Receptionist Service psychiatrist regarding the case. All three of the professional people were concerned about Billy's impending court appearance. The psychologist characterized Billy as "bristling with anxiety." The social worker agreed. "He is so frightened," she said, "that it took me almost half an hour to reassure him so that he could even talk to me about himself." The psychiatrist raised the question of whether or not Billy might be suffering from an anxiety neurosis. It was pointed out that for many years, since he had been a toddler, Billy had been motherless, but there seemed to be even more to it than that. The psychologist found some of the test results on the father suspicious and with the judge's permission he was interviewed by the psychiatrist who found these suspicions confirmed. The psychiatrist later reported to the judge. "Billy," he said, "is living with a father who is walking a thin line between reality and psychosis. He is one of those people who may truly be said to be living their lives on the brink of insanity. The kind of trouble that Billy was getting into is that which might be expected from a boy who not only felt unloved but lived in constant terror of the disturbed father and his own frightened fantasies."

It was these fantasies that the Reception Service social worker had to deal with in preparing Billy for his court appearance. She succeeded in some measure so that by the time Billy appeared before the judge, although not entirely convinced that the proceeding was designed to help him, he at least no longer saw it as a chamber of horrors with the judge as the chief ogre.

The Reception Service report assisted the judge to understand Mr. Rodriguez as he listened to his protestations of his love for Billy and his promises to take better care of him. The judge was able to recognize that despite Mr. Rodriguez's sincerity, he was a very sick man and that there were real limits to what the community might expect from him in the care of his child. After making a finding of delinquency, as a means of further evaluating the situation the judge arranged for a full probation and investigation procedure, for which Billy and his father had been prepared in their interview in the

Reception Service. The Reception Service report was passed on to the Probation Department to facilitate their investigation.

At a hearing some weeks later, the judge, on the basis of the information derived from the court hearing, the probation investigation and the Reception Service report, instructed the Reception Service representative and the probation officer to begin the job of straightening out this highly complicated situation. Billy and his father were both referred to the treatment division of the Mental Health Service of the court, where after a period of several months of brief psychotherapy it was possible to refer father and son to a privately sponsored child guidance clinic. For several months the court, through the Probation Department, kept in touch with the clinic to see that progress was satisfactory. At last reports things were going well and the case has now been discharged from the court. Thus, through the collaborative efforts of the judge, the probation officer and the clinical team of the Reception Service, the court was instrumental in assisting in the productive resolution of one of the many thousands of similarly complicated and difficult situations that pass through its doors. This was achieved through the court's use of its clinical personnel to aid its other departments in evaluating and scientifically planning the disposition of this case.[13]

This case story illustrates several aspects of the project's activity as it seeks to:

1. Provide data of value in arriving at an interim disposition on the day of a first hearing (detention, parole, hospital observation, etc.)

2. Prepare children and parents to understand the courtroom experience and use it constructively

3. Initiate a relationship which, where appropriate, may be sustained as the child is referred, after disposition, for continued service in the Treatment Clinic

4. Identify gaps and defects in community agencies and services which become apparent in the nature of situations referred to and from the Court or in the efforts of the Court to serve clients

5. Assemble data which will contribute to somewhat broader understanding of the problems of the children and families that come to the Court

[13] New York City, Domestic Relations Court, *Annual Report*, 1952, pp. 28-31.

6. Develop and test techniques appropriate for brief psychological and psychiatric evaluation of court cases, individual and group intake interviews, individual and group treatment.

On the basis of preliminary description of its work, the project has obtained financial backing for a second year of operation. It plans to evaluate the first year's efforts systematically, to determine the values of the procedure and the patterns of operation most likely to yield the results sought. It will seek also to relate what have thus far been independent and, in a sense, parallel operations to routine court procedures, and to determine how its processes may become part of standard practice. In addition, specified research interests relating to remedial reading, psychological tests, the psychosocial determinants of maladjustment, and so forth, will be followed in further detail. Particular attention is to be given to validation of brief psychological test batteries, further experimentation with group tests and interviews, as well as to improvement both of the content of the case studies per se and of the form of the reports made available to the Court, the probation officers, and community agencies. The Presiding Justice has, for his part, expressed his intent to utilize project data as they become available, to demonstrate to city authorities the need to provide for all clients, as part of the regular court routine, the kinds of services being developed by the Reception Unit.

At the time of this writing it was not yet clear how the proposed realignment of treatment and diagnostic resources and the several procedural changes would be applied outside Manhattan, scene of the experiment. Yet to be determined, too, were the attitudes of the judges as a group to the long-range goals of the project, the effect of the Reception Unit on probation operations, or—of primary importance—whether, on the whole, those served by the Reception Unit fared better than those handled by the routine court procedures.

Central to the entire Reception Unit concept, it will be noted, is recognition of the need for an intake service charged both with preparing clients for the courtroom and with providing the judge with available data relevant to interim disposition. The project's experience must, therefore, be examined with particular care in relation to success in developing this function and its effect on court services. While eventually, if found valid, Reception Unit services should be incorporated into regular court routine so as to be available to all cases, only a small portion of the petition cases can be included for the demonstration period. Moreover, to date, the project has been aligned with the Bureau of Mental Health Services rather than tested as a function of the entire court process for all clients. Bureau of Adjustment clients are, naturally, not screened at present; and the relation of the proposed procedures to the information clerk and the petition desk has not yet been explored. The legal complications inherent in any interview prior to a formal hearing before a judge have apparently been avoided by stressing that the interview is voluntary and avoiding discussion of the evidence per se.

Should the basic screening operations be shown to yield improved services, the project will have presented evidence of the validity of the Bureau of Applications concept developed independently by this study (Chapter XI). However, it will perhaps have carried that concept a step further in its definition (a) of the composition of the units and (b) of the tie between the reception function and the clinical services. For, while the proposal for a unified Bureau of Applications includes much of what the Unit has sought, and also stresses the inclusion of information desk, petition desk, and court reporting functions, the Bureau of Applications is conceived as essentially a social service unit. The Reception Unit has, instead, taken the form of a clinical team and has sought to bring a battery of diagnostic instruments and skills to bear on case situations. It has not yet, however, found its place in the total pattern of routine court operations as distinct from the mental health services. In addition to demonstrating the effectiveness of the instruments used, the Unit must establish the feasibility of requesting psychiatrist-psychologist-social work teams for all court offices and must indicate the appropriate balance of the professions in each team. Recognizing the difficulty of obtaining and financing psychiatric time, the leadership of the demonstration has considered use of the psychiatrists more in a consultant rather than service capacity and may thus change the emphasis somewhat.

In regard to the second point, the tie between the Unit and the clinical services, great value may be expected to derive from a plan which moves clients rapidly from screening to hearing to treatment, without the long periods of discussion, consideration, request, and waiting which now prevail. Moreover, with clinic personnel thus in a position, given the cooperation of the judges, to influence in major measure the choice of cases referred to the Treatment Clinic, there is some likelihood that the limited number of Treatment Clinic cases will be selected in the most strategic manner.

Summing up, the Reception Unit demonstration has been designed to blaze new trails and to introduce new levels of service—and may prove able to do so. New concepts are combined with considerable devotion by a research and operations team which is dedicated to increasing the effectiveness of clinical personnel in particular, and of the Court in general. The planned follow-up studies are yet to be undertaken and other evaluations are projected. Results must be watched carefully and, if favorable, followed by incorporation of major proposals and procedures into normal routine; for this demonstration could be the much-needed first step in a general strengthening of the Children's Court.

IX. SERVICES AND RESOURCES

When the juvenile court movement began, it was assumed and sometimes required that probation services would be provided by private agencies. Probation officers, at first unpaid volunteers, later received their salaries from private benevolent societies. As probation services were accepted as a public responsibility, some existing voluntary (often sectarian) agencies undertook to make social work and psychiatric facilities available to the court, and some new agencies were created for this purpose. Courts could refer families to these facilities, whether or not there had been formal court action. Other private agencies developed panels of volunteer "big brothers" or "big sisters" who would attempt to help children known to the court, in lieu of, or parallel to, probation efforts. Both these patterns developed in New York City and have continued.

VOLUNTARY AGENCIES IN THE COURT. The Children's Court, of course, draws on many voluntary and public social welfare and institutional resources; but several voluntary social agencies are by tradition particularly closely connected with it. These agencies are provided with office space in each borough for liaison, conference, and interviewing activities and relate to court operations through probation officers, Bureau of Adjustment personnel, and sometimes the judges themselves. Their activities vary from those conducted solely by volunteers to those depending largely on professionally trained personnel.

One of the two largest programs, by tradition *in* the Court, is maintained by the Guidance Institute of Catholic Charities, Youth Counseling Service, Archdiocese of New York. Since its inception in its present form in 1944, it has maintained a court consultant who developed a pattern of work in Manhattan which, at the time of this study, was being duplicated in the Bronx. The Brooklyn Children's Court is served in similar fashion by a court representative of Catholic Charities, Diocese of Brooklyn. The court consultant functions as a liaison worker between the Court and the agency and is responsible for screening referrals made by the Court, handling the agency's intake study, and notifying the Court of the agency's action on cases. She receives referrals of the following cases: those which appear in the Bureau of Adjustment and in which official court action is not considered desirable or necessary; those in which the judge dismisses the petition and makes a direct referral; those in which the judge postpones adjudication and asks the Youth Counseling Service to study the case (the case is usually dismissed on acceptance by the Service); cases similar to these but referred after adjudication and prior to disposition (the agency sees the child for a period of exploration while he is on parole); those in which the child is on probation but the probation officer remains inactive while the agency assumes responsibility for treatment and reports regularly to the probation officer. The Youth Counseling Service prefers to receive cases in this latter group at the beginning of probation rather than after a period of active probation. The practice of working with such cases is less common in Brooklyn, where Catholic Charities does not have a Youth Counseling Service.[1]

The assumption of full responsibility for treatment while the Probation Bureau remains technically active is a relatively new departure for the Youth Counseling Service. Its development follows a pattern long successfully demonstrated by the Jewish Board of Guardians, which is represented in the courts of the three largest boroughs by paid professional staff and ten volunteers who perform

---

[1] More detailed description is to be found in a three-page mimeographed (undated) circular describing the service, issued by the Youth Counseling Service. Detail re Brooklyn policy is summarized in an unpublished manual of Catholic Charities, Diocese of Brooklyn.

similar functions and who also, where appropriate, provide a liaison service between the Court and other voluntary Jewish social agencies. In addition to these services, Jewish Board of Guardians representatives interview all Jewish clients before they go before the judge and appear with them at hearings. They prepare these clients for the courtroom experience and assemble sufficient background data to enable the judge to determine whether remand to a shelter or detention facility or parole in the community is the best temporary plan, while awaiting the case study by the probation officer. The assembled information is, of course, quite helpful to probation officers as they begin the investigations. Moreover, the knowledge which these representatives have of other Jewish social agencies and institutions enables them to prepare clients when direct referrals are made by the judge as well as to assist probation officers in selecting the most appropriate resources. The contact with the client is often sufficiently intensive so that the court representative is the one to whom he returns if, for instance, difficulties arise in connection with placement plans.

In both of the above instances, the acceptance of a case may mean the inauguration of a period of treatment by trained caseworkers who function under psychiatric guidance. Where desirable as a supplement to, or in place of, intensive treatment, the agencies arrange contacts between the child and a "Big Brother" or "Big Sister" of the same sectarian group. The Catholic program also emphasizes referrals to the parish priest since many of the court clients are considered to be lax in religious observance. The Youth Counseling Service's directives state, however, that there are instances and occasions when casework considerations make such referral unwise.[2]

Protestant welfare agencies are not represented in the Court by a similar single coordinating and liaison service, and coverage is, in general, less complete. For the most part, probation officers have made direct referrals to nonsectarian or Protestant welfare agencies where indicated; but in these instances the probation officers have

[2] Undated mimeographed circular, Youth Counseling Service.

usually continued their responsibilities and contacts until case closing.

Over the years, the Protestant Big Brother Movement and the Protestant Big Sisters in particular have worked with the Court in varied ways. At the time of this study each organization assigned either voluntary or paid workers to all the courts part-time or sporadically and, at the request of judges and probation officers, attempted to arrange a child's contact with a "Big Brother" or "Big Sister." The Big Sisters maintained trained social work staff in one borough for case evaluation, referral, and introduction of children to "Big Sisters," and plans were under way for expansion in another borough. The Big Brother Movement employed paid staff in their own borough offices and referred cases to their panels of "Big Brothers." Their services were, generally, not available for Protestant Negro boys, and individual probation officers sought to make their own arrangements through personal contacts. Efforts were under way to recruit fully trained staff, and to increase the number of Negro "Big Brothers."

Both the trained and untrained representatives of the sectarian groups have contributed to court operations in many other important ways, several of which deserve mention. At times of staff turnover, the Jewish Board of Guardians representatives in particular have assured a certain amount of continuity in work with children. Experienced Catholic Charities and Jewish Board of Guardians workers have contributed to the orientation of new probation officers and judges, and have even, informally, supplemented efforts of supervisors. All the voluntary agencies have been excellent friends of the Court, interpreting court needs when it has been necessary to turn to authorities or to the public at large in connection with court problems or budget.

The activities of these agencies have not been studied in any detail; however, there is general agreement that since they assure prior evaluation of cases by fully trained staff members, the Youth Counseling Service and the Jewish Board of Guardians programs are likely to use volunteers where they can truly serve and to provide trained staff for cases requiring professional skills. The promise of similar efforts to provide service for more of the Protestant children is therefore a hopeful sign.

In view of the demonstrated values of services made available through all the voluntary agencies mentioned, few doubt the wisdom of the Court's continuing to call upon them. Questions are raised, however, about those few cases in which a representative of a private agency is in effect designated as fully responsible for a child who is officially under the Court's jurisdiction but remains only technically on probation. Witmer, who most forcefully expresses the objection to such practice, stresses that, once adjudicated, a child should deal with the representatives of the public whose law was evaded or violated;[3] in this perspective, the Court should not delegate its authority in cases in which continued probation is considered necessary but can, of course, use voluntary resources as a supplement to probation status and contacts.

Thus, without yielding its responsibility, the Court could, as the *Standard Juvenile Court Act* states, "follow the example of the best private agencies in cooperation with others, taking advantage of the resources they offer in helping to work out the complicated and difficult problems often presented." [4] Even at the present time—and surely as the New York City Children's Court recruits more fully qualified staff—judges and probation officers should be able to decide on the basis of a child's treatment needs whether he is best served through a court-based relationship with a probation officer, by a caseworker in another public agency, or by a volunteer or staff member in a privately supported guidance agency (with or without concomitant probation status and reporting). Referral should not be made on the frequent but unjustifiable assumption that *any* voluntary group provides services superior to that of the Probation Department. Referral should be made only where it is believed that the voluntary agency rather than a public one, whether or not the setting is authoritarian, would assure the appropriate service. Where, for legal or treatment reasons, a formal re-

---

[3] Witmer, *Social Work*, p. 414.
[4] National Probation and Parole Association, *A Standard Juvenile Court Act*, comment on pp. 35-36.

lationship to the Court is considered essential after adjudication, the case should remain within the court structure, served by court clinic or Probation Department through frequent or only occasional contacts, as needed. If, at some point, therapeutic value is seen in the full transfer to a private agency of a child already on probation, probation officers, judges, and voluntary agency representatives should make it clear that referral is an alternative to probation and that while representatives of such agencies may bring cases to court, they do not function as probation officers.

Study of court intake activities demonstrates clearly that all clients before the Court require the kind of service currently, and competently, provided for a minority of cases by one sectarian agency: the assembling of background data and preparation of clients for the courtroom, whether or not the petition comes via the Bureau of Adjustment. Provision must, therefore, be made for qualified court staff to undertake this responsibility. In brief, services essential to all clients, as an intrinsic part of court operations, should gradually be assumed by the official court staff.[5] Given such a development, the freeing of voluntary agency staff members and resources would permit expansion of the extremely important liaison and treatment services through which voluntary agencies could join with the Court in seeking to assure a system of community services designed to meet varying individual needs.

DETENTION AND SHELTER. The daily work of the Court requires the ready availability of facilities where children can be "sheltered" (a term used for the care of those allegedly neglected) or placed in "detention" (a term used for the care of those allegedly delinquent). While it was outside the scope of this study to evaluate the quality of available facilities, it was necessary to consider their adequacy in number and the uses made of them.

The Court's leadership has adopted the criteria of the National Probation and Parole Association in defining the groups of children considered to require detention:

[5] See recommendation for a Bureau of Applications in Chap. XI.

1. Children so beyond control that parents or guardians may not be able to prevent a repetition of behavior which is menacing to themselves or the community, such as repeated offenses, armed robbery, serious assault and certain sex cases.

2. Children who are in physical or moral danger in their own homes or who are temporarily stranded and for whom no other immediate emergency placement (such as with friends, relatives or neighbors) is possible.

3. Children whose presence in court, return to another jurisdiction or community, long-time placement or uninfluenced testimony in another court can only be assured by detention.[6]

This study could not systematically review all aspects of the use made of detention. It did not try to verify or to disprove the claim made by some that detention facilities—Youth House and Girls' Camp—are being used improperly in the community. Since such practice might violate basic rights and, hence, be of concern to the Court, it is relevant, however, to mention the allegations. Those who raise questions, on the basis of available statistics, as to whether New York City is using detention in accord with recommended standards call attention, for instance, to the fact that only about a fifth of the boys detained in Youth House are eventually committed to institutions by the Court, while the rest remain at home after court disposition. They note, too, that almost as many children are brought to Youth House by the police evenings and weekends, when court is not in session, as enter following the judge's evaluation of the appropriateness of detention. When such cases are reviewed in the courtroom, the judge decides against continued detention in more than half of all cases originally detained by the police.[7]

Those with contrary opinions note that the statistics disclose decreasing proportions of children detained at the suggestion of the police when court is not in session or accepted by Youth House from sources other than the Court or the police. Moreover, with few exceptions, children are not held in detention over the week-

[6] Norman and Norman, *Detention for the Juvenile Court.*

[7] These data are in the fifth, sixth, and seventh annual reports of the executive director, Youth House, New York City.

end at the request of the police unless their parents are unwilling to sign them out. More important, they stress, careful review of the circumstances around each case discloses few cases in which detention might have been dispensed with, at least pending a first court hearing. The crucial criterion, they note, is whether or not the detention facility itself can provide constructive experience and the detention period be used to study the child and contribute to developing and initiating a helping plan.

This study did not undertake any quantitative estimate of the extent to which judges in the Children's Court may themselves use detention facilities when not necessary in the light of the above criteria, but a substantial number of instances were noted in which detention was inaugurated in what, to the child, must have seemed like a quite routine and punishing way even though it may have been a wise plan. It was found also that Youth House and Girls' Camp are almost always overcrowded, and the judge is often placed in the position of choosing from among the children before him on a given day those who most require remand to detention facilities. At times the police have had to decide, when court was not in session, who of the children apprehended should use the available Youth House beds and who could, with the least risk, be sent home to await an appearance in court. Occasionally, children permitted either by police or by the Court to remain at home for lack of detention space have become involved in further difficulty.

Sound community planning requires careful study of these contentions and observations. Although decision to expand Youth House and to construct more adequate quarters has already been taken, on what seem like sound grounds, and while it is clear that its new facilities will, when available, be of great value, there must be continuing concern with, and alertness in the community to the use of, detention. Basic appraisal both of the decisions to use detention and of the manner in which its use is inaugurated by the Court are, therefore, proper matters for further investigation.

The Court faces an even more vexing problem in coping with temporary shelter for neglected or dependent children. The procedure has been for court representatives to telephone detailed data about the children involved to the Allocation Unit, Division of Children's Placement Service, Department of Welfare. The children remain in the waiting room or nursery of the Court while the Allocation Unit attempts to make arrangements with one of the fourteen public and private agencies providing shelter care for dependent and neglected children. Quite often the shortage of facilities or the specific limitations placed on available beds are such that children must be sent home, despite the existence of an emergency requiring shelter, and returned the next day or several days later. The Department is frequently obliged, under such circumstances, to shelter some children in long-term-care institutions, in well-baby wards, and in other wards of city hospitals.[8] Siblings are often separated from one another for lack of foster care arrangements under which family members might be kept together.

Only solution to the problem of insufficient long-term foster care facilities (see below) will make it possible to end completely the resultant overcrowding of temporary and interim facilities. As a helpful parallel step, the city should provide expanded facilities assuring immediate shelter for a child who needs it, so that plans for the night will not be delayed while the Allocation Unit tries to obtain details and then to "fit the child to the bed." During the period of this study the city experimented with, and then discontinued, a limited reception facility supplementing the regular resources and able to accept twelve children of specified ages referred by the Court and to shelter them for seventy-two hours while further arrangements were made. Under new arrangements there is to be experimentation with provision of similar "emergency beds" in several of the regular shelter facilities.

No attempt is made here to record the many liaison problems which have arisen in connection with court referral to shelter facilities through the Department of Welfare.[9] Note must be made, however, of the fact that representatives of public and private

---

[8] Beck, *Simple Arithmetic about Complex Children*. The response of the Commission for the Foster Care of Children to Mr. Beck's report and the Commission's proposed actions are described in the New York *Times* (February 18, 1952).

[9] Beck, *op. cit.*

shelter facilities, detention facilities, and the Court have had important differences of opinion in recent years about temporary shelter and about so-called "brief" remands which last months or years and are, in effect, long-term commitments. On the one hand, agencies have called attention to the difficulty children have in adjusting in institutions, knowing that their cases will be reconsidered in court in a short time; quite often, moreover, a different judge with a different attitude toward commitment hears the case at the presumed end of the remand period, thus defeating continuity in planning. In some instances, however, judges prefer remand—which involves retention of jurisdiction and the possibility of continuity in planning—to a commitment and the closing of the case. On the other hand, the complaint has been registered that some foster agencies, wishing to evaluate a child's adjustment, insist on temporary remand rather than accept commitment, although the child's need is for commitment and the Court is prepared to commit. This is a serious handicap to a child's adjustment; some children have been known to remain in institutions for one or two full years under these so-called "temporary" arrangements. Such policies would seem to be unnecessary since agencies accepting children for placement examine reports in advance and can return to court, within sixty days, any child who does not adjust. In addition, an institutional transfer can be requested at any time in cases of children adjudged delinquent (although legislation to include neglected children is necessary).

Youth House has also called attention to the fact that, because of the difficulties the Court has in finding placement facilities and completing case action, there are some allegedly "delinquent" children who are remanded for a five- or six-week period of detention (the maximum permitted), although there has been no request for case study in Youth House or the court clinic. (Under current plans of operation, some children are remanded for custody and care only, while the remand of others is accompanied by the judge's request for social, psychiatric, and psychological study.) To the child who must remain so long in a detention facility for no apparent purpose, while others come and go, "the placement must

be construed as punishment."[10] The waits in shelters, which do
not have the six-week maximum, are considerably longer for neglected children, to whom waiting for one, two, or three years can
only seem punitive; the experience is known to be severely damaging.

These are problems which have many aspects no more than
touched on in this report, but which come to the fore in the Court.
They represent permanent obstacles to effective work by the Court
and agencies associated with it in its endeavors. They can be dealt
with only on a community planning basis by such bodies as the
Commission for the Foster Care of Children and other groups.
They can be solved only if planning is followed by implementation by the responsible agencies.

FINDING PLACEMENT FACILITIES. Arranging long-term
placement for children to be committed by the Court poses even
more perplexing and equally urgent problems. Unless the placement problem is solved, the Court will never be able to discharge
its responsibilities with maximum effectiveness; yet it has no direct
power to remedy the situation. The work of the Commission for
the Foster Care of Children, appointed "to concern itself with the
many problems relating to the foster care of neglected, dependent
and delinquent children" is, therefore, of greatest importance.

The Court's annual reports indicate that in 1950, 489 boys and
girls were committed as neglected and 954 were committed as delinquent. In 1951, there were 541 neglect commitments and 1,065
delinquency commitments, while in 1952 the neglect totals rose
to 624 and the delinquency commitments declined slightly to 999.
About as many neglected girls are committed as are boys, but there
are more delinquency commitments among boys than among
girls.[11]

In 1950, 53 percent of those delinquent boys and 46 percent
of those delinquent girls who were to be placed away from home

[10] Youth House, *Sixth Annual Report*, p. 13.
[11] Details in Tables 16 and 17 in New York City, Domestic Relations Court,
annual reports, 1950-1951, and Tables 24 and 25 in the 1952 report.

were committed to the New York State Training School for Boys and the New York State Training School for Girls (Warwick and Hudson respectively). By 1951 these totals had risen to 54 percent for Warwick and 58 percent for Hudson, and the upward trend continued into 1952 as far as the former was concerned (Hudson, 59 percent and Warwick, 53 percent). These are the only institutions to which the Court can automatically commit delinquents without regard to religion, race, or case quotas and without prior clearance as to a child's acceptability. Such clearance, usually obtained by submitting a request and a copy of the probation record, is required in all other institutions serving the Court which accept delinquent and neglected children. While Warwick and Hudson are the Court's first choice for some of the children committed, they tend to become places of last resort for many others whom the Court wishes to send elsewhere but who are not acceptable.

In addition to the 59 percent ultimately committed to Warwick in 1952, 22 percent of the delinquent boys who were committed were sent to Lincoln Hall, a Catholic institution. Four percent of those committed were sent to the Children's Village, which, in the main, serves Protestant children; slightly more than 4 percent to Hawthorne-Cedar Knolls School of the Jewish Board of Guardians; and 3 percent to the Wiltwyck School for Boys, a nonsectarian institution. The remaining 47 boys (over 7 percent) were committed to nine different institutions.

In addition to the 142 delinquent girls (53 percent of the total) who were committed to the New York State Training School in 1952, 50 were sent to St. Philomena's Training School and 39 to St. Germaine's Home (both Catholic institutions), 13 to Hawthorne-Cedar Knolls School of the Jewish Board of Guardians, 13 to St. Anne's Institute, and 9 to five other institutions. Fewer institutions are thus involved in commitment of delinquent girls than of boys.

Since with few exceptions a different group of foster care agencies and institutions is involved in long-term care of neglected children, all of them privately controlled though receiving public

subsidies, and all of them highly selective in their admission policies, it may be sufficient for present purposes to note that in 1952,
36 different institutions and agencies took part in the commitments of boys and 37 in the commitments of girls. In addition,
mentally defective children were committed to four different state
institutions. No two or three programs dominated the picture of
neglect commitments.

These data serve to suggest the complexity of the task of match-
ing child to agency or institution but do not, in fact, indicate all
aspects of the placement problem or give an accurate total of the
Court's commitments. A substantial number of deliberate long-
time remands in institutions and boarding homes (see above) are
in effect commitments, though they are technically and legally
remands used to permit an agency time to evaluate a child's adjustment or to enable the Court to retain jurisdiction in the interest
of long-range planning.

The 152 probation case records reviewed in detail revealed attempts to arrange placement for 65 children, 20 of whom were
sent to the New York State Training Schools, apparently as the
judges' first choice of a plan, and an additional 10 after one or more
refusals by other institutions. There were 47 rejections and 37
acceptances of children by 21 of the institutions and agencies
which could exercise the right of refusal. Several of these 45 children were rejected by as many as four agencies, finally to be placed
on probation or sent to the New York State Training School.[12]

If it is recalled that these figures, based on a sample of 152 cases,
are multiplied ten- or twentyfold in the course of a year in the
Court as a whole, the scale and complexity of the problem become
more obvious. Involved in these numbers are children—under stress
from the start—judges, probation officers and supervisors discussing
suitable institutions, attempts to prepare families and children for
the idea of foster care and for the particular agency or institution,
extensive correspondence, consideration of cases by the institu-

[12] Long-time remands, commitments to state hospitals, and commitments
arranged at Bellevue or Kings County hospitals are not included in these
totals. Nor are cases included if, after clearance by a probation officer and
case acceptance by the agency, the judge decided on another disposition.

tions' intake machinery, the rejection of the majority of requests, and the development of new plans with clients. Rejections often mean a series of court rehearings until an effective plan is made— or until the judge decides to try probation or the New York State Training School instead. In the interim, delinquent children wait for weeks and neglected children for weeks, months, or even years in so-called "temporary" facilities, unable to settle down to a routine which permits a feeling of relative stability or to have the advantages of much needed services and programs prescribed for them.

The shortage of facilities, the restricted intake policies of many institutions, the inability of certain institutions to assure psychotherapy, casework help, proper grade placement, remedial reading, all represent obstacles to treatment plans considered essential for children. Particularly questionable too is the procedure which converts every probation officer into one who "shops" for facilities suitable for a child and tries to convince an agency to take a child. Moreover, institutions do not receive these requests through one channel in the Court. While expected to consult with his supervisor, each probation officer, with no idea of the "shopping lists" of his colleagues, sets out, as a matter of practice, to plan for the children on his case load. Certain officers, particularly those with more experience, have developed personal contacts with child-caring agencies or have learned what kind of presentation makes a child acceptable, while other probation officers are less successful in this respect.

To remedy this situation, central direction of long-term placement has been considered in the Court as a means of conserving the time of probation officers, but particularly while case recording is inadequate and typing lags behind, personnel assigned to centralize placement could hardly get to know a case well enough to interpret it to agencies. Central allocation will not, in itself, in any sense eliminate the basic lack of adequate foster care facilities.

Those experienced in work with children in temporary shelters and detention facilities have questioned the wisdom of having a court probation officer handle all aspects of the long-term placement of a child who spends months in a temporary placement, for quite regularly it is the staff of the temporary facility who know the child best and have a relationship with him. Yet often, on the basis of only superficial acquaintance with the child, the probation officer is expected to make plans and to prepare him to accept a new placement, whereas those in the temporary facility who know him far better are not at all involved in these plans. With some exceptions, most probation officers reveal little skill in helping the child and his family prepare for placement, although admittedly the uncertainty about obtaining institutional acceptance often precludes preparation of any kind. Some of the judges do all they can to introduce the plan at the time a decision is made, but little real preparation is possible at this late stage. As already mentioned, two judges have complicated the matter by forbidding probation officers to prepare children coming before them for placement.

Though the problems are complex and the objections serious, this may, nonetheless, be the time for the Court to experiment both with centralized responsibility for planning placement of children and with allocation to temporary facilities of responsibility for preparing for placement those children who become well known to them. Under this system, the staff members in the Court handling centralized placement would have to rotate from borough to borough to consult records. Since too few places are available, a suitable system of priorities could be developed in lieu of the present system based on fortuitous personal relations and chance. In designating a person to experiment briefly with placement of "difficult" cases, the Probation Bureau made a beginning in this field several years ago but was unable to continue. As such experimentation is renewed and experience is accumulated, it may be necessary to ask whether a considerably strengthened Department of Welfare should not eventually assume the total responsibility from the time long-term separation of child from parents is decided upon. Such a plan would make possible a central intake system—the only full solution to the difficulties described.

OTHER RESOURCE NEEDS. While temporary and long-term

placement facilities require the highest of priorities in a consideration of which community resources must be made available to the Court to assure its more effective functioning, placement is by no means the sole problem. The Court is plagued by many lacks of resources, which hamper it in its day-by-day attempts to serve children. Extensive tabulations would be necessary to give exact dimensions to all the needs, but it may be useful to refer to those which assume major proportions.[13]

PSYCHOLOGICAL AND PSYCHIATRIC DIAGNOSTIC SERVICE. The Court requires readily available diagnostic service in evaluating many of its cases and in making plans, yet Youth House and the court clinic constantly have long waiting lists. Long-range planning with children is often delayed and expensive use of temporary detention and shelter overextended because of inadequate diagnostic resources. There is, therefore, urgent need for improved and expanded diagnostic facilities. In this regard, several possible approaches suggest themselves: First, the development of brief psychological and psychiatric screening devices within the Court, such as those currently being tried in the special project in the Manhattan Court, might assure more appropriate referrals for intensive diagnostic study, although there is no expectation that it would decrease the number of referrals as such. Success of some of the project's newer techniques might, however, make full diagnostic study unnecessary and thus increase the coverage. Second, expansion of its psychiatric and social work staff would make Youth House available for more studies. Beyond this, an over-all examination of other resources which provide diagnostic and treatment services to the Court and to other community agencies would be needed to establish their potential for better use and expansion. The existence of waiting lists in many of these agencies is a well-known fact, yet there is no current estimate of the extent of unmet need, nor are there definite plans to expand resources.

INTERMEDIATE INSTITUTIONS. There are children requiring placement through the Court who need a kind of group living and treat-

---

[13] For a more complete review of these problems and their historical and social backgrounds, see Polier, *Everyone's Children, Nobody's Child.*

ment that the New York State Training Schools cannot provide. However, they are not so ill as to require commitment to a state hospital. Some of these children are served in voluntary institutions; but others have been inappropriately returned home or sent to available public shelter or long-term facilities. The Commission for the Foster Care of Children has recommended to the Mayor that one of the existing shelters be converted into an interim treatment facility for a small group of children and that residential treatment facilities be made available by the state. As a result of a recent study, New York State, through the Department of Social Welfare and the New York State Mental Health Commission, is making grants to several sectarian agencies to launch limited experimental programs for this group of children. This, however, is only a beginning and will have to be supplemented by other publicly financed facilities.

VOCATIONAL GUIDANCE. A significant number of the children known to the Court seek part-time or, having reached the age of sixteen, full-time employment. Some probation officers exercise ingenuity in establishing contacts with potential employers, referring children for aptitude tests, or using employment agencies. Others know less about such resources or work in areas where resources are lacking.

While finding a probationer employment when he is sixteen is by no means the whole answer to his problem, though it is often so regarded, in a significant number of cases finding a job may be an important part of a young person's plan. The probation officer must then have access to good vocational guidance and employment agency resources. The lack of such resources for teen-agers is apparently city-wide, but further appraisal is necessary before the nature of required facilities can be specified. Planning groups must eventually clarify whether the school system (which surely has responsibility for those under sixteen), the State Employment Service, or the several voluntary agencies should take major responsibility in helping those over sixteen develop employment plans and find jobs.

RESIDENTIAL UNITS. This need is more pronounced in courts serving adolescents, but it is also marked in the Children's Court. Young people who have been institutionalized because of conditions in their homes may adjust well while at the institution, only to return to the same home atmosphere and come back to court after new offenses—often intentional in order to assure apprehension and removal from the home. Others, not previously institutionalized, can make better adjustments if they are enabled to live away from their families. Experience has suggested the validity of providing residential units to serve as the transitional residences for teen-age children until they are established vocationally and able to live alone. Such resources are available to a very limited extent. The Y.M.C.A. and the Y.W.C.A. have been willing to make such arrangements at the suggestion of judges and probation officers; the Community Service Society provides residences and treatment in Dosoris and Boys House; the Jewish Board of Guardians has recently opened a similar facility to serve those who leave the Hawthorne–Cedar Knolls School and other institutions. Additional facilities are available through such agencies as St. Vincent's Home of Brooklyn and the Girls' Service League. The P.A.L., with Youth Board aid, has recently established a recreation center for graduates of the New York State Training Schools which, while not a residence, promises to provide valuable help in the transition back to the community. Since all these facilities, however valuable, serve relatively few cases and thus meet only a small part of the total need, further community planning is necessary in this area.

These and other resource lacks which seriously handicap the Court in its attempts to serve children effectively have been long recognized and improved public and private services long urged. In some instances the problem has been largely financial, and services have been provided as soon as financing could be assured. In far too many instances, it must be honestly stated, the inability of agencies to develop long-range perspectives, to move outside the grooves of traditional patterns, or to put aside self-interest has delayed much-needed services unreasonably long. This is reflected in court case loads in the appearance of families who have not been

well served—or served at all—by schools and other community
agencies. It is seen statistically in the Court's totals for case rehearings while reports are awaited and alternate plans explored. It
is reflected in probation case loads, particularly in the many pending cases (Table 14). Behind these statistics are the children who
wait in temporary and interim care facilities; the families labeled
"not accessible to treatment" by voluntary agencies; the families
who return to court week after week because there are no placement resources or because reports necessary for planning are too
long delayed; the judges and probation officers who act without all
the diagnostic information they would wish; and, finally, planning
which represents less than the highest levels of professional knowledge and skill.

LIAISON AND COORDINATION PROBLEMS. Agencies in
the community can best serve and use the Children's Court as it
succeeds in establishing widespread understanding and acceptance
of the services it offers. This, in turn, requires agreement within
the Court about basic policy and practice. For, while the vast majority of Court personnel would probably subscribe to a general
statement of the philosophy of the juvenile court movement, and
while judges and Bureau of Adjustment personnel are consistent,
for example, as to which cases should, under court rules, be enter-
tained formally, there are fundamental disagreements and incon-
sistencies in other areas. Different approaches to the Court on the
part of personnel may be a sign of vitality in so far as they guarantee flexibility and change but are self-defeating to the extent
that they imply inconsistent attitudes and contradictory practices.
The result is that clients and community groups experience varying
emphases and interpretations of the Court's role and cannot be
sure which truly represent the Court.

There are, in particular, a number of questions pertaining to the
community's best use of the Court which require clarification but
which cannot be resolved except in the context of official court
guidance. For instance:

Should a private guidance clinic, which has decided with family and child that a child can be effectively treated only in an institution, bring the child to court for formal commitment or arrange commitment voluntarily?

Who should be the petitioner in different types of cases?

When should a "neglect" case come to court?

In which parent-child difficulties should a court intervene and in which should other public or voluntary agencies?

When is it appropriate for a parent to file a petition about his child, rather than an agency representative or a police officer?

In which school maladjustments should the Court intervene and which ones ought to be resolved by school adjustment services?

These and related fundamental questions may all be answered with the statement: "It all depends." What is needed is guidance as to the factors to be considered at a given moment. Obviously, these cannot be identified once and for all time, nor is complete consensus to be expected or desired. However, those within and without the Court who would work to strengthen it cannot expect to succeed without an area of agreement in their basic conceptions. It may be noted too that while the Court is able to evaluate and refer elsewhere those cases which come to it improperly, successful clarification to the public of its services might bring to it others requiring, but currently failing to use, court process.

If issues of policy were clarified within the appropriate group— within the Board of Justices, between probation officers and judges, within the Probation Bureau—the Court might then share in exploring those matters which concern its operations less directly but not less significantly. For example:

Court personnel currently deal with many categories of school representatives for different purposes, and there is need to clarify the proper liaison channels and to specify the situations in which a direct approach to principals and teachers is considered appropriate. Current arrangements involving, in various ways, attendance officers, court liaison workers, community liaison representatives, teachers, principals, and others are confused and inefficient.

Out of their experiences, judges come to question the quality of certain institutions and their appropriateness for specific cases.

They note gaps in the network of available institutions and find they must often choose one because it is deemed appropriate for all children of given ages on the basis of religion or seriousness of offense. Consequently, judges have an important role to play, together with representatives of institutions, the State Board of Social Welfare, and other public and private agencies, in clarifying or defining the special treatment value of each institution, eliminating substandard facilities, and working to make fully adequate the total institutional pattern.

Voluntary social agencies and public bodies often have a far from satisfactory understanding of court philosophy and procedure and consequently use the Court less effectively than possible, making referrals poorly. When called upon to testify, agency representatives have difficulty in adjusting to court procedures and requirements. At times they hesitate to file needed petitions for no reason other than fear of how such action might affect relationships with other clients. These and related problems are ultimately traced to voluntary agencies' conceptions of their relationship to clients, the responsibilities they are willing to assume, and the clients' conception of the Court. A court aware of these problems and able to devote staff time to liaison activity would be in a position to help agencies clarify their philosophies about use of the court and prepare their staffs to act in cooperation with it.

TRANSPORTATION AND FEEDING. In the course of the daily work of the Court, the problems of transporting, feeding, and detaining children loom large. Prior to the closing of the shelters of the societies for the prevention of cruelty to children, and the gradual curtailment of their activities, beginning in April, 1944, the respective S.P.C.C. groups took full responsibility (although there was considerable dissatisfaction with the quality of the service) for custodial care, care of children in the court building, feeding and transportation, with assistance from the court staff in emergencies. Since that time, these responsibilities have been met under only partially satisfactory arrangements improvised by Youth House and Girls' Camp, the Board of Transportation, Department of Welfare, Department of Public Works, the Board of Education, and court staff. Although details change from time to time, the persistently haphazard, irrational, and inefficient character of current provisions makes a strong case for the advisability of having *one* agency, perhaps the Department of Welfare or a new bureau within the Court, undertake responsibility for transportation, feeding, and custodial service and for equipping and staffing nurseries for the use of children in the court buildings in all boroughs.

THE ROLE OF NEW YORK STATE. While the broad question of state-local relationships is outside the scope of this report, it is necessary to stress the basic responsibility of New York State for services to neglected and delinquent children. Legally and historically, the state has the obligation to provide care, support, and protection to children in these and several other groups. The state may, however, at its discretion, delegate this responsibility to its subdivisions, and New York State has done so extensively in the case of New York City, making the city financially responsible for the care of large groups of children. The situation that has thus been created is a rather confused one. For instance: at the time of this study (see below re new provisions) the city received state and Federal reimbursement for the care of dependent children in their own homes but not if these children had to be put in foster care. The city alone was responsible for the foster care of neglected children; while the state was financially responsible for delinquents under its own care, but did not reimburse localities for payments to voluntary institutions serving delinquents. Particular objections have been leveled at statutory wording which makes it possible for situations to arise in New York City in which state institutions cannot accommodate "delinquents," authorized agencies or institutions lack suitable facilities, and the public welfare authorities cannot (as they can elsewhere in the state) assume responsibility for developing services. Also, while it is assumed by many that the state will provide directly for emotionally disturbed children, it does, in practice, provide for mental defectives and for only some of the emotionally disturbed.

In brief, great confusion has existed as to whether the state has retained direct responsibility for services in all instances where it should, whether suitable delegation has taken place, and whether localities have been reimbursed in all appropriate instances and in sufficient amounts. Finally, there are other states known to carry at least part of the cost of local probation services, and the question has been raised as to whether New York State might not, in like fashion, contribute toward the cost of improved services in the Children's Court.[14]

A 1953 amendment to the New York State Social Welfare Law increased state participation in foster care programs and, in its provision for state reimbursements to subdivisions, pointed the way to relieving some of the resource lacks. More specifically, provision was made for 50 percent reimbursement of the amount spent for foster care, provided that the expenditure was made through the New York City Department of Welfare.[15] While this represents an important contribution to the foster care program in New York City, it fails to solve court resource problems since reimbursement is not available for the bulk of delinquency and neglect cases for whom foster care facilities of a temporary or long-range nature are not now arranged through the Department of Welfare. It has been estimated that more than three million dollars of additional aid would be forthcoming if Youth House and Girls' Camp could be operated by, and all court neglect and delinquency placements channeled through or assigned to, the Department; the matter was being discussed at the time of publication of this report. Such arrangements would definitely represent an important new state contribution to services for children who come to court.

An even more active role for the state is outlined in the recent

[14] State assistance to, or supplementation of, services has, generally, developed to encourage probation services in rural areas; but a Virginia law, passed in 1950, provides for state payment of half the salaries of probation officers in juvenile and domestic relations courts in cities over 10,000. National Probation and Parole Association, unpublished memorandum on "Probation Services in Rural Areas" (1952) and Rubin, "Legislation and Court Decisions," in National Probation and Parole Association *Yearbook, 1951*, pp. 249-250.

[15] New York State Social Welfare Law, Art. 5, Title 1A, Sec. 153-154.

policy recommendations of the United States Children's Bureau:

In every State government a single department should have authority and responsibility for coordinating services for delinquent children, developing standards for such services, establishing new services, relating these services to those of other agencies in the State, using the services of other agencies in the State, and stimulating leadership in local communities.

This State agency should have responsibility for aiding political subdivisions of the State in providing probation service and detention care.

This State agency should make consultation service available to the various agencies providing care and treatment to delinquent children and should have responsibility for promoting the development and use of social services in juvenile-court cases.

This State agency should have a clear responsibility for giving leadership and assistance in developing in-service training programs in all State and local agencies that operate programs for delinquent children.

Programs of service to children, including delinquent children, should be coordinated at the State and local levels by some form of planning and coordinating body.[16]

While the statement appropriately stresses state obligations for much needed coordination, standard setting, consultation, training, and so forth, and implies the importance of reviewing New York State reimbursement policy with regard to delinquents, it may not be sound policy to select delinquency per se as the unifying factor in planning services. Attractive as this may seem strategically in a situation in which the state has continued considerable direct care of delinquents and justifiable as it is for an interim period, it is important to emphasize that good community planning must ultimately involve the development of services in relation to special needs rather than for symptom groups.[17] In New York City and New York State, the improvements must be for all children in need of care and protection, including those now labeled as "delinquent," but not excluding children in other categories as well.

[16] "Recommendation for Every Community," The Child, XVII (December, 1952), 65.
[17] See Chapter I.

X. A DREAM STILL UNREALIZED

The juvenile court movement presented society with a dream and a challenge: A social institution was to be created which would protect and help, rather than punish and embitter, children in trouble. A court was to be developed which would guard legal rights and represent the community's interests, but at the same time yield the idea of a fixed penalty for each offense and avoid losing the individual in a maze of technicalities. At first the emphasis was on a kindly attempt to understand a child's problem and to plan helping measures, while at the same time separating him from adult offenders. Later the task became understood as planning dispositions in the light of causes of disturbances and meanings of behavior. Humanitarianism and the best available knowledge were to join forces to rehabilitate, because such an approach was seen as most economical, humane, scientific, and effective.

This study has found that the New York City Children's Court, considered by some as an illustration of what a successful court should be, has only begun to move in the expected direction. A minority of children are served with both kindness and skill by those judges, probation officers, and other staff members who have understood the purpose of a children's court, are equipped to perform their tasks competently, and have at the same time had available to them needed community resources. The majority of children before the Court, however, receive service which does not reflect the juvenile court movement's aspirations or the kinds of help that fully qualified personnel with adequate community resources at their disposal would be able to provide. For some of the children, the Court represents a well-intentioned but inadequately prepared, pressured group of individuals who cannot achieve what they strive to do. For many, it is the insensitive instrument of an indifferent or hostile social world. Thus, in most instances, the Children's Court in New York City fails to act as a "good parent" or as a skilled counselor; far too often it does not even appear as a kind friend. Indeed, it is as though an ambivalent society created a new institution and then, not being sure about what it had wrought, permitted old practices and failings to continue and provided so few new resources that the institution could not flourish.

FINDINGS. Each phase of the court program faces major problems. A brief summary of the findings in the various aspects of the study may serve to present these in fuller perspective and to indicate what might be done by way of improvement.

THE LAW. The law is, in the main, framed in the spirit of the juvenile court movement and places emphasis on protection, treatment, and rehabilitation of children. Certain of its provisions, however, are not consistent with its underlying philosophy or fully adequate to its purposes. Of vital importance is the fact that, given statutory amendments by the state legislature and/or appropriate action by the Board of Justices, those aspects of the law (and of established rules) which do require reconsideration and change could well be corrected within the framework of the present statute. Among them are such matters as the use of the labels "delinquency" and "neglect," the method of selecting judges, and the assignment of probation officers by religion. Lacking in the statute is provision to terminate parental rights where parents are hopelessly psychotic or severely defective, or under such other circumstances as justify plans for the adoption of a child. Rules relating to giving notice and clarifying clients' rights also require review.

COURT AND COMMUNITY. While the services provided individual parents and children are found to require major improvement, the Court's contributions to community standards and facilities are nevertheless significant. Mention has been made of the pioneering developments in diagnostic and treatment facilities by the court clinics; activities of judges as members of various official and semi-official planning bodies; the effects on other agencies of the treatment plans developed in the clinics or courtroom; the investigation of the societies for the prevention of cruelty to children; and the report on the New York State Training Schools. As they sit in the Children's Court, judges become aware of the many lacks and weaknesses in the community's resources for treatment and service. Some of the judges have effectively interpreted and reported what they have thus learned and, often under the leadership of the Presiding Justice, have worked actively for improvement. This kind of contribution could be increased if the entire Court were to consider such reporting a regular responsibility.

Though the Court has made steady progress in recent decades, it must be noted that its many efforts to improve its facilities and to add to diagnostic and treatment resources in the community have achieved a far from satisfactory situation. Many of the weaknesses in the court program reflect the community's failure, despite urging by the Court and many civic and professional groups, to provide personnel fully qualified for complex professional tasks and to equip them for competent service. Although it is asked to serve the most deprived members of the city's population, often the very individuals who have not been successfully served by many other agencies and groups, the Court is given inadequate equipment, placed in unsatisfactory work settings, and, most important, not even supplied with necessary personnel.

INTAKE. Individuals come to the Court via the information desk, the Bureau of Adjustment, and the petition desk. Sometimes only one of these services is involved; in other cases, all three play a role; but these services are neither under unified direction in the Court nor do they reflect a consistent philosophy. Particularly the information-giving and petition-preparing tasks seem to be considered almost completely in their clerical aspects, and the need for more individualized services associated with them seems little understood. Although children and parents are dealt with face to face at the petition desk, the process is conducted without sensitivity to the meaning of the experience to the child and is not used as an opportunity to prepare him for the courtroom. Moreover, the offense rather than the child is the unit for petition-writing purposes.

The Bureau of Adjustment gives better service to clients than most of the Court, but since it is understaffed and able to secure only partially qualified workers much of its work is below its own best standards. The best of the Bureau's informal processing of cases, referral activity, and preparation of clients for the courtroom might well be considered minimal service to be made available to all who come before the Court, whether or not an immediate petition is necessary.

Planning for the future must consider, in addition to those deficiencies, other problems found current in court intake services: the use of the Bureau of Adjustment as a channel to the petition desk under circumstances in which a petition will doubtless be drawn; the kinds of data to be forwarded by the Bureau to the Court and to the Probation Department; the role of the Bureau's receptionist.

Even if the rest of the Court were operating in ideal fashion, the failure properly to screen, refer, prepare, and support people at the Court's entrance would be a major impediment to effective service. In a court with many other limitations, the intake service is a particularly strategic point at which to introduce improvements. The Court's new Reception Unit experiment (Chapter VIII) is built on this concept. If successful and if ultimately converted into a pattern of regular court services, the experiment might well inaugurate noteworthy remedial measures in all aspects of the program.

THE COURTROOM. Although significantly different from those of the adult courts, Children's Court hearings only rarely achieve the informality and spirit of helpfulness which are proclaimed as their goals. The exceptions are due to a favorable combination of judge, attendants, and physical setting. The physical aspects of several of the courtrooms themselves are not conducive to what is sought. Some of the attendants do not share the conviction that an informal atmosphere should be created in the Children's Court. The routine court procedures and the necessity that probation officers wait for their cases to be called require the presence of enough people to make the hearings public. The fact that attorneys who appear in a minority of cases are by training and background unprepared for this court's special procedures and are determined to "win" a case may obscure the issues, block treatment planning, and further complicate efforts to create an informal atmosphere. The heavy calendars and the long delays, for all concerned, in crowded and generally unattractive waiting rooms only add to the difficulties. Most of the judges are unable to overcome the obstacles in the present situation as they adjudicate and plan dispositions; indeed, the majority give no indication of requiring an atmosphere other than that which exists.

Court rules and procedures do not, in themselves, offer adequate protection to the rights of clients. In some instances procedural provisions are ignored or modified by judges, and hearings are held with too great dispatch. This is a court with few legal safeguards, where an all-powerful judge typically functions in the absence of attorneys or representatives of the press. Under these circumstances, it fails to protect individual rights unless the judge sitting is particularly alert to the inherent dangers. Many of the judges are not.

The judges' activities in the courtroom are so widely varied in pattern and so different from one another in underlying premises that one is left totally perplexed as to what it is the Court means to do. There are judges who are extremely careful about procedure, individual rights, evidence, and the separation of adjudication from disposition. But there are also judges who fail to verify the petition with the petitioner, to inform clients of their right to counsel, to review evidence justifying the assumption of jurisdiction before making plans—in sum, to safeguard the rights of all those involved. Some judges conduct hearings with full consideration for the feelings of children and parents and the meanings of the court experience to them. Other judges seem to be insensitive, punishing, unconcerned, or too harassed to care.

There are several judges who initiate use of temporary detention facilities in a punishing way, having decided on remand because of the nature of the offense which has brought a child to court. Others consider parole to parents or remand only after appraising the child and considering what may achieve the best long-range rehabilitative effect.

In planning case dispositions, a small but significant group of judges ignores completely, or almost completely, the costly and time-consuming probation investigations, each judge trusting instead to his own courtroom impressions and impulses. Several, similarly, pay little attention to psychiatric studies. Such judges do not see themselves as team members or team leaders in an effort to arrive at considered judgment as to the best disposition for a child. Rather, in too many instances, consciously or by implication, they see themselves as *the Court*. The disposition case conference in which judge, probation officer, and/or supervisor pool their thinking, in an atmosphere of mutual respect, and together evaluate reports of examinations and tests is only an occasional occurrence. Lecturing, moralizing, routine dispositions, superficial "assembly line" processing of cases, are all far more common in the Children's Court than the exercise of the best team judgment in planning dispositions. Because the majority of judges respect and review psychiatric recommendations, planning for large numbers of children is saved from being wholly inadequate; but the fact that facilities are often lacking and that, where they can be followed, recommendations are sometimes accepted by the judges unwillingly, and often interpreted and implemented unskillfully, decreases their worth in considerable measure.

The court reporting officers perform valuable liaison and enabling services, but no procedures have as yet been worked out to avoid the unproductive time that probation officers spend waiting in the courtroom, or to eliminate from the daily court calendars the large groups of adjourned cases requiring only routine postponement to later dates, when disposition will be possible.

Most judges and probation officers strongly feel the need to avoid converting the courtroom and probation work into instruments to enforce religious participation. While eager to protect a

child's religion, they honor the wishes of parents and avoid infringing on a province proper to the family and religious bodies.
However, several judges and probation officers show no such re-
straint, apparently believing that religion can be effectively promoted by lectures and "orders." In so doing, they are acting beyond
their legal rights, and are ignoring all that is known about how
children are helped or, for that matter, how spiritual values are
conveyed.

Fundamentally, the courtroom reflects the failure of the community to develop an adequate pattern of social welfare resources
as much as its reveals the Court's own failings. The Children's
Court clearly cannot meet its obligations without access to a complete range of facilities: detention facilities; shelters; institutions
for children of varying degrees of disturbance who require different
types of treatment; resources for psychological testing and psychiatric examinations; vocational guidance facilities; transitional residences for teen-agers unable to return to their homes after periods
in institutions; liaison channels to school adjustment programs;
and so on. In its every action, the Court functions in a framework
defined by resources such as these; yet some of the basic facilities
are more adequately provided than others, and some are completely lacking.

PROBATION. The findings relative to probation work in the Children's Court were readily predictable from a review of: staff shortages, a long history of inadequate salaries, high staff turnover
rate, unserved case loads, employment of a large number of provisional workers, job definitions, lack of patterns for staff supervision, and unsolved administrative problems. The level of staff
qualifications required by civil service, although above the general
level attained in most jurisdictions throughout the country, is still
below that which the Court itself would wish and which necessary
services require. Recent attempts to organize in-service training
have yielded some results, but the personnel replacement rate is
too high to assure development of a staff with minimal training.
The use of community educational resources has not been suffi-

ciently extensive to improve levels of performance. Some of the Court's supervisors have begun to train personnel in their own probation units, but they have been defeated to a large degree by the need to provide emergency services for unserved cases and to begin anew as new probation officers are assigned.

Effective disposition of cases assigned to the Probation Bureau for study requires competent investigation and collaboration of the judges and the probation staff. Yet, to the inability or unwillingness of certain judges to respect the probation officer's potential contribution must be added the fact that most probation investigations do not reflect available knowledge and skill in case study and appraisal. Probation officers, as currently qualified, perform useful services in providing facts about home and family essential to court action, but they are not able to complete the kind of case study fundamental to optimum planning. This has serious consequences for many children because their situations and needs must be understood before proper dispositions can be selected and initiated. Under present circumstances, court actions are characterized by expensive trial-and-error manipulations; the rule is a drift into dispositions.

Without appropriate treatment, variously called "probation," "parole," "supervision," and "counseling," the entire Children's Court intent is nullified. Yet, although more than 60 percent of all cases disposed of in the Children's Court are assigned for probation or supervision, very few of these are really adequately served. Children are seen in extremely brief, occasional interviews in reporting centers or offices by probation officers who, in stressing the "checking up" phase of the work, lose the treatment intent; occasional contacts with parents in under-care cases are hardly more meaningful. While it is possible that longer and more frequent interviews under more favorable circumstances would reveal more skill on the part of the probation staff, current contacts do not demonstrate ability to understand and develop a relationship in a manner to sustain a helping process or to make effective referrals to other agencies. The Court labors mightily to bring children to a point where they are to be placed on probation, but probation usually proves to be a feeble attempt to police their activities or an inept introduction to a community resource.

There are some cases in which probation officers have demonstrated professional competence and skill—this is all the more admirable in the light of present circumstances; there are also cases in which a particularly favorable coincidence of probation officer and child, perhaps encouraged by a judge, has had valuable results. The former are rare because there are not many fully qualified or skilled probation officers; the latter are few because they derive not from professional ability and plan but rather from the chance that the personality of the probation officer and that of the child may complement each other in a manner which has socially desirable results.

Despite continuous efforts, the Court has been able to do little to help probation officers organize their work better and raise their standards. In addition to unserved case loads, staff instability, and frustrated efforts to train and supervise staff, there are other specific factors which defeat earnest attempts to organize the workday. Completely inadequate office space for more than half the staff and insufficient clerical facilities for all are major problems in probation work, yet the Court has not been granted adequate office space, clerical staff, or supplies despite repeated requests. Field work is constantly sacrificed to other priorities; the inability to predict when a case will be reached on the calendar, the need for a probation officer to be in the courtroom to obtain case adjournment or to request legal process, are very real impediments. Yet, some of the failings also derive from the probation officers' concepts of their tasks and of how their time should be apportioned. The range of demands by the judges and the consequent attempts of probation officers to meet requirements geared to different philosophies of the Court add to the confusion, pressure, and frustration. As though this were not enough, many of the community resources necessary to planning are often lacking, and an officer must quite regularly "go shopping" for placement facilities for children needing long-term care away from home; in planning for

Negro children or in an attempt to keep several children in a family together in one foster-care facility, he faces particular obstacles.

In reviewing the Court's total performance it must be recalled that its task is exceedingly difficult and that many people come to it because of the failings or lacks in other agencies in the community. What is more, the Court's actions to remove children from homes which endanger them, or from a community in which they are incapable of adjusting, represent highly important activities. Referrals are regularly made to many public and voluntary agencies and institutions—and these too may positively affect children's lives. The basic fact which remains, however, is that many children and parents known to the Court require a complex range of services and facilities, but only a minority are well served. Hence, from the perspective of the aspirations of the juvenile court movement and the expressed goals of court leadership, the accomplishments are outweighed by the inadequacies. It is this which represents a challenge to all who would see the Children's Court play its role fully and with maximum effect.

THE ROLE OF A CHILDREN'S COURT. A BASIC PERSPECTIVE. If the New York City Children's Court is to make significant progress in coming years, a consistent strategy must be developed. What concept of the court's role is to guide such efforts? What should be the court's place in the pattern of services for children in trouble?

Several centuries of repeatedly undesirable results from treatment of children in trouble in less humane fashion serve to nullify those attacks on the juvenile court which see it as "coddling" youthful offenders who should be punished as "incipient criminals." Nonetheless, those convinced of the basic idea do not always agree as to the court's optimum role.[1] Some who maintain

[1] For a summary of attempts to curtail the function of the juvenile court and a list of major sources, see Teeters and Reinemann, *The Challenge of Delinquency*, and footnotes, *ibid.*, pp. 338-343.

that a children's court should have a protective rather than a punishing function, and that informality and understanding should pervade proceedings, are opposed to expansion of the court's activities. They differentiate "judicial and law enforcement" functions (i.e., deciding about the right to intervene in a child's life, making decisions about a child's legal status, granting custody, etc.) from what they term "administrative" functions (i.e., providing social services for children in need of material or personal help, planning treatment, placing children in foster homes, etc.). They hold that the day when the juvenile court had to assume social service functions, for lack of other resources in the community, is passing; that a program of specialized social services for each community should become available and also serve the court. They contend that the court is by its very nature a poor setting for social services since it must stress fact, due process, and adjudication and should avoid becoming involved in activities for which social work must assume responsibility.[2] They feel that persons trained in judicial functions are incapable, by orientation and interest, of operating a social service program. They believe, too, that perhaps children and parents can better accept social services from other agencies than from courts which have called them in on petition.

Because of these considerations, it has been held that when "compulsory commitment or removal from the home is necessary . . . a court instead of an administrative agency must decide the question"; but that "we should not continue to ask a judge to decide what should be done for children requiring not legal but psychiatric and social treatment." [3] Similarly, an expert in the United States Children's Bureau has urged that the juvenile court find its place not as the central agency in the community for dealing with juvenile delinquency, but as a juridical agency which functions in a more limited field and depends upon other youth agencies, better equipped, to study and treat the child whose behavior is not acceptable. Whatever their current lacks and inadequacies, public welfare agencies and educational groups are

---

[2] Rappaport, "Social Work and the Court," *Child Welfare*, XXVIII (November, 1949), 15-17.
[3] Abbott, *The Child and the State*, II, 338.

considered more suited to provide the kinds of services required and should, therefore, be made available as needed in the community pattern.[4] Another student of the subject has urged that "the relative functions of the judiciary, and of the administrative machinery for the treatment of the delinquent, should be thoroughly reorganized and further separated." Courts should, by this view, be limited to ascertaining guilt or innocence. Once the fact of an offense has been established, "the court having served as safeguard of citizens' rights and of public interest, the offender should become subject under certain general regulations . . . to an administrative machinery independent of the courts and entrusted with the task of custody, education, rehabilitation and eventual release of the offender." [5] Children found guilty of breaking laws should be seen as "children," not as "delinquents," and transferred to "such public welfare bodies as are organized for the care, protection and support of dependent children." [6]

None of these experts has suggested the more extreme practice, adopted in Denmark, of placing cases of children under the age of fifteen in the care of Child Welfare Committees, with optional arrangements for the fifteen-to-eighteen age group and other processing for some of those between the ages of eighteen and twenty-one. Under such a plan, qualified members of the community take major responsibility in most cases, but procedural and appeals safeguards are provided. It has been urged, however, that juvenile courts seek to perfect their work with youthful lawbreakers and not attempt to concern themselves with behavior not clearly delinquent or to become social agencies serving many kinds of maladjusted or neglected children.[7]

[4] Alice Scott Hyatt develops her point of view in her various articles and reports, listed in the Bibliography.

[5] Klein, "Next Steps in Dealing with Delinquency," *Bulletin*, New York School of Social Work, July, 1945, pp. 7-8.

[6] *Ibid.*, p. 10.

[7] Rubin, "The Legal Character of Juvenile Delinquency," *The Annals*, American Academy of Political and Social Science, CCLXI (January, 1949), 3; Tappan, *Juvenile Delinquency*, pp. 196-200, 222. The Young Committee suggested that perhaps neglect and dependency cases should be removed from Children's Court jurisdiction. New York State Joint Legislative Committee, *Young People in the Courts of New York State*, pp. 29-30.

The contrary point of view, which favors rather extensive development of facilities and resources in the Children's Court for "delinquent" and "neglected" children, or which at least envisages an active role for the Court in encouraging the development of such services and in providing some of them, is represented by Judge Schramm, who says, "It seems almost self-evident to declare that the juvenile court, protector of children needing help, should follow through in providing this help."[8] In this view, the Court's exact role should vary with community resources and experience, but the Court should take the lead in assuring development of needed services and in helping integrate them.

The quite common tendency to see the differences between social agency and court as analogous to those between administrative agency and judicial has itself been challenged. It has been pointed out that many adult courts have administrative functions and that if treatment through an authoritative agency (probation) is necessary, it can properly be administered within court structure.[9] There is no strong body of opinion which would favor restricting the Children's Court to functions of a purely administrative nature, yielding its legal framework. Roscoe Pound expresses the basis for retaining the Court's judicial orientation in the following statement:

There are . . . special advantages in a juvenile court as a judicial tribunal rather than a purely administrative agency, such as a board of children's guardians, which was at one time much advocated as a substitute . . . experience is making us appreciate the importance of the ethics of judicial adjudication, of hearing both sides, fully, of acting on evidence of logical probative force, and of not combining the function of accuser, prosecutor, advocate of the complaint, and judge; of a record from which it can be seen what has been done and how and on what bases; and of possibility of review. . . . The juvenile court as a means of dealing with juvenile delinquency is better adapted than a purely administrative agency to keep the balance between justice and security.[10]

[8] Schramm, "Philosophy of the Juvenile Court," *The Annals*, American Academy of Political and Social Science, CCLXI (January, 1949), p. 102.
[9] Teeters and Reinemann, *op. cit.*, p. 342.
[10] Pound, "The Juvenile Court and the Law," in National Probation and Parole Association *Yearbook* (1944), pp. 14-15.

True, it is unrealistic at this time, in most jurisdictions in the United States, to talk either of curtailing court functions to a major degree in favor of social agencies or of promoting expansion of court facilities to include a full range of social services. Communities have nowhere so completely developed their treatment and adjustment facilities that they can urge the court to limit itself to adjudication and then turn cases over to other agencies for help; similarly, courts have in too few places successfully geared their basic judicial activities to the intent of juvenile court statutes to be able to encompass a wide range of treatment activities in addition. Nonetheless, choice of ultimate and ideal objectives must be made, since the aggregate day-by-day decisions cumulatively shape a court's direction.

It is clear that, even within a juvenile court concerned with arranging treatment, the process which considers intervention (judicial steps) must be carefully separated procedurally from treatment planning (disposition) since the court properly should assert jurisdiction only in clearly defined situations and not simply because a judge considers a particular child to need treatment. It does not follow from this, however, as some have claimed, that all phases of planning and administering treatment must be removed from the court structure. A court limited to consideration of whether or not to intervene in a child's life, and entirely unconcerned with the degree and nature of the intervention, could not be expected to make wise findings about the need to intervene. A judge who is not acquainted with the implications of intervention into a child's life and the quality of subsequent services cannot balance wisely the many considerations which enter into adjudication.[11] The basic question is the extent of a court's jurisdiction; once jurisdiction is defined, it must be accompanied by responsibility for disposition.

[11] Judge Jerome Frank has taken the argument a step further and suggested that in all modern law "there is no standard of sufficiency of evidence to induce belief" for "the feeling of probability is subjective." To ask a judge to look only at "facts" as evidence, leaving all else to a disposition body, is to ignore the vast variation in the way facts are seen and the desirability of a court which will, even in adjudication, approach facts in the light of the juvenile court's objectives. See Frank, *Courts on Trial*, Chap. IV.

None of this means, however, that in an ideal plan the judge must necessarily select the particular agency or institution to which a child is to be committed or the clinic in which he is to be treated. It may be, as resources are developed in a given community, that welfare departments or youth authorities may increasingly be able to receive cases on court referral and make expert disposition arrangements. The court would, however, even then remain responsible for primary disposition decisions: Should the case be discharged? Must child be separated from parent, or should treatment be tried while the child remains in the community? Further experience with qualified staff would indicate whether or not a court should, in an ideal plan, retain under its own aegis a casework treatment (probation) agency. It seems highly probable that, apart from carrying responsibility for case studies, probation departments may always represent the treatment agency of choice for some children. A juvenile court would thus remain basically a judicial agency rather than a social service center, but would make basic decisions about the direction of dispositions, delegating implementation of disposition specifics to appropriate agencies outside the court and probably retaining a probation treatment service for children best served under court auspices. To protect the rights of children referred to administrative agencies and institutions for treatment planning, the court might be empowered to request reports on treatment at periodic intervals and to concur in discharge plans—as it usually does in most jurisdictions now when children are assigned to probation officers for help.

USING THE COURT. It is hardly necessary to assert that courts have roles in social control and protection. Nor does it take long debate to indicate that children are sometimes involved in situations requiring court intervention in some form. More immediately relevant are the attempts, within the current definition of the role of juvenile courts, either to expand or limit their jurisdiction.

With some exception, the central concepts of the children's court movement are no longer seriously criticized: the State must act as parent-surrogate for certain children; the child is neither morally nor legally responsible for his acts; the State must therefore seek to protect and correct rather than punish; procedure must not be too technical since probation and clinical facilities must be used, nonpunitively, to discover and resolve the child's needs. However, because of the gap between the aspirations and the operations of many courts and the assumption by some that delinquent children are to be treated as a group apart, the right of a children's court to be concerned with any except allegedly delinquent children has been questioned. Tappan, for example, sees as absurd the tendency of some courts to deal with all manner of social and behavior problems. Since "social science cannot predict from a behavior problem to delinquency with any degree of accuracy . . . the community may not safely, therefore, employ the potentially injurious techniques of court treatment upon nondelinquents in the hope that here and there some good may be done." [12] What is more, even with regard to delinquents, the greatest care must be exercised to preserve the basic conceptions of due process of law in the face of attempts to disregard such safeguards and to subject a child to "quasi-criminal facilities simply because he is deemed in need of special care." A large part of the remedy is seen in precise definition of situations justifying assumption of jurisdiction by a court—combined with procedural safeguards:

The child should be adjudicated by the children's court only when his conduct has already assaulted community welfare in some clearly defined way. Beyond this, to deal with incipient problems or predelinquency, society cannot justifiably go at the present stage of behavior "science" and of judicial facilities. This is not, of course, to say that the *community* should shirk preventive efforts against delinquency; rather, anti-social behavior should be attacked by a broad program of child-welfare activities that are not concentrated merely upon delinquency per se but upon optimum child adjustment. Work of this scope and complexity cannot be performed by court methods. "Preventive adjudication" and informal probation merely

[12] Tappan, *Juvenile Delinquency*, p. 201.

discourage the development of resources designed for child welfare, the community being deluded that the work of prevention is being taken care of by the courts.[13]

It is quite possible to heed such cautions, while visualizing a somewhat broader role for the court. Thus, while agreeing that conditions for adjudication must be defined by statute, it is not necessary to eliminate from court consideration so-called "neglect" cases. Society has long decided that child welfare and community protection require formal court intervention in situations other than delinquency. Indeed, the "delinquency" and "neglect" labels are, as has been indicated, not essential and are often arbitrary. A court which is to protect children and the community has the right to build on the considerable amount of empirical evidence and scientific research showing that specified actions of parents as well as specified juvenile behavior constitute threats to community welfare and to a child's future adjustment and well-being. This is, in fact, more reasonable than to revert to an attempt, urged by a few, to identify juvenile equivalents of adult crimes. If statutes explicitly spell out such conditions and behavior, and if procedures are strengthened to require that their existence be objectively established in a manner guarding individual rights, it is legitimate to make a finding that a child requires the State's care and protection.

Under such an orientation, a children's court would be called upon in all those instances where a child demonstrated specific behavior indicating need for court intervention to protect him and/or the community; or where parents demonstrated inability to protect and care for children, or such clearly harmful handling of children as to require the court's action. The court would then not be a weapon used against children by parents who have failed in child rearing or by aggrieved citizens seeking retribution through punishment; it would become instead a refined instrument of

[13] By permission from *Juvenile Delinquency*, p. 210, by Paul Tappan. Copyright, 1949. McGraw-Hill Book Company, Inc. For his full position, *see ibid.*, particularly Chap. IX, and also *Delinquent Girls in Court*.

social control and treatment, used only when appropriate and then with adequate legal safeguards.[14]

The Children's Court in New York City can serve the community in this manner under the Domestic Relations Court Act. If it is to do so, the act must be implemented by adequate procedural safeguards in court rules, efforts to achieve increased understanding and definition of the nature of parental behavior considered harmful to children,[15] a gradually accumulated body of knowledge and legal opinion describing more specifically the various conditions requiring the Court's intervention, and a readiness to use the law in accord with its full intent.

It is assumed that the child manifesting deviant behavior or the parent providing questionable care would not inevitably come before the Court. The full range of public and private welfare resources might be brought to bear initially in the attempt to achieve voluntary adjustments. The Court would under such a plan be asked to consider, but not necessarily to serve formally, only cases in which:

1. A member of the community demands court intervention in a situation and, therefore, has the right to be heard.

2. A child's behavior or a parent's mishandling of a child are such as to require immediate court intervention, i.e., they represent clearly defined situations or acts included in the statute because they are known to be associated with conditions requiring court review.

3. Voluntary or public agencies attempting to help individuals have decided that the particular case situations are among those included in the law as justifying the Court's intervention and, on

[14] Such statutes are, of course, difficult to write but are inherently no more complex than statutes defining a court's right to intervene in any person's life. The Standard Juvenile Court Act, Art. II, illustrates how it is possible to use descriptions of circumstances justifying assumption of jurisdiction and including all children generally called "delinquent" and "neglected," without recourse to labels.

[15] An expanded definition of "neglect" to include the more subtle psychological and emotional aspects has unsuccessfully been suggested to the New York State Legislature several times in recent years.

the basis of experience with the family, are seen to require more authoritative treatment measures in the community or in an institution. Thus, the Department of Welfare might under a new definition of its responsibility, carry all initial responsibility for service in so-called "neglect" cases but be free to come to court when it seemed necessary.

4. A plan involving separation of parent and child must be considered, and there is no voluntary and complete agreement of all parties to such a plan. Of course, only such situations currently within Domestic Relations Court jurisdiction could be included, and not those now assigned to the Supreme Court or the Surrogate's Court.

The Court, under this conception, would entertain cases: because citizens wished to exercise their rights to present complaints; because the welfare of the child, the protection of the community, or the failure of other public or of voluntary agencies demanded the action of a body able to use authority; because diagnostic understanding suggested the value of authority and objective data justified it; or to safeguard individual rights where authoritative measures (partcularly separation of parent and child) were contemplated.

Not all such cases referred to the Court would reach the courtroom under this plan, since a properly functioning Bureau of Applications would both screen cases in the light of the Court's right to intervene and make informal case adjustments and voluntary referrals to public and private welfare agencies where such an approach gave indication of better meeting a client's needs. Nonetheless, petitioners would on their insistence be heard and clients would not be subject to authoritative dispositions of any sort (including informal probation) without prior formal determination by the Court of its right to intervene.

It is thus suggested that the Court, as part of the community's adjustment resources, come into play in certain well-defined situations, screen cases, arrange certain voluntary dispositions, and then, finally, plan authoritative dispositions competently for the remainder of the cases. The Court would continue to use many public and private social agency resources, while maintaining its own casework bureau, i.e., probation, for cases best served in this manner. Such a role could not be successfully fulfilled in New York City without substantial improvements in community resources as well as procedural, personnel, and administrative changes within the Court. Although changes in the law, previously touched on, would strengthen the Court and are, indeed, essential for its maximum improvement, even as presently written the law provides adequate framework for implementing the suggested view of the Court's responsibility.

LEGAL SAFEGUARDS. Those who use any court are protected best where the nature of the court's authority is well defined and where it assumes jurisdiction only when proper and appropriate. In this sense, the discussion on utilization of the Children's Court has many implications for guarding the rights of clients. Beyond this, however, certain improvements in the New York City Children's Court structure and procedure would be helpful.

A careful separation of the adjudication from the disposition phase of the court hearing is already observed by many of the judges and should become standard practice. The daily implementation of all the law's provisions and of court rules by several judges who now fail to do so would in itself represent considerably increased protection of the rights of respondents.[16] These include permitting the petitioner to verify the petition and informing respondents that they may take time in considering their situation, in lieu of holding immediate hearings—whether or not they wish to engage attorneys. Granted a Bureau of Applications (see Chap. XI), procedures might readily be modified to obviate the need for adjudication hearings immediately after a petition is filed. The judge might have a preliminary "hearing" at which shelter, detention, or parole could be decided upon with the help of Bureau of Applications data; however, the hearing to determine the Court's right to assume jurisdiction could in all

---

[16] It has been reported that, since completion of this study, observers have noted care in having the petition verified and the right to counsel announced. Judges do not yet, however, explain the right to adjournment for other reasons.

instances, except parental petitions, be scheduled for a day or more later if postponement were requested, thus properly "giving notice," in the due process sense.

Court procedure must include review of the petition allegations to determine whether specific conditions requiring court intervention exist, and must also offer opportunity for evidence to be challenged and witnesses questioned. The respondent must constantly be informed, by the manner in which the judge conducts and interprets procedure, of the status of the proceedings and the meaning of the steps taken. Although an attorney's contribution to cases and to court atmosphere is currently questionable, and although the facts are disputed in only a minority of cases, the right to attorney must still be maintained. Law schools should seek to prepare their students to function in the spirit of this special court and to be aware of the context in which it operates.[17]

Given such developments, the Court might, while guarding legal rights, succeed more regularly in conveying its protective and helping intent. What is more, granted safeguards in adjudication to resolve the technical matter of jurisdiction firmly, the disposition phase of the hearing could evidence greater flexibility in the planning of treatment. It remains vital, however, that the search for legal safeguards be regarded only as one phase in the effort to improve the Court; for, despite such safeguards, without careful case study, qualified probation officers, good judges, and sufficient community facilities, the Children's Court idea would be lost.

[17] See the excellent presentation for attorneys by Justice Dudley F. Sicher in "Socialized Procedure of the Domestic Relations Court of the City of New York: the Lawyer's Role in Its Children and Family Court Divisions." Tappan, *Delinquent Girls in Court*, p. 192, has also discussed the need to clarify the attorney's role in a socialized court.

XI. NEW DIRECTIONS

Once the Court's basic role is determined, it becomes possible to discuss specific means to strengthen the various aspects of its work. In this sense, the recommendations which follow are a direct outgrowth of the study's view of the functions of the Court. Their essential intent may be preserved even as modification of detail becomes necessary in practice.

A BUREAU OF APPLICATIONS. The deficiencies noted in the information services, at the petition desk, and in the Bureau of Adjustment would be largely overcome by a unified court intake service, staffed by probation officers, petition clerks, and clerical personnel, under the administrative and professional direction of the Probation Department, and provided with the regular consultative guidance of a judge. Such a service might be referred to as the Bureau of Applications. It would then be possible to have one or more trained receptionists give information to, and refer elsewhere, the more obviously misdirected people, obtain and record basic information, pull old records and petitions from files, and control the distribution of interviews to the three or more special probation officers required for the Bureau of Applications intake assignment in each borough.

In instances where the law or the Court's rules required a court hearing, the task of the interviewer would be to obtain such information from the petitioner and respondent as is necessary for preparing a petition and, to the extent possible in the course of a limited interview, orient parents and children for the courtroom proceedings to follow. He would then provide the petition clerk with data for the text of the petition and review it with the petitioner, who would be urged to verify it before affixing his signature. In addition, the interviewer would dictate a supplementary statement summarizing social data in the court files or assembled in the brief contact, and any other information which would help the judge make a wise interim disposition, i.e., remand, parole to family, psychiatric study, physical examination, and so forth.

This manner of use of a skilled person in court intake for all cases would yield many advantages:

1. The skilled interviewer would provide the petition clerk with data enabling him to formulate the allegations more exactly than do the clerks who currently complete petitions.

2. Arrest cases and other cases which must come before the Court would be provided with maximum preparation for the courtroom. As has been indicated, the majority of clients do not, under present court rules, pass through the Bureau of Adjustment; hence they enter the courtroom without a clear concept of what may follow. Remand, examination, even answering questions becomes less threatening as the Court's intent and processes are understood.

3. The Court, following its adjudication, would have available more extensive data as a guide to interim disposition for the period of case study than can usually be brought out in the courtroom. The choice between parole to parents or use of a shelter might then more readily reflect the child's needs, and clues to the need for psychiatric study would often be picked up. The use of a separate memorandum to relay such Bureau of Applications data to the judge would make it possible to achieve this end without adding to the petition material irrelevant to immediate adjudication. None of this need in any way influence the "evidence" in the case or affect the judge's responsibility to establish the "preponderance of evidence." Such a memorandum could later also serve to relay to the Probation Bureau a more complete

picture of case background than is currently available through a mere carbon copy of the petition.

4. The Bureau of Adjustment worker would be known to children and parents and, after the judge had made his decision, would be in a position to interpret and prepare the way for long-term disposition plans in situations not referred to the Probation Department.

Cases not requiring petitions automatically under the court rules would also be served in the new Bureau of Applications; that is, the function of the current Bureau of Adjustment would be continued. Where such contact eventually showed a petition to be necessary or desirable, the interviewer would take responsibility for providing data for the petition, supplying a supplementary memorandum, and preparing all concerned for the courtroom experience.

To carry out such assignments, the Bureau of Applications must be staffed by skilled probation officers who, functioning at its gateway, would determine the Court's tone. The combination of effective decisions about content of petitions, skilled preparation of clients for the courtroom and subsequent procedures, careful evaluation of the wisdom of a court appearance—where alternative possibilities exist—and good referrals elsewhere, when proper, would inevitably improve court service considerably. By the very nature of their task, these interviewers would be in constant touch with community agencies which refer cases to court and which accept referrals from the Court. They would meet with many complainants and petitioners, to whom they would have the opportunity to convey and to demonstrate the Court's intent.

Under the general supervision of professional personnel and staffed by specially selected clerk-receptionists or probation officers whose age made them unsuited for strenuous field work, and as a part of the Bureau of Applications, the information desk could become a far more sensitive reception and information instrument than it is at present. To be fully effective the Bureau of Applications would also require ready access to the judges for consultation purposes; this could be met by continuing the

present arrangement whereby the judge in the adjudication Part
(Part I) is available for consultation in the Bureau of Adjustment
in each borough. Time for such consultation could be made available more readily if courtroom calendars were separately scheduled
for early morning or late morning sessions, thereby allowing
greater flexibility for all personnel.

Court leadership has developed the Bureau of Adjustment,
has continuously stressed its importance, and might well be prepared to take the next logical steps in attempting the broader
intake program here described; personnel and resources not
currently available would, however, be prerequisite.

A UNIFIED PROCESS. Determination as to whether the State,
through a court, has reason to intervene should precede the considerable intervention involved in case study. Adjudication prior
to case study also avoids the danger of using hearsay evidence in
making legal determinations. Unlike that in many other jurisdictions, the New York City Children's Court's present practice
of assigning most cases for full investigation only after adjudication is, hence, sound and should continue; but this principle need
not preclude pre-adjudication case studies in certain instances
as at present. For example, neglect charges are now often made
by agency representatives or community members who are unable
to present adequate substantiating data in the courtroom. Until
such time as another community agency (logically the Department of Welfare, perhaps the Juvenile Aid Bureau) is able to
conduct further case study when a judge lacks data sufficient for
adjudication, referral for probation study remains proper. In such
instances, probation case studies represent simultaneously "investigation," in the evidence-seeking sense, and planning endeavors.

The Bureau of Adjustment also meets situations, which may
or may not eventually reach the courtroom, too complex to solve
on the basis of office evaluation alone, supplemented by agency
reports. It has become increasingly clear that, like the courtroom
procedure itself, court intake could be strengthened by a field
arm. While not of highest priority, the provision of field staff for

work in the Bureau of Applications structure would prove valuable in contributing to sound action in cases now often incompletely evaluated in office interviews and, at the same time, in assuring data invaluable to treatment planning, should the Court eventually assume jurisdiction.

The reporting officer, a significant link in the chain of court services, has proved his value and might be permitted to go even further, following courtroom dispositions, in helping parents and children understand both what has occurred and what will follow. At the present time, in the larger boroughs, this probation officer is too busy to enlarge the area of his operations to such an extent. However, consideration should be given to placing court reporting within the Bureau of Applications as a logical extension of that concept, thereby permitting the total load to be shared by several persons and more extensive service to be given by each.

As part of a general effort to render the courtroom more effective, attendants must be helped to understand the Court's objectives and to appreciate the importance of the manner in which they fulfill responsibilities. Serious effort must be made, as well, to eliminate the coming and going of unnecessary personnel during hearings and to promote a friendly and helpful atmosphere. To a considerable extent, the Court will remain permanently handicapped in these respects until the city provides more adequate quarters.

In sum, if all clients were introduced to the courtroom via a Bureau of Applications, if adjudication and disposition were regarded as distinct phases in procedure, if the judge had the benefit of all data possible before arriving at an interim disposition for the period of probation case study (when a petition cannot be completely disposed of in an initial hearing), and if basic rights were more carefully safeguarded, the courtroom would doubtlessly become far more helpful than at present. All of this can be accomplished through strengthening of the present structure, clear definition of optimum procedure and of responsibilities, and provision of limited additional staff and facilities.

PROBATION — THE COURT'S CASEWORK ARM. It is obvious by now that the recommendations of this study are meaningless unless the standards of performance of probation officers and judges are raised. Suggestions in this regard are interdependent; for judges will remain severely handicapped as long as case studies are of the present caliber and as long as probation per se remains the meaningless gesture it often is. On the other hand, incentive for improvement on the part of probation officers depends to a great extent on how judges use investigation reports, discuss cases with probation officers, and encourage efforts to achieve staff competence and stability.

FROM "PROBATION" TO "COUNSELING." Recommendations for improving probation are intrinsically concerned with salary scales and qualifications. The findings of this study demonstrate, however, that changes in these areas alone will not suffice to bring the probation program completely up to standard.

The character of probation cannot be expected to be basically transformed except in the context of agreement about the Court's role in the community and the functions of its component parts. Considerable discussion is necessary in the Board of Justices, among probation officers, and between probation officers and judges before a consistent outlook is established. Thus, if the premise of the Children's Court as a judicial body closely related to the community's pattern of helping agencies is rejected, this study becomes less meaningful and its recommendations have no point — but in that case, the state law must also be questioned. If, instead, the intent is, indeed, to develop the kind of court envisaged by the juvenile court movement but not yet achieved, the responsibilities of judges and probation officers and the ways they work together are very much to the point.

It is here suggested that the Probation Bureau gradually develop and recruit fully trained social work staff and discard for all time the policing, checking-up, and routine clerical completion of case studies. As fully trained workers holding graduate degrees, probation officers in the Court could be expected to:

1. Man the Bureau of Applications, except for its purely clerical functions and those technical aspects requiring expert help in completing petitions and preparing other forms for legal process.

2. Conduct, after adjudication and prior to disposition, case studies, i.e., "investigations," with emphasis on the understanding essential to planning effective treatment measures. When so directed by the judge, studies might be made prior to adjudication, but evidence so assembled and used in adjudication must be challengeable in the courtroom.

3. Carry through effective casework contacts with clients from the time a case is assigned for study until its disposition. This implies ability to prepare a client for the courtroom, to develop and maintain adequate professional relationships with community and agency sources of information and assistance, to provide emotional support when necessary, to help a client clarify his situation and begin to do something about it, and to implement dispositions. Involved in casework skill is also the ability to initiate case referrals for tests, examinations, and placements, to prepare parents and children for such referrals, and to follow through.

4. Serve as court liaison officers, performing somewhat expanded functions, as described.

5. Provide extended casework help in instances where the disposition calls for probation or supervision. Meaningless "reporting" would be replaced by an effective helping process.

Clearly, the Court cannot properly organize its intake, study and evaluate cases within its jurisdiction, or provide meaningful dispositions, including probation treatment, unless its Probation Bureau is converted into a qualified casework agency. The belief that incomplete training in casework or experience alone can be an adequate substitute for graduate classwork and supervised field experience is no more valid than the expectation that a partially prepared doctor, lawyer, or engineer can assume full professional responsibility. Reforms in civil service procedure, job qualifications, and salary scales represent the major and highly necessary, but not sufficient, conditions toward achieving a Probation Department made up of qualified staff members. Achievement of a minimal consensus within the Court about the direction of probation services is another fundamental step, and other elements, particularly administrative improvements, also enter into consideration.

Given staff stability and more personnel, to man the Bureau of Applications, it would be possible to bring probation case loads within manageable proportions. A small increase in probation field staff would be needed immediately to accomplish this purpose, and a greater increase eventually, to permit more intensive case study and treatment. Substantial additions to the staff could be justified (and the exact number estimated) only as qualifications were raised, currently authorized positions used with maximum effectiveness, and specific objectives, in the form of new levels of diagnosis and treatment, undertaken. As one of the immediate next steps, parallel to modest expansion of the Bureau of Adjustment and the first, small, increases in the probation staff, it is highly important to develop a pattern of supervision and consultation essential to effective operations. Staff training as well as efforts to improve probation administration would benefit considerably from regularly scheduled conferences between the unit supervisor and the individual caseworker, devoted to analysis of performance in specific case studies or treatment cases, total job organization, unusual planning problems, and related administrative matters. It might be expected, too, that qualified supervisors would supplement individual conferences with occasional unit meetings concerned with teaching and administrative matters. Despite their value, these measures need not consume more time than that currently required for a less satisfactory mode of supervision.

Present incumbents among the supervisory staff, with few exceptions, are not trained for such individual supervision, and the regular occurrence of emergency situations together with the existence of uncovered case loads defeats attempts in this direction by those who are qualified. A series of steps under the leadership of the assistant chief probation officer in charge of the Children's Court might prove helpful. Consideration might be given initially to general discussions of the Court's role and the place of probation within the Court, to the planning of uniform systems of case reporting and case control (there are already some beginnings), and to case seminars conducted by Probation Bureau leadership with the help of court clinic staff and outside expert consultants. Such seminars, designed to give concrete meaning to the more theoretical discussions of probation's role, might include discussion of: types of case situations and services offered by probation; case study, referral for placement, and preparation of a child for placement; long-time casework help to the so-called "neglectful" family; and the probation treatment relationship with a "delinquent" child. Clinical psychology, casework, and psychiatry have long established that such seminars are among the most effective means of teaching case analysis; through participation in such seminars, unit supervisors gradually learn to assist staff in similar analyses of their own cases.

Such efforts within the Court would require supplementation from outside; despite many unsolved problems in this field, social casework has had considerable experience in supervising caseworkers, which could be made available to unit supervisors as they attempt to develop patterns of supervision. The New York City Youth Board, for example, might be urged to allocate a portion of its training budget to draw on local social work schools for organizing special seminars in supervision for staffs of agencies working with children in trouble and might help the Court in this manner.

The training of probation officers would not, of course, be limited to the efforts of individual supervisors, although they would be key elements in the process. Further in-service lecture-discussions of the kind recently conducted, regular and special part-time courses at social work schools, and a liberal policy of educational leave are all necessary to raise the level of knowledge and competence in this area.

Steps to organize and train supervisors so that they can supervise are, however, only transitional measures. Eventually, the Court must recruit and retain fully trained graduate social workers as probation officers and as supervisors. Then, like many agencies, it will be in a position to utilize seminars and meetings to clarify policy, raise the level of case analysis, and supplement individual supervision, relieved of the overwhelming task of completely training unprepared staff.[1]

Another element, not to be overlooked in training supervisors and probation officers and raising the level of case appraisal, is the need for increased consultation with psychiatrists. In recent years, guidance clinics and family service agencies have found that making psychiatrists available to consult with caseworkers about case analyses and treatment plans has introduced new professional insights and improved services to clients. The Court has already used its own clinic psychiatrists for consultation as much as possible, but their time is limited. A long-range plan for the Court should therefore include provision for additional psychiatric staff so that case consultations may become more regular; for example, the assignment of a psychiatrist to each of the two large borough offices one day a week and to the smaller offices half a day a week would have a profound effect on case study and treatment. The participation of the unit supervisors in consultation conferences of their supervisees in the initial months would, in addition, assure a consistent approach to the probation assignment.

This is not to suggest that a family casework agency or a child guidance clinic provides the perfect model for the Probation Bureau and that all developments can analogously be mapped for the future. On the contrary, an experimental orientation must govern any program which intends to incorporate casework concepts and methods within an authoritarian setting; but the casework profession is in a position to offer guidance in the fundamentals of case study, disposition planning, treatment, supervision, consultation, staff training, working with members of other professions, and job organization. A probation program

---

[1] The first step in this direction was taken as the study went to press: a graduate degree or two years of experience will be required of all candidates.

could build on this base a superstructure appropriate to the Court. Those acquainted with developments in casework education will recognize, in this point of view, the opinion that generic casework has meaning in the probation job, but that court workers, once having qualified in generic casework, must take responsibility, in cooperation with judges, psychiatrists, and others, for gradually developing the form of casework specific to the Court.

STAFF STABILITY AND QUALIFICATIONS. The effort to improve probation standards must contemplate measures to increase staff stability, improve morale, and gradually professionalize the entire service. Increases granted since the completion of this study assure a salary scale (including cost-of-living bonuses) which begins at a level adequate to attract fully trained social workers as probation officers, but increments are low and salary maximums inadequate. Salaries for unit supervisors also begin at a reasonable level, but rise too slowly and assure only two mandatory increments. Scales at the higher supervisory levels are even less satisfactory. Thus, although there has been significant improvement, particularly for beginning probation officers, further adjustments are necessary. Standards of supervision and conditions of work remain important considerations, as indicated above, and combine with the scales to create a situation under which the Court is still not in a position to attract and hold graduates who have been awarded master's degrees after two years of training in a graduate social work school and have also had some social work experience. County courts, requiring only slightly higher qualifications, offer considerably more attractive salaries.[2]

[2] In January, 1953, for instance, when the vastly improved Children's Court probation salaries summarized in Chapter VII were going into effect (although they would not be fully effective for six months), the following salary scales prevailed in county courts:

General Sessions	$3,800—$6,065
Kings County	$3,900—$6,675
Bronx County	$3,940—$5,360
Queens County	$3,550—$5,400

When examinations for these positions were announced in September, 1951, the requirement was college graduation or its equivalent, as well as one of the following (or an equivalent combination): a two-year graduate course in

The inequities in civil service salary scales in New York City are many and require major adjustments. Extensive proposals presented to the Mayor's Committee on Management Survey by Griffenhagen and Associates during the period of this study reflect an approach which, with modification, would in many, but not all, respects initiate improvements too long delayed.[3] The salary recommendations per se are outdated both by increased costs and by the new probation scales, but the Griffenhagen emphasis on a rational structure of positions and on raising requirements at the same time that salaries are increased is sound and should be applied to the Court. The proposals are limited, however, in that they are essentially based on classifying jobs as they exist and do not take into account future developments. Because attempts must now be made to recruit professionally trained staff, and because there are relatively few supervisory positions in the Children's Court, so that promotional opportunities are limited, the salary scales should be revised and made considerably wider than those current or suggested in the Griffenhagen plan; proposed qualifications should correspondingly be raised.

Plans for the development within the next few years of a staff of more highly qualified probation officers and supervisors cannot be implemented until requirements are changed, examinations held, and lists promulgated. Until then, the Court will have to go on hiring provisional probation officers who do not qualify at the levels here suggested; such employees, who are hired at

---

social work; a two-year graduate course in psychology; two years of social work experience in a recognized agency; two years of clinical psychology experience in an approved setting. In contrast, it will be recalled, the Children's Court probation officer was required to have thirty credits in casework or allied subjects before or after college graduation, plus one year of experience.

[3] Examinations for the position of probation officer would be open to college graduates who had a year of graduate social work education, a year of social work experience, or an equivalent combination. Unit supervisors would, in addition to the educational requirement, have four years of casework experience, at least two of which would be in probation and parole. Those in charge of borough probation work would have five years of social work experience, including one in supervision in probation or parole. Mayor's Committee on Management Survey, *Classification and Compensation of the Service of the City of New York.*

times when there are no civil service lists or when those on the list refuse positions, might be permitted to progress within the salary scale at the same rate as permanent staff, with the result that upon passing subsequent examinations they could be engaged at the salaries actually reached. This step, which has adequate precedent in the educational system, might make it possible to recruit provisional workers who would have incentive to learn while on the job, would qualify for subsequent civil service probation examinations and continue as regular staff members thereafter. From the Court's point of view, this source of increased stability would justify investment in the form of intensive supervision and in-service training for provisional workers.

Similarly, it would be valuable during an interim period to implement the proposal made some time ago by the Presiding Justice for providing incentive to staff for further training; namely, that a bonus be paid those who complete more than a stated minimum of professional courses and in-service training and demonstrate grasp of relevant material. It might be desirable, too, during an interim period before graduation from a social work school was required as a minimal prerequisite, to appoint new staff members as probation aides, at a salary level one grade below that of fully qualified probation officers.

It should also be possible to open the competitive examinations for all levels of supervisory positions to those who have not worked in probation and parole at all but who are graduate social workers with supervisory experience in agencies employing trained staff (guidance clinics, mental hygiene clinics, Youth Board referral units, etc.). There is urgent need in the Children's Court for pioneer action in the development of a pattern of supervision, but there are few probation and parole services in the geographic area which can serve as models. The new scales are already adequate to attract a competitive group to the unit supervisors' positions. Fully experienced supervisors would be drawn to other positions as well, once adequate salaries were offered, and all would doubtlessly introduce a fresh approach to the entire court casework program. These "outsiders" could be expected, in connection with their preparation for the examination, or in subsequent in-service orientation, to master the pertinent statutes and court policy and procedure. The latter, particularly, can well be taught within the court framework in the course of special in-service programs.

JOB ORGANIZATION AND EMPHASIS. Far too many uncontrollable factors currently defeat probation officers as they seek to organize their jobs. Judges, supervisors, and probation officers will have many specific improvements to suggest in this direction, given staff stability and more highly qualified personnel. The assistant chief probation officer in charge of the Children's Court might, even at the present time, inaugurate certain improvements, granted sufficient authority to do so. The following are, therefore, only suggestive of the kinds of measures which flow from this study and which might be considered in the Court. General strengthening of administration in probation and in the Court as a whole would, almost of necessity, lead to review of these and related possibilities.

The Probation Bureau leadership has implied readiness to experiment with a schedule of only one day a week for courtroom and office duties for probation officers. Under such a plan, all cases due for investigation reports or other reports requiring court review would be scheduled for one particular day during a week, permitting more flexible use of field time for investigations and activity on under-care cases. An alternative might take the form of retaining the system of two court days, but instituting early morning and late morning calendars; this would facilitate an officer's work schedule, decrease his waiting around in the disposition Part of the Court, and minimize aimless waiting by others with business in the Court. Under such a plan, with its somewhat longer workday, the judge would inevitably have more time "in chambers." During this time he could be available for consultation with the Bureau of Applications and for discussion of particularly complex cases with supervisors and probation officers.

Each of these alternatives merits experimentation; but at this stage, the latter system seems more promising. Probation officers

probably need two court days a week for appearance in the courtroom with reports, for regular conferences with unit supervisors,
occasional opportunity for psychiatric consultation, and clerical
responsibilities. The continued scheduling of two days for each
officer would, moreover, avoid further complicating the task of
the judge and the court reporting officer as they place cases on
the calendar, while separating the calendar into two sections
would decrease waiting by probation officers, clients, and witnesses.

Although there is value in having a probation officer in the
courtroom during the first hearing of a case, that advantage is
outweighed by the extent to which it interferes with his work
schedule. It would be far wiser instead to make modest staff
increases to assure the courtroom presence of a reporting officer
as able as the most experienced of the court reporting officers
currently assigned. Equipped with adequate secretarial help such
a well-prepared officer might record, at the end of each day, especially significant observations based on the first hearings, or instructions from the judge that might be helpful to the probation
officers to whom a case would be assigned. As indicated previously,
each probation officer would, under this plan, receive Bureau of
Applications reports with background detail.

Changes are also necessary to eliminate the major administrative
obstacles to planning a probation officer's work week, i.e., the
many routine courtroom appearances necessary to request process
(subpoenas, warrants, etc.) or to secure permission to make referrals to new agencies and institutions, to report on progress in
seeking placement, and so on. It should be possible for the Board
of Justices to specify which case situations do not legally require
the presence of respondents in the courtroom. Generally, children
and parents should not have to appear in the disposition Part of
the Court for routine procedure, as contrasted with instances
where new substance, disposition, change in disposition, or new
orders for examinations may be involved.

A period might be set aside daily, perhaps at the end of the
morning in the disposition Part of the Court, during which unit
supervisors or an augmented group of reporting officers would

confer with the judge about such matters and make necessary reports. Such planning, representing as it does a far more efficient use of staff time, has considerable precedent in other courts and is quite feasible, given staff stability, since supervisors must be adequately informed of the status of cases in their units; as an alternative measure, an adequate staff of reporting officers could be properly briefed.

The law as written requires that a child be assigned to a probation officer of the same religion, a practice which hampers case allocation by geography. As a result, probation officers may cover widespread territories, consuming considerable time in travel. Because court cases show marked geographical concentrations, an officer frequently makes visits on the same streets or in the same houses as other probation officers of different religions. On administrative grounds alone, therefore, particularly when there is so little time for case treatment, it can well be asked whether the arrangement is "practicable," in the sense of the law. Beyond this, professional personnel such as child welfare workers, teachers, doctors, and judges of a wide variety of religions have established their ability to act in their trained capacities regardless of their own or the recipient's religion. There is no reason to assume that probation officers could not render services similarly. No other state has a law which embodies such specifications with respect to the provision of probation services. Finally, assignment by religion requires employment by religion (and, as a corollary, refusal to hire those not of the "appropriate" religion), a questionable practice under New York State's antidiscrimination law and policy. Steps to change this practice are therefore in order.

All these measures are in the direction of preparing probation officers to serve as trained and competent professional workers, able to fulfill their roles in case study, planning, and treatment. Such strengthening of staff should result in major changes in the neglected area of service to under-care cases, i.e., probation and supervision. Instead of occasional ten-minute contacts, probation officers must be in a position, where indicated, to have weekly or biweekly interviews with children, of half-hour or hour duration.

The reporting center and all devices connected with reporting should be abolished and the kind of treatment relationship essential to the needs of particular children substituted. Families supervised because of questionable care for their children should be seen regularly and helped through the use of social casework's best skills, as modified to meet the specific problems and characteristics of the authoritarian setting.

To symbolize the new outlook, the probation officer in a strengthened Probation Bureau might be called a "counselor," his superior a "unit supervisor" and the chief probation officer a "director of casework." Counselors would conduct not "investigations" but "case studies," and they would "confer with," rather than "report to," the judges. Children and families would be assigned not for "probation" and "supervision" but for "counseling and guidance," after having been found to be not "delinquents" and "neglected" but individuals in need of the Court's care and protection.

CASE DISPOSITION. As shown earlier, a substantial number of cases are disposed of at the first hearing. If a petition's allegations are not sustained, or if they are sustained and previously available background data permit full planning, there is no reason why the judge should not act at once. In arriving at his disposition the judge might, at this point, on the basis of a review of data from the Bureau of Applications and when deemed necessary, suggest a voluntary contact with a family welfare agency or referral to any of the available public or private community services. (Reporting back must be requested by the Court, lest cases requiring service be lost.) In instances where immediate steps are taken to place a child in an institution, previous court and Bureau of Applications data—made available through the reporting officer—could be used as a source of leads for decision-making and interpretation of the plan finally arrived at.

Most long-range dispositions, however, are made following the probation officer's study. The questions then arise: By what procedure can the Court arrive at the best possible plan once its legal responsibility for disposition has been determined? What can be done to reflect the interests of child and of community as defined by the best knowledge currently available? What, in short, should be substituted for a disposition procedure which, far too often, drifts into plan?

The argument has already been made for retaining the disposition function within the Court, despite occasional suggestions from some quarters to the contrary. No juvenile court has, in fact, completely relinquished its disposition function, limiting itself to adjudication. Within this framework there are, however, several alternate proposals currently being advanced as means of improving juvenile court disposition. Each has merit and each raises complex issues: one plan would retain the present system of responsibilities but would assure better selection and preparation of judges; another would turn responsibility over to a special disposition panel; while a third would introduce the use of referees.

Whatever their differences, all these proposals imply that the assumption that the delinquent can be "reformed" in the courtroom has been abandoned and that, at most, one might seek to use the courtroom experience for discussing decisions and to create a favorable orientation toward further treatment. It is assumed, too, that unlike some criminal courts this court should not permit the nature of an offense or attendant circumstances to predetermine a disposition. If the Children's Court properly regards actions behind specific allegations as symptoms of trouble or virtually as cries for help, its planning must be based on sound consideration of insights yielded by case study and examination, focused on understanding needs and appraising possible remedies.

The system of referees may be briefly dismissed as inappropriate where there is no lack of judges; its distinct advantages apply only in rural areas where judges cannot attend to all cases and in certain other limited circumstances. Under the present New York City plan, particularly if the proposal for a Bureau of Applications were implemented, informal adjustments would be made at intake, while the remaining cases would tend to be those which, even under a referee system, would require review or a formal hearing before a judge.[4]

The proponents of the disposition panel argue that treatment decisions should be in the hands of experts representing several different disciplines, rather than entrusted to judges generally unprepared for the many ramifications of their complex assignment. Leonard Harrison, who has done much to elaborate the idea and to urge its adoption in New York City, believes that, in addition to judges to conduct hearings, the Children's Court should have special disposition panels meeting in each borough five days a week. Made up of members of such professions as education, medicine, the clergy, psychiatry, social work, and psychology (the exact composition varies with the proponent), and drawing upon the social investigations by court counselors (probation) and clinical examinations as needed, the panels would be responsible for the basic decision as to the advisability of probation, foster care, referral for out-patient treatment, and would plan pertinent details.[5]

The disposition panel, as a full substitute for the judge's disposition role, is more difficult to evaluate than is the proposal for a referee system as a potential plan for New York City. Theoretically, a panel of three or four fully qualified and well-selected experts should be able to decide on dispositions better than Chil-

[4] Referees are provided for in about one third of the juvenile court statutes throughout the country and are designated by judges in other courts. Although results of using referees are spotty, there are some jurisdictions in which the referee system has eased the burdens of judges, creating a children's court career service independent of political pressures and providing personnel skilled in dealing with behavior problems. In most such courts, referees conduct initial hearings and are also responsible for subsequent disposition planning. The judges sit on rehearings from referee decisions, generally supervise and review the work of referees, and conduct more formal hearings in cases where offenses are considered particularly serious or where the child denies the offense. For details see Killian, "The Juvenile Court as an Institution," *The Annals*, American Academy of Political and Social Science, CCLXI (January, 1949), 96, and Sussman, *Law of Juvenile Delinquency*, pp. 54-55.

[5] Leonard Harrison, of the Bureau of Public Affairs of the Community Service Society of New York, has made his extremely useful files on the Children's Court available to the writer. Included in these files is a description of, and a chart illustrating, a proposed disposition panel. See also Van Waters, "Adult Offenders," in *Social Work Year Book, 1951*, p. 38.

dren's Court judges currently do. Sitting in a special disposition Part of the Court and provided with the good social studies and clinical reports essential under any effective disposition plan, members of the panel would carefully review reports, discuss cases with court staff and with clients, decide upon dispositions, and initiate them. Panel members could, after a period of time, develop full acquaintance with the range of disposition facilities and might also help the community gradually identify the need for new resources.[6] Although at first glance this ideal picture is extremely inviting, practical aspects of implementation present overwhelming problems. First, at least five panels of experienced and qualified specialists would be needed to serve the court case load throughout the week. Assuming the availability of these specialists, the considerable cost of such a venture can hardly be overlooked in a court which has long suffered from totally inadequate budgets. Nor, apart from financial considerations, is there any guarantee that one could avoid, in the appointment or civil service designation of panels, the many political and sectarian factors currently operative in the appointment of judges. Indeed, the energies which would be necessary to promote the idea of disposition panels and the merit system selection of highly qualified experts would be of such magnitude, and the results so uncertain, that perhaps equal or better results would redound from similar efforts to guarantee that only well-qualified judges be selected and that they themselves be expected to conduct disposition procedures.

A disposition panel of more limited functions, i.e., taking responsibility only for specifying details of foster care after the judge has made the basic decision, hardly meets the major disposition problem. Its value is questionable at this time in view of the limited alternatives once the Court decides on commitment. In lieu of this, careful discussion within the existing court framework and the services of personnel to centralize placement may achieve

---

[6] England has had considerable success with lay participation in the disposition phase of juvenile cases. See Teeters and Reinemann, *The Challenge of Delinquency*, p. 318, and Archibald, "Some Services for London's Difficult Boys," in Eissler, ed., *Searchlights on Delinquency*, p. 407.

better results for the present. Long-range, a comprehensive and flexible public child care referral agency might be able to accept responsibility for a child from the Court and, by drawing upon both voluntary and public services, assure welfare services and supervision by skilled social workers, psychiatrists, and doctors while that child is in his own home or in a suitable foster care facility. Such an agency would receive a large number of court cases, but the Court would still need its own disposition machinery to decide whether to transfer a child to that agency, assign him to probation, refer him directly to a voluntary agency, or discharge him without further plan.

All things considered, the most hopeful and realistic approach to the matter of court disposition suggests neither a disposition panel nor a system of referees but a combination of changes in procedure with revisions in qualifications of judges within the existing structure. Introducing a minimum of disruptive changes and the least added cost, such changes are far less difficult of achievement than other alternatives. Current performance indicates that well-selected judges, working together with well-prepared probation officers and provided with necessary resources and community facilities, can very effectively indeed arrive at and initiate case dispositions. This procedure has the added advantage of avoiding the creation of a truncated court in which the adjudication phase would, for lack of relationship to disposition planning, have difficulty in sustaining the Court's intent.

It is proposed, therefore, that a judge sitting in the disposition Part of the Court regard the planning session more as a case conference than as a formal hearing. Most of the routine actions, such as process, adjournments, postponements, could then be attended to in a brief series of conferences with unit supervisors or reporting officers at the start of the day, leaving nine or ten cases a day on the average requiring full consideration after completion of initial study. There would also remain a group of cases, previously discussed in disposition conferences, requiring briefer handling.

Assuming a period of experimentation, it is suggested that on the day a case study is to be completed, the counselor (probation

officer) and a (probation) supervisor appear for a case conference
with the judge, while a psychiatrist-consultant—or school and
social agency representatives in appropriate instances—is invited
to participate in especially complex situations. At such conferences
all reports would be reviewed and the counselor's recommendations discussed. The conference would end with a tentative decision and plan to be made by the judge. While considering material
submitted or after formulating a preliminary plan, the judge would
have the parent, child, and others involved called into the conference, separately or together depending on the case situation. Attorneys would, as appropriate, be called in during preliminary
discussion or at this point. In joining the conference, the family
members, like the judge, supervisor, counselor, and court stenographer, would be seated around a table. The judge would direct
the questioning and discussion. All material entering into the planning would be reviewed. He would then decide to continue with
the plan initially arrived at, formulate another plan, or postpone
action to permit opportunity to rediscuss the plan. Major emphasis in the final phase of the conference would be on interpreting the plan to all involved and helping initiate it.

All these factors—the prior acquaintance of the judge with the
case, the informality of sitting at the table, the presence of a
counselor who had conducted a thorough case study, the absence
of unnecessary court personnel (attendants would wait outside)
and formal trappings—might well convert even the disposition
procedure itself into an instrument of treatment. In instances
where there had been no adjudication prior to assignment of the
case for study, the hearing would more closely resemble the initial
hearing as described earlier, since adjudication procedures would
be followed and the presence of more individuals would be required at the time evidence was weighed. It might then be feasible
to recess the case for a discussion of plans or to provide opportunity for the judge to review reports.

The various suggestions made herein in relation to preliminary
hearings, assumption of responsibilities by supervisors and reporting officers, and the role of the judge would require scheduling of

the judge's time to permit such diverse activities. This would be quite feasible under a system of early morning and late morning calendars and the inauguration of an appointment schedule for judges, a relatively new departure. The following outline illustrates one possible approach to this:

POSSIBLE CALENDAR IN COURT WITH ONE PART	POSSIBLE DISPOSITION PART CALENDAR IN COURT WITH DISPOSITION PART AND INITIAL HEARING PART
Early Calendar	*Early Calendar*
1. Begin by having routine conferences with unit supervisors or court reporting officers re adjournments, process, and other nonappearance situations.	1. Begin by having routine conferences with unit supervisors or court reporting officers re adjournments, process, and other nonappearance situations.
2. Hear new cases—both preliminary hearings in re remand, etc., and full case adjudication hearings.[7]	2. Conduct scheduled disposition conferences to discuss reports of newly completed studies and to see clients involved.
3. Conduct scheduled disposition conferences to discuss reports of newly completed studies and to see clients involved.	3. Conduct scheduled conferences for reports, new dispositions, case closings, etc., in cases discussed in previous conferences.
4. Conduct scheduled conferences for reports, new dispositions, case closings, etc., in cases discussed in previous conferences.	
Late Calendar	*Late Calendar*
Repeat items 1, 2, 3, and 4, except that other supervisors and other counselors would be scheduled, so that each one could know whether his would be a morning or an afternoon conference.	Repeat items 1, 2, and 3, except that other supervisors and other counselors would be scheduled, so that each one could know whether his would be a morning or afternoon conference.

The conference would be enhanced to the extent that the opinions and knowledge of an experienced unit supervisor would be assured. It might prove feasible to have unit supervisors rotate in this assignment; it would be simpler to assign one full-time unit supervisor to the disposition Part of the Court, just as there would

---

[7] This would constitute the sole activity of one Part of the Court in boroughs which have two Parts.

be a reporting officer in the Part of the Court conducting first hearings. In the smaller boroughs, one person could assume both roles.

The question might well be raised as to whether the disposition conference procedure properly safeguards the legal rights of children and parents. Some have considered the conference approach as far too informal, particularly in so far as it limits the possibility of challenging data on which decisions are made, but further consideration reveals that this need hardly be the case. While the judge may often wish to review the available materials, reports, and recommendations with "team" members before calling in a parent, child, or attorney, the basis for planning would always be discussed again in the presence of the latter, subject to full objection and review. As they come to understand the Court's treatment intent and their contribution within that framework, attorneys might more often be called in for the entire conference. Only medical, psychological, and psychiatric data considered by their sources particularly inappropriate for sharing would be withheld from clients or, at least, from their representatives.

In relation to these issues it might be added that only in a court which relates dispositions to offense rather than to rehabilitative plan is it possible to weight exactly the evidence justifying certain actions. Where treatment planning is at stake, it is reasonable to permit, in fact to require, that the judge draw on advice of experts and results of examinations as well as on his own experience and that of the probation staff in utilizing community resources, and then make the best possible decision. The basis for his judgment must be placed on the record and must be challengeable on the merits or on the accuracy of the data from which it derives; but the disposition process is not fundamentally comparable with that of adjudication, where the right to intervene, and hence its justification in objective fact, is at stake.

Medicine, psychology, psychiatry, and casework have learned the use of case conferences in planning treatment measures. It is here suggested that a conference in which the total "community team" pools thinking and arrives at a plan, together with those whom it will affect, is the most fruitful approach for Children's Court dispositions. However, a disposition case conference can only be conducted by a judge who sees himself as a team member—in fact, as team leader, since he must make the final decision—but who recognizes that when he acts without considering the information, knowledge, or views of others who are qualified or affected (as expressed verbally or in reports), he negates the entire intent of the Court.

As team leader in this sense, the judge requires very special qualifications. He must be equipped to question clients skillfully, to know who should be in the conference room at a given point and who should not. He must balance various considerations, evaluate disposition resources, and, finally, formulate a plan for which he will assume responsibility. Then, he must take the first steps toward interpreting and initiating the plans with parents and children. Because many judges are not at present equipped to play such a role, the selection and preparation of judges becomes a most crucial issue in efforts to improve the Court.

HOW SHOULD CHILDREN'S COURT JUDGES BE SE- LECTED? In its examination of the Children's Court in New York City, the New York State Citizens' Committee of One Hundred for Children and Youth concluded that:

> The judge is the keystone of the court. No matter how honest or well intentioned he may be, if he does not possess the wisdom, understanding, patience, and common sense essential to his job, the work of the court, and the welfare of the children who are before the court, inevitably will suffer.
>
> The statute provides that the judges of the Children's Court shall be appointed by the Mayor. The wisdom of leaving the selection of the judges in the hands of one man, particularly one as busy, harassed, and subject to pressure as any Mayor of New York City must be, is questioned.
>
> A search must be made for a mode of selection which will furnish better assurance of obtaining judges with the proper qualifications. Exploration of the idea of limiting the Mayor to appointment from a list of candidates submitted by a carefully composed panel, on which

panel there should be substantial representation of agencies interested in the field of child welfare, is suggested.[8]

While the proposal for a panel with "substantial representation of agencies" requires fuller consideration, it is clear that the statement places proper emphasis on the method of selecting judges. The Committee of One Hundred, a representative group of experienced lay leaders and professional practitioners in the field of protective and correctional work, who incorporated the thinking of a large group of judges, saw this as a crucial beginning point in the attempt to improve courts in the state. This entire report has demonstrated both the key role of the judges and their many inadequacies. The proposals made herein assume a general level of performance at present typical only of a minority; yet, appointment procedures now emphasize political considerations at the expense of the skills and personal qualities necessary in the Court.

While agreement with the idea that "something must be done" about the methods of selecting judges is readily won, devising the details for a more satisfactory plan is a far more complex matter. One author lists the following variety of methods used in selecting judges for work with children:

Designation by judges of one or more of their number to serve in juvenile court

Popular selection

Appointment by the governor

Appointment by the city or county government

Appointment by the mayor (only in New York City)

Appointment by a local juvenile court committee

Appointment by a state commission

Mixed systems.[9]

To this may be added such variations as appointment by the general assembly on the governor's nomination, as in Connecticut; by the state department of public welfare, as in Utah; by the gov-

---

[8] New York State Citizens' Committee of One Hundred for Children and Youth, *The Four Million*, p. 141.

[9] Discussed by Consulich in *Juvenile Court Laws of the United States*, Chap. XIII.

ernor on nomination of a juvenile court board itself appointed by the county legislative delegations, as in two South Carolina counties. To date, bills which have been introduced for merit system selection of judges have nowhere been adopted.[10]

The New York City and New York State systems of government automatically eliminate several of the alternative plans; several others (popular election, for instance) give little promise of a more careful sifting of candidates according to qualifications for a complex job. Merit system selection, however sound in principle, is not possible in the light of current political realities. It is generally agreed that no one system of selection is universally applicable and that state constitutions and traditions would of themselves require considerable variation. Most serious consideration is, however, currently given, in discussion of improved systems for selecting judges, to a modified Missouri Plan, as described in the Standard Juvenile Court Act and endorsed by the American Judicature Society, the American Bar Association, and some state bar associations.[11] This plan calls for appointment by the governor (in New York City, by the mayor) from a list submitted by a panel consisting of representatives of the bar or judiciary, and of local or state welfare, health, and education departments. (The Standard Juvenile Court Act specifies that a group of three from which the choice must be made shall be nominated by a panel of seven persons.) The panel is to propose individuals who have been admitted to legal practice and who "shall be selected with reference to their experience in and understanding of problems of family and child welfare, juvenile delinquency and community organization."

Whether even the proposal in the Standard Act is a sound means of improving the qualifications of judges in New York de-

[10] National Probation and Parole Association, A *Standard Juvenile Court Act*, comment on pp. 11-12.

[11] *Ibid.*, Sec. 3; Sussman, *op. cit.*, pp. 51-55; Teeters and Reinemann, *op. cit.*, pp. 313 ff.; and Killian, *op. cit.* Under the original Missouri Plan, appointments must be ratified in a general election. The background for the original plan is described in Winters, "A Better Way to Select Our Judges," *Journal of the American Judicature Society*, XXXIV (April, 1951), 166-173. See also *Report on Consideration of New Methods to Select Judges*, a recent publication of the Association of the Bar of the City of New York.

pends, of course, on the level of political morality prevalent. A nominating panel chosen to balance sectarian and political interests might advance the effort to obtain more qualified judges no further than the present system. Indeed, the very balancing of interests and the process of "trading" might eliminate the occasional appointment of an outstandingly qualified judge, which is possible even when a mayor attempts to reconcile diverse considerations. However, all possibilities considered, statutory provisions which spell out the composition of a panel, assuring it a membership not subject to any one interest, give greatest promise of introducing improvement. Modification of the provisions of the Standard Act to include representatives both of appropriate legal bodies (a higher court, a bar association, a law school) and of interested functional fields on a city-wide level (welfare, education, mental hygiene, and medicine) is, therefore, a prime recommendation of this study. The group thus comprised might be called the "Children's Court Judicial Commission" and would be expected to nominate three names for each position, from which the mayor would be required to choose one.

Whatever the particular system of judicial appointment, political rewards should hardly take precedence over capacity for understanding and evidence that a potential appointee has in the past shown concern with the kinds of problems known to the Court and is willing to learn to work effectively in such a setting. Readiness to reach out to, and work with, members of other professions is surely a minimal requirement. The selection process must also explore a potential judge's identification with the Court's philosophy and goals, items far more relevant than party regularity or personal connections.

Several leading juvenile court judges have stressed that no appointee can be fully qualified initially and that many are poorly qualified, by virtue of the failure of law schools to prepare students in relevant areas. In this light, "eagerness to learn" and willingness to devote the beginning of one's term to learning become important prerequisites for a judge.[12] One New York City judge has

<hr />

[12] A *Standard Juvenile Court Act*, personal opinions of committee members quoted on pp. 12-13.

commented that part of the first year of the ten-year term could very profitably be used for self-preparation; from the community's point of view, this would be an excellent investment of time. In this and other courts some judges have, on their own initiative, arranged elaborate orientation programs of conferences and visits to institutions. The Court might well consider a formal program of several months' duration for new judges, consisting of visits to institutions, professional reading, sitting in on agency case conferences, followed by some time in court as observer with opportunity for discussion with an experienced judge. In developing such a program, the New York Children's Court could pioneer in "field work" training or "internship" for judges, a concept accepted in medicine, social work, and many other fields but thus far not familiar to the Court where, at present, judges are expected, it would seem, to be fully prepared upon appointment to assume all responsibilities.[13]

Judges selected and prepared on this basis and working with more adequate and fully qualified staff might gradually begin to record and make available, as a matter of course, opinions pertaining to the adjudication and disposition phases of their work. Their influence would extend well beyond the courtroom and their chambers as they increasingly contributed to the growing field of child welfare law and social practice.

At the present time, the monthly rotation of judges from borough to borough, or from Part to Part within one borough, has the advantage of avoiding the subjection of any one section of the Court to continuous exposure to some of the most questionable patterns of practice. On the other hand, the lack of continuity in teamwork and case planning has obvious disadvantages. While rotation of judges has become traditional in many courts in order to avoid the abuses which appear in "one-judge" courts, such potential abuses hardly match the disadvantages of frequent rotation and need not be expected, given improved methods of selection

---

[13] Judge Jerome Frank has made even more drastic suggestions about preparation of judges through "something like" psychoanalysis, special training for trial judges, apprenticeship and a "stiff examination." *Courts on Trial,* pp. 250-251.

of judges. Therefore, following revision of the method of appointing judges and attainment of satisfactory standards in all boroughs (but not before), it should become possible to consider relatively permanent assignments or far less frequent rotation.

RESOURCES AND FACILITIES. COMMUNITY RESOURCES. As repeatedly noted, Children's Court activities are seriously hampered for lack of community resources. Facilities to handle emergency situations as well as resources for long-range treatment must be available to judges and probation staff (counselors) if the Court's efforts are to be more than well-intentioned gestures. The Court itself can do little more than indicate which resources it finds lacking, while it falls to other public and private bodies to attempt to meet such needs. However, because it is so well situated to identify needs, the Court should conduct regular statistical reporting activities and research with this end in mind. Specific proposals about statistical and research operations to achieve these results have been made in a special report (see below); the Board of Justices might itself assume the responsibility for annual reports to the community about resource needs.

Although many needs might be listed, the following require immediate attention:

1. Expansion and improvement of temporary shelters for "neglected" children along lines suggested by the Commission for the Foster Care of Children [14]

2. Development of more psychological testing and psychiatric diagnostic facilities, to give timely service to the Children's Court

3. Expansion of public and voluntary community resources for out-patient casework and psychiatric treatment of children known to the Court and requiring such help under other than court auspices

4. Development of group residences and residential treatment homes in the city for teen-age boys and girls who cannot return to their families after institutionalization or who need such help in the transition to full adult responsibility for their own care

[14] See Beck, *Simple Arithmetic about Complex Children.*

5. Development of more extensive intermediate treatment facilities for children whose needs are not met by existing institutions or in the state hospitals

6. Development of adequate vocational guidance and job placement facilities for boys and girls of school-leaving age (there is need for more facilities in the school system proper as well as for facilities independent of the schools)

7. Clarification of the range of resources in the schools which are available to the Court and of the best system of liaison between school and court

8. Expansion of foster homes to serve many kinds of children, with particular emphasis on facilities for Negro children.

The Court, in turn, must give high priority to experimentation with the possible use of centralized responsibility in effecting long-term placement of children.

THE MENTAL HEALTH SERVICES OF THE COURT. Whatever their ultimate role when the Probation Bureau shall have been transformed into an effective casework agency and the lacks in the out-patient treatment resources of the community largely met, the court clinics must in the predictable future continue their extremely useful work and attempt to balance attention and skills among the following:

1. Expansion of diagnostic services either through staff additions or further development of group and individual screening techniques, with which there has been experimentation. Increasingly, should results prove satisfactory, the approach now being developed by the clinic Reception Unit teams, as part of a special project, might become the routine pattern for diagnostic evaluation and screening of all cases and be integrated into court intake services

2. Provision of a larger full-time casework core for the Treatment Clinic, to permit an increased case load and insure less interruption in cases now completely served by social work students, assigned to different agencies after nine months

3. Organization of a plan for psychiatric consultation with probation staff and eventual participation in disposition conferences, when called upon

4. Continued contribution to staff training in the **Probation** Bureau.

FACILITIES FOR THE COURT. As each section of the Court has been described, the difficulties created by poor courtroom and office facilities as well as by inadequate clerical help have been emphasized. The Court itself has confronted the community with these problems on many occasions, to little avail. Within the scope of this study it was not possible to determine the exact number of additional secretaries, clerks, and messengers needed or to describe the basic equipment required. It is clear beyond doubt, however, that the Court is handicapped, even at its current level of practice, by inadequate clerical help, and the many improvements recommended assume added facilities.[15] Dictaphone cylinders must be on hand when needed and must be transcribed immediately if court hearings and conferences are to proceed rapidly and profitably. Secretaries must be available to type referral letters and necessary summaries. Good switchboard operators are needed to assure efficient service. Sufficient clerical and service personnel must be provided so that expensive professional time is not used on clerical routine. These are all matters of moment in day-by-day court activity. It is obviously false economy which, for example, keeps a child in a detention facility for even an extra day for lack of a typist to transcribe a report needed in the court hearing.

While building restrictions during the present emergency period have slowed down major improvements of physical facilities, which handicap work in several counties, long-range plans must be made for all boroughs. The authorized Brooklyn building will constitute a significant improvement, renovations in Manhattan would be helpful, and a more flexible interpretation of the law to make parts of the beautiful Manhattan Family Court Building available for Children's Court work (the School Part meets in that building) would contribute markedly to court atmosphere.

The need for a professional library in each borough has long

---

[15] Following the completion of this study, and continuing at the time of publication, the Court found it necessary to require extremely curtailed probation reports as a way to conserve typist time.

been indicated by the Court, and means must be sought to finance it. The budget should also include an item to permit staff attendance at conferences and workshops which give promise of clarifying court issues or raising levels of performance.

AN ADVISORY COMMITTEE. On several occasions over the years, surveys and reviews of various aspects of the Children's Court have been made by the Bar Association, the Welfare Council, the New York Academy of Medicine, and the Community Service Society of New York. Other community groups have also been interested in specialized aspects of the Court's work or have attempted to assist the Court in specific instances. In 1951, during the period of this study, the three large sectarian welfare groups appealed to the mayor on behalf of the proposed Children's Court budget, and a remarkably large group of agencies participated in the public hearing on probation salaries organized by the Citizens' Committee on Children of New York City, Inc. Despite such active concern, the Court has not fared well. It has reported in no uncertain terms its need for more adequate staff and resources, yet it has never succeeded in conveying dramatically to the community what the lacks mean in terms of the lives of children.

There is great need, therefore, to channelize all the existing lay and specialist interest in the Court, to assure for the Court continuing support and understanding in the community, as well as to provide for periodic examination of its operations. Such a program might result in long-due consideration of court budget needs by the city and proper backing on specific issues arising from time to time. It might also result in a body which the Court would consider as representative of the public and to which it would wish to report. The public at large can never be sufficiently informed about the Court to know whether it is achieving its goals, nor can the legislature follow the Court in detail, month by month; but a smaller representative citizens' group could become well aware of the Court's needs, limitations, and problems.

In short, the Children's Court requires a representative advisory committee. There is considerable precedent in other states for the appointment of a committee; it is, in fact, often required by the law. At best, such a committee serves "as a necessary link between the juvenile court and the community at large, in interpreting the juvenile court, its functions, and needs, to the community, and conversely in interpreting community needs to the juvenile court judge."[16] With a slightly different emphasis, the New York State Citizens' Committee of One Hundred has suggested a Committee on Children's Courts to study "the Law under which the court operates," as well as "the court and its operations" from time to time.[17]

An advisory committee might be constituted by the Presiding Justice in consultation with the mayor and civic and professional groups concerned with the welfare and protection of children. The objectives of the group and its continuity might be promoted by staggered appointments for three-year terms, with the group designating its own chairman every two years. Should it later be found necessary, to advance the committee's objectives, it might be given formal status under the statute.

ADMINISTRATION AND FINANCES. It was not within the purview of this study to examine all of the Court's administrative problems. It is clear, however, that, long-range, a plan for improving the Court must consider the relative rights and responsibilities of the Presiding Justice and the Board of Justices, the role of the director of administration, the need for a staff member in each borough to relieve the court clerk of his many administrative and custodial duties, and so on. One immediate problem, that of inadequacies in probation administration, would be lessened by charging the assistant chief probation officers in charge of the Children's Court and of the Family Court with the responsibility for professional operations and staff development in their respective courts and for coordinating activities effectively. Subject to the

---

[16] Sussman, *op. cit.*, pp. 61-62.
[17] *The Four Million*, p. 142. A broader concept of advisory committees is summarized by Boswell, "Citizens Help a Juvenile Court," *The Child*, XV (March, 1951), 127-129.

leadership of, and responsible to, a chief probation officer, each must be permitted to take the lead in clarifying and teaching professional standards and giving direction to the fundamental task of raising the quality of services to clients. Confusion as to relative roles and responsibilities over a period of many years has handicapped both courts. The fact that the administrative structure currently assumes that the Family Court, primarily a "support" court, is effectively integrated with the Children's Court, although this is not so in practice, has had repercussions in the form of weak probation administration.

A minor illustration of the general need for administrative "tightening up" is found in the problem of supervising warrant officers assigned to deliver process, as ordered, or to bring specified individuals to court. Since they are police officers, warrant officers are not included in the court system of staff controls; they are independent of the Court except for the occasional inquiry of a judge about outstanding actions. A regular system of responsible supervision is necessary to increase effectiveness of their work and to assure that they reflect the Court's objectives in their practice.

While the Court's needs for statistical controls, card files, regular reports, and continuous research have been discussed in a separate study,[18] attention might particularly be called to the need for trained statisticians and research specialists who would make possible: a regular child count (in place of the case count); more accurate and consistent statistics; the tabulation of more extensive data; study of the interrelationship of factors which are currently tabulated independently; special studies of unmet needs; reports of case activity of probation officers to supplement present data about cases assigned or closed; uniform systems of case control for the use of supervisors; as well as a blueprint for more basic research in the areas of prevention and treatment.[19]

[18] Detail in Kahn, *Proposals for the Development of a Statistical and Research Service in the Domestic Relations Court (Children's Court).*

[19] The "basic research" activity might not be possible as part of the Court's regular budget, but good statistical reporting is essential to operations. Many other matters need be considered. Thus, both administrative and professional staff in the Court should systematically examine the organization and use of

Children's Court plans have often been soundly based and well developed, only to be set aside by the city's budget authorities and the mayor. Many efforts to improve the Court have failed because budget requests have won verbal support but not necessary funds. The exact costs of the improvements outlined in this report cannot be specified, since alternatives are posed at several points and since salary scales are changing rapidly, but it can be affirmed that a court which assumes the major role allotted to the Children's Court and which seeks to raise standards of service continuously must have an increased budget. The higher investment would not only yield dividends in improved public service, a worthy enough objective, but would also eventually mean less destructive activity in the community, fewer cases in youth and adult courts, and (as out-patient efforts are more successful with new cases) far less costly institutionalization.

The problem of how all the courts serving parents and children are to be organized, related to one another, and administered both efficiently and with concern for all involved is beyond the scope of this report. A special Bar Association study is expected to present recommendations in this general area.[20] It is, however, to the point to stress in these concluding pages that all phases of this report reveal the arbitrariness of serving cases involving custody, separation, or divorce in one court, violent quarrels between parents in another, support in still another, the welfare of children in a fourth, and adoption in a fifth. Substantial numbers of cases come to the Bureau of Adjustment, for instance, because there is a custody or visitation issue or because a parent wishes reconciliation. The Bureau is now permitted to effect voluntary visitation agree-

---

probation records. There is agreement about the need to change from the clumsy legal to the standard folder size; to eliminate the many carbons of investigations and under-care contacts (retained as the sole means of providing agencies with court data), and to find ways of preparing case summaries to serve the requirements of institutions and agencies and contribute to proper service to clients simultaneously.

[20] The study, under the direction of Professor Walter Gellhorn of the School of Law, Columbia University, is expected to present a report in 1953 to the Special Committee to Study the Administration of Law Relating to the Family, Association of the Bar of the City of New York.

ments, but litigation must be referred elsewhere. The strategy for general unification of courts serving families and children is complex; this report does not seek to spell out details of a sound approach to such unification, since its ramifications were not studied. It is noted, however, that the problem is a recurrent one in the Court and must eventually be resolved. Meantime, the Family Court and the Children's Court could surely seek better to integrate their efforts in the interest of more effective service.

WHOSE RESPONSIBILITY? The recommendations of this report call for a major effort to improve the Children's Court in New York City. Although all that has been said is firmly rooted in realistic perspective, it is nonetheless proper to ask whether there is any likelihood of action along the lines proposed—and just where initiative might be taken.

INITIATIVE WITHIN THE COURT. Of major importance is the fact that within the Court there are judges, probation officers, and other staff members who, although they perhaps differ in their emphases, have raised basic questions about the Court's effectiveness, have seen many of the Court's weaknesses, and have begun to develop plans and take steps toward improvement. The Presiding Justice, in his addresses and representations to public authorities, several of which have been quoted herein, has emphasized his concern with probation salaries and levels of qualification. He has encouraged efforts to provide in-service training in the Court and to facilitate educational leaves. He has, in a series of speeches, indicated a readiness to expand the Court intake concept along the lines of the best Bureau of Adjustment practice. In the light of this interest, it is to be expected that the broader recommendations of this report, which appear to be in harmony with the Court's policy, may expect serious consideration.

Particularly important evidence of court initiative is seen in the demonstration-research project under way in the Court under the leadership of the court clinic, with the cooperation of the Probation Bureau, the enthusiastic support of the Presiding Justice, and the financial backing of several philanthropic foundations. Described in some detail in Chapter VIII, this special project represents not only an extremely promising development for the New York City Children's Court but, in effect, the pivot around which all the necessary major improvements might be planned. It may, in fact, contribute important knowledge and administrative suggestions of value to the juvenile court movement as a whole. For, should the project prove successful, the concept developed in the discussion of the Bureau of Applications would have been carried a step further in that an even more complete evaluation of cases prior to hearing would have been assured, while the transition from case evaluation to clinical treatment would have been made less abrupt.

An important step has already been taken in aligning all of the Court's psychiatric and psychological diagnostic facilities with the Reception Unit scheme. The long-term success of the project requires favorable action by the city on the request of the Court that the Reception Unit personnel, now provided for by the special foundation grants, be placed on the regular Children's Court budget. The project, in turn, must successfully demonstrate how it can translate its knowledge and procedures into daily operations on a more economical basis, it being recognized by all that the permanent Reception Unit team must use psychiatric time more economically. While the present efforts are limited to Manhattan, it is essential that the plan eventually include the other boroughs.

Also involved in the permanent effectiveness of this plan are: review of legal considerations (to assure that clients who are worked with prior to, or without, adjudication are acting voluntarily); incorporation of the present Bureau of Adjustment into the scheme (the Court should have only one intake channel and offer uniform services to all); and the relating of the project to petition desk and information desk activity (the Court must have a consistent tone). Given developments in these directions, it is highly likely that the educational values of the project vis-a-vis judges and probation staff (reported by the Court after the completion of this study) will be multiplied severalfold, and the general improvement of all Children's Court operations will be facilitated.

RESPONSIBILITY OF THE STATE LEGISLATURE. Several recommendations for the improvement of the Children's Court proposed herein require consideration by the New York State Legislature. It is quite likely that amendment by the Board of Justices to the Rules of Practice could achieve the sharper differentiation between adjudication and disposition here urged. Civic groups, the bar associations, and court leadership could deal with the misuse of their position by a few judges who compel participation in denominational religious activity. Other steps proposed, however, require careful review by a legislative committee and, upon agreement, legislative action. More specifically, to substitute for the delinquency-neglect labels specific statutory definitions of situations in which the Court may intervene in a child's life, and to make such definitions broader than offenses which would be crimes if committed by adults, will require careful study by a committee of the legislature. The choice of a new method for selecting Children's Court judges and its incorporation into the law and the problems arising from the hiring and assignment of probation officers by religion also require legislative action. The legislature must, further, consider the possibility of substituting, for the current loose advisory relationship of the Court's Probation Bureau with the Division of Probation, Department of Correction, a more intensive relationship with a state agency able to evaluate probation practice continually and to assist in raising standards. The legislature and the Governor's office must review the entire question of state responsibility for supervision and subsidy in the fields of child welfare and probation. Other possible statutory changes suggested in the text of this report require consideration as well, particularly those having to do with termination of parental rights in specified and well-defined circumstances.

CIVIC GROUPS. The Court may, of its own initiative, launch certain internal improvements. If optimum objectives are to be attained, however, the Court requires continued evidence of community interest in, and insistence on, improvement and, where necessary, major change. Progress will be made if civic groups in New York City carefully evaluate the picture of the Children's Court drawn here in the light of their own experience and act accordingly. An important first step might take the form of urging appointment of an advisory committee to examine court operations in some detail and of providing leadership for community support of the Court. Proposed statutory changes will also require the evaluation and backing of such groups.

OTHER PUBLIC AGENCIES. To the extent that the Court seeks to determine its own direction, it will be possible to resolve certain of the problems of liaison and relations with other community agencies and services. The matter of how and when the Court is to be used by Police and Welfare departments should be both formally discussed and demonstrated in action, but on the basis of the Court's new clarity of philosophy. Such clear understanding and articulation would also provide the point of departure for court efforts, together with the Commission for the Foster Care of Children and the Department of Welfare, to estimate resource needs and determine their requisite qualities. As has already been suggested, the Court might also at that time approach the school system with the view of improving liaison and mutual cooperation. Finally, the Court, other public bodies, and major voluntary agencies could, under the Court's initiative, meet to plan a strategy for dealing with certain other major gaps in facilities which continue to hamper operations.

The New York City Youth Board could very properly serve as a resource for these many efforts. Established to "prevent" and "remove causes" of delinquency, the Youth Board has partially financed the Court Treatment Clinic and has assembled valuable data through its Central Register. As the Court begins new efforts to train staff, to seek treatment facilities in the community, to raise the level of initial case evaluation, the Youth Board must be prepared to contribute of its knowledge, its experience in coordination, and its funds to the support of these efforts. There is little doubt that such action by the Youth Board would be in accord with the intent of the state and the city in establishing the agency. The very extensive and useful experience of the Youth Board's referral units which, since July, 1949, have devoted themselves to case study and referral might well help a new Bureau of Applications in the Court develop its initial intake policies and improve its channels for case disposition.

SOCIAL WORK EDUCATION. There has been important evidence recently that local schools of social work are interested in the problem of preparing social workers who can serve in police, attendance, parole, and probation agencies. Special courses and institutes contributing to in-service training efforts have been helpful. Full-time scholarships have aided a few individuals to complete a program of professional training. These are significant way stations; two major goals yet to be achieved by social work education in its attempt to prepare staff members for protective settings remain to be seriously approached: schools must (a) incorporate material from such settings into generic casework education and (b) encourage practitioners to enter such work.

The implementation of proposals of this report for court improvement may in itself offer a method for achieving the second of these objectives. If the recently established salary scales for probation officers could be followed by the hiring of supervisors who have had experience in professionally competent agencies and by the development of a pattern of court activity and teamwork in which the court social worker is a respected member with a clear-cut area of activity, these facts in themselves would almost assure the readiness of newly graduated social workers to compete for court positions. The improvements would also make it more likely that social work school faculties would become acquainted with the Children's Court and its needs and would present court work to students as a challenge for public service as well as an opportunity for personal professional development.

Trained supervisors and probation workers would gradually develop suitable casework methods and produce illustrative case records. As these records became available for the teaching of all caseworkers, they would both encourage men and women to see probation as a casework career and help identify those elements of probation which are generic casework and those which are specific to the court setting.

As now constituted, the Probation Bureau is not a suitable setting for internships (field work training) for social work students. The establishment of special student training units in the Children's Court Probation Bureau would, however, be a valuable means of raising the prestige value of probation work and would make it possible to acquaint students with the work, clarifying the nature of probation casework, demonstrating new methods, and developing teaching records. If each of the three local schools of social work were to establish a unit in one of the boroughs (quite independent of the New York School of Social Work unit in the Treatment Clinic), a major step would have been taken. The assignment of special supervisors and the assurance of a satisfactory range and level of operations would, of course, be prerequisite. The New York City Youth Board might consider making supervisory and financial resources available for the experimental periods of such work.

THE BAR ASSOCIATIONS AND THE LAW SCHOOLS. The findings of this study have raised important questions about: the relationship of adjudication to disposition in an individualized system of justice oriented to treatment; the role of the attorney in a children's court; the safeguarding of individual rights; the functions of witnesses; the possibility that the child rather than the event be the petition unit; the method of selection of judges; and other possible statutory changes. Particularly valuable service could be performed by the various bar associations in bringing expert legal thinking to bear on these and related issues and in inaugurating action deriving from their consideration. Implications for legal education might also be explored, with some attention to the possibility that at a much later date it might be feasible to offer preparation to those who would compete in civil service examinations to become juvenile court judges. It might also be appropriate for the bar associations to consider whether this report's findings justify reviewing the entire area of practice by judges in the Children's Court.

The Children's Court has been created and must be maintained by the entire community. Its failings are as much a matter of inadequate budget, poor diagnostic and treatment resources in the community, and the level of standards demanded of court personnel as they are of professional failings in the Court itself. There is little likelihood that the Court will completely reform itself and, without substantial backing, fully embody the hope and promise of the juvenile court movement. Civic groups must therefore seek to improve it by supporting considerable changes in the Court. Public and private agencies must be prepared to cooperate in the major effort required. The city administration must be prepared for necessary expenditures. The state legislature must recognize and assume its own responsibility, while bar associations and graduate social work schools study court practice, clarify concepts, and help develop personnel for the court program.

The New York City Children's Court is, in short, a community endeavor. To the extent that it is neglected by the community, it cannot be expected to work well. Only if court and community see it as a joint venture and strive truly to give form to the promise, will it become all that it was meant to be—a sensitive and effective court for children.

APPENDIX: THE METHOD

OF THE STUDY

The methods adopted in this study of the Children's Court are based upon the author's experience in studying the Bureau of Attendance of the New York City Board of Education and the Juvenile Aid Bureau of the New York City Police Department (reported in Kahn, Lash, *et al.*, *Children Absent from School* and Kahn, *Police and Children*). In brief, those and other studies indicate that evaluation of professional practice involves a logical process of several component parts:

A yardstick must be selected or devised to represent the criteria by which practice is being judged.

A cross section of agency activity must be examined in the light of that yardstick.

The results of the examination must be formulated and considered.

Recommendations must be developed as needed. This includes priorities, strategy, etc.

THE YARDSTICK. The choice or development of the yardstick, clearly the starting point of the entire process of appraisal, is particularly crucial in evaluating protective and correctional services where lack of agreement on many basic issues is characteristic. What can and should be expected of a probation officer? What type of training does a policeman require if he is to work effectively with children? Should police officers undertake casework treatment of children? Do attendance officers require teacher training? By what criteria does one evaluate an intake interview in the Court, a probation officer's home visit, the way a judge conducts a courtroom session?

Where agreement exists, the problem is less complex. There is general consensus, for instance, that family service agencies should be staffed by caseworkers who are graduates of social work schools. Hence, in a study of such an agency one can seek to establish whether it is adequately staffed by determining the level of staff education. Similarly, there are standards for case load size, performance by caseworkers or psychologists, agency structure, staff job definitions, agency personnel practices developed by groups such as the American Association of Social Workers, the Family Service Association of America, the Group for the Advancement of Psychiatry, the National Probation and Parole Association, and so on. However, even criteria offered by these and similar sources must sometimes be discarded because they are founded on questionable data or values not appropriate to a particular study. There are few unchallengeable standards in the social welfare field comparable to engineering criteria for the range of variation allowable in construction, education criteria for the number of children in a class, housing criteria for minimum standards; nor are there clear criteria for good performance in some aspects of social welfare, such as exist for the musician, the surgeon, or even the ballplayer, whose "average" can be computed.

Where there is no agreement about function or where a function is new, the problem of a yardstick is particularly challenging. It is here that the researcher embarks on a creative task. He must review the history of the particular agency and analyze its functions from all relevant aspects. Eventually (after this preparatory phase, and preferably with the cooperation of advisory committees and consultants), he must take the responsibility for formulating the yardstick. To the extent possible, the postulates, assumptions, and values which underlie the yardstick and which determine key choices should be uncovered and specified.

The yardstick thus formulated must be subjected to examination, for the reader of the study must be permitted to appraise the criteria before he is presented with conclusions flowing from the application of such criteria. Where the development of a yardstick in a new area has been successful, its very articulation may well represent that phase of the study of interest and value beyond the immediate needs of the agency involved.

Criteria must, in fact, be defined on several levels. There are, first, the *ultimate* criteria, better described as the values and postulates on which the yardstick is based. They must be isolated even though they are so related to the cultural milieu and so colored by personal prejudice that their complete identification is probably never possible. (In this instance, the relative responsibility of public and private bodies for the protection of children; the proper approach to delinquency and neglect, etc.) The next level pertains to *intermediate* criteria, those which often draw on experience in fields closely related to that being examined, but of such a degree of generality that they do not allow specific judgments to be made about practice (for instance, the quality of relationship essential to treatment). These intermediate criteria form the basis for selecting from among the *immediate* criteria offered by various sources or for establishing such immediate criteria independently. The latter define the yardsticks used in examining the specifics of professional practice. It should be added that in the completely or relatively uncharted field one must sometimes be content with the identification of characteristics shown by experience to be predictably related to bad practice, although one is unable as yet to specify in detail exactly what assures good practice.

This study of the Children's Court began with certain attitudes and values, implicit in the entire approach of the Citizens' Committee on Children, developed more specifically in the two prior studies referred to above, and part of the professional orientation of the author. To the extent that they can be made explicit, particularly in relation to areas of difference of opinion, they have been sketched in Chapter I. For intermediate and immediate criteria, it was possible, to some extent, to draw upon standards existing in, and accepted by, the juvenile court movement, the probation movement, the fields of social work, psychiatry, and criminology. The Domestic Relations Court Law of the City of New York, the New York State *Manual for Probation Officers*, the Standard Juvenile Court Act developed by the National Probation and Parole Association, and standards suggested by the Welfare Council of New York City were to a considerable extent helpful. Finally, the addresses and published papers of the Presiding Justice and other justices of the New York City Domestic Relations Court were valuable in clarifying the level of performance to be sought.

In no instance was it possible to accept any one criterion without evaluation, and no single guide has been followed completely. Preliminary study of practice was itself a source of guidance in making choices. It was ultimately necessary to select between alternative standards and to indicate the values justifying such selection. To some degree, too, it was necessary to draw upon the experiences of the helping professions and to take responsibility for the complete development of criteria to be used in certain phases of the study.

The reader's acceptance or rejection of the findings rests, to a considerable degree, on his acceptance or rejection of the yardstick. The effort has therefore been made at each stage of the appraisal to clarify standards sought. In discussing the juvenile court movement and the Court's development in New York, the early chapters seek to clarify the basic values assumed and the intermediate criteria applied. Each of the subsequent sections states and attempts to justify precisely what was sought in looking at court intake, hearings, probation investigations, supervision, and all other phases of court operations. Generally, each chapter begins with the intermediate criteria, while the subsections develop the more immediate criteria. The logic of the presentation does not always permit this approach, however, and in some instances (Chapter VI) selected details of standards applied are presented in the context of a summarization of findings. In one of the sections, namely, the discussion of the judges, the appraisal rests largely on "negative criteria" since it is easier to obtain agreement as to what conduct is inconsistent with the Court's intent than just what balancing of roles would be appropriate and optimum in such a court.

THE MEASUREMENT OF RESULTS AS A YARDSTICK.

This entire procedure would, of course, be quite unnecessary in a study concerned with follow-up of cases or an estimate of results. Such a study might devote itself to an attempt to find out what has occurred to all Children's Court clients a given number of years after case closing; it might explore the relationship between outcome and such factors as the Court's disposition, the identity of the judge, the training of the probation officer. Results in one court could be compared with those in another. Control groups might be instituted, where possible, to separate elements of improvement resulting from a child's maturation from those specifically attributable to court action. The families and friends of former clients might be interviewed to obtain their evaluation of the experience and its helpfulness.

Studies which seek to follow up and test results are extremely important, posing many difficulties and unsolved technical problems described elsewhere.[1] The mere completion of such studies leaves unanswered the question of whether results which are discovered are, quantitatively speaking, good or bad, or whether they are obtained at a price which is socially defensible. Despite this, such study of the New York City Children's Court in the near future is highly desirable. The choice of the different method of this study, rather than the measurement of results, derived from two sources:

a) Consideration was given to the type of study which would obtain cooperation in the Court, be undertaken with available resources and time, and be completed by one person with limited

---

[1] See, for instance, Blenkner, "Obstacles to Evaluative Research in Casework," *Social Casework*, XXXI (February, 1950), 54-60, and *ibid.*, XXXI (March, 1950), 97-105; Hunt, Blenkner, and Kogan, *Testing Results in Social Casework*.

research assistance, but with the full cooperation of an advisory group and expert consultants.

b) Weight was given to the considerable amount of empirical evidence, based on preliminary examination of court records and information from other courts and community agencies, that the Children's Court was missing its opportunity in many cases and was obviously in need of greater support from the community. The method chosen gave promise of identifying the weak spots in the total professional structure and suggesting specific measures for improving services to children and parents. One might not be able to describe quantitatively the amount of improvement needed or, given changes, to be expected. On the other hand, the task of planning changes would be advanced further under this method than through a study limited to statistical specification of the Court's rate of failure.

It might be added, of course, that in developing a yardstick in the manner specified and in not following up results, this study draws upon criteria and bases itself on values which have been elsewhere established, empirically in practice or by research, as relating to achievement of results sought. To introduce an analogy: if it is not possible to evaluate a hospital by its mortality and recovery records for given patient groups, since some patients cannot be followed up and there is no agreement as to what is a good recovery rate for certain patients, it is feasible to seek, instead, and to apply criteria for surgical and medical skill, nursing care, physical facilities, diet, and so forth which have been previously shown to correlate with good results.

A CROSS SECTION OF PRACTICE. A proper appraisal of an agency's professional performance requires an examination of a representative sample of practice. In this study, the writer was able to employ the following techniques in examining a cross section of practice:

1. OBSERVATION. In the year devoted to the data-gathering and analysis phase of the study it was possible to observe for periods of one to three calendar days the work of twelve of the eighteen

judges in the Domestic Relations Court. In addition, many days were spent observing all phases of the probation officer's assignment (office interviews, home interviews, courtroom appearances, record dictation, etc.) in all boroughs except Richmond. Workdays were spent with seventeen of the sixty-odd probation officers; the seventeen were selected by the probation officers-in-charge in each borough to provide a group stratified by length of experience, training, approach to the job. In addition, all except a handful of the probation officers on duty were observed as they presented large numbers of cases in the courtroom and in their daily office routines.

The observation technique was also employed in the Bureau of Adjustment in the three largest boroughs and in relation to the work of the court reporting officer, information window, petition room, and clerical departments.

Results of these observations were recorded, yielding several hundred typed pages of material and case illustrations which have been drawn upon in the preparation of this report.

2. CASE ANALYSIS. In order to make it possible to apply consistent criteria in evaluation of the Bureau of Adjustment and of probation, cases were analyzed and recorded on two different schedules. Tabulations were made on the basis of these schedules.

Bureau of Adjustment cases, which are of short duration, were obtained by choosing the intake of a month shortly before the arrival of the case reader (in one case an earlier month was selected because dictation was lagging). In two boroughs, a month's intake was too large to be covered completely, and a random selection was made by using the docket book. (Chapter IV gives details as to the total case load and the number of Bureau of Adjustment cases read.)

Probation cases were chosen according to time closed; that is, the reader selected all, or a proportion of, cases closed during a given month in a given borough. Only this method of sampling would assure inclusion of cases investigated and closed, cases investigated and placed on probation, School Part cases, short cases, long cases. Selection from cases closed in a given month was made in a random manner. An exception was made in one small borough where this procedure, because of a particular dictation situation, omitted the work of two probation officers. The sample taken was, therefore, stratified by officer. (The text of Chapters VI and VII gives detail as to the total number of probation cases, the number read, the number of probation officers represented by these records, and the totals from each borough.)

The court case load is, of course, so large that only a sizable research team could have read a very large proportion of the records. It was discovered during the preliminary phases of the study, however, that in all aspects important to the study the records were remarkably homogeneous, the range in quality of work relatively narrow, and the conclusions from record reading similar to a remarkable degree to those derived from observation and conferences. The sample of cases evaluated is, therefore, clearly adequate in size and representative in composition.

3. ANALYSIS OF PROCEDURES AND REPORTS. The results of the analysis of administrative, clerical, and statistical procedures and relevant reports have been presented in a separate document.[2] This analysis was also valuable to the remainder of the study in that it provided data for estimates of case loads and court loads, and was the source of leads followed throughout the appraisal. Experience with the Court's administrative procedures gained in the course of the analysis made it possible to envisage implementation of various recommendations in realistic detail.

4. CONFERENCES AND DISCUSSIONS. A considerable amount of time was devoted to discussion of the Court's problems, needs, limitations, relationships, and possible directions of improvement with judges, probation officers, and supervisors on all levels, representatives of agencies dealing with the Court, clinic personnel, administrative and clerical staff. An attempt was made, in an informal manner, to assure coverage of all points of view.

The Court's cooperation must be stressed, for that alone made it possible for the observer to spend a large portion of his time

---

[2] Kahn, *Proposals for the Development of a Statistical and Research Service in the Domestic Relations Court* (*Children's Court*).

during the year in the Children's Court in the various boroughs and to develop a relationship with staff on all levels. Records, docket books, statistics, and reports were made available freely. The author's attendance during court sessions, interviews, and conferences and his regular presence in the buildings made it possible for him to experience the Court's atmosphere and operations as they really are rather than on the basis of the "best foot forward." From information desk, to Bureau of Adjustment, to petition desk, to waiting room, to courtroom, to Probation Department, he was permitted to see fully and to experience the nature of the Children's Court in New York City and its impact on children and their parents.

OBSERVER BIAS. In studying an agency's impact on a community, one is constantly faced by the temptation to identify with the views of one or two critics or proponents and to adopt their formulations, since it is difficult to grapple with the many intangibles involved. The only reasonable protection under the circumstances is a deliberate attempt to obtain the views of a cross section of community groups and to seek, where possible, to verify the statements made.

Observer bias has, however, even wider ramifications. Assuming that a schedule has been developed for case analysis, how is one to know that another reader of the case record would note the same facts on his schedule? If judgments are called for about a client's needs or about the level of service reflected in a record, how is one to be sure that another reader, using the selfsame criteria formulated in the yardstick, would make the same judgments? Where the study method calls for accompanying individual probation officers on their daily rounds for the purpose of clarifying for oneself their conceptions of how to do case studies and how to "supervise" children, how is one to know that independent observers would arrive at the same conclusions?

The research worker will recognize in these questions the familiar problems of reliability and validity. It would be out of place here to dwell on these problems and the particular difficulties they pose for social welfare research. It is necessary only to stress that the standards which hold for other research are not irrelevant in the field of agency evaluation. The application of these tools may pose complex problems of technique and theory, but they must be resolved in the development of sound methodology.

In this study, a series of devices was introduced to cope with such problems. As a preliminary step in the development of the schedule, the case reader had a number of "trial runs" to be sure that he could complete all sections and had clear definitions of data called for by each one. A number of research specialists examined the schedules in this light. Then, after being trained in the use of the schedule, an independent case reader with the same professional background completed twelve analyses of probation cases (the Bureau of Adjustment schedules being far more simple) which had been analyzed by the original case reader. An item-by-item comparison was made of the schedules of the case reader and the independent reader with respect to the detailed factual items as well as the judgment items in the schedule (for instance, disposition at first hearing, school record, whether the probation officer attempts a formulation about the child's personality or simply lists what the child says, whether the recommendation follows an appraisal of the situation or only a listing of facts, etc.). Extremely high agreement was obtained. In six instances (referring to items, not cases), the independent reader provided more detail than the regular case reader, but this detail did not alter the nature of the conclusions. In one instance, one of the readers failed to record dates correctly. There was disagreement on only one evaluative item. While such rate of agreement appears remarkable on the surface, in view of the number of items in the schedule, further consideration suggests that it might have been expected since most items required mere summarization of corresponding items in probation records, while judgment items (see Chapters VI and VII for detail) required relatively simple judgments on which one could expect trained social caseworkers to agree.[3] The judgments drawn from the schedules and the classification of cases according to level of services offered were also reviewed in the many drafts of this study by members of the Advisory Committee and con-

[3] Mrs. Freeda Taran was the independent case reader.

sultants, thus introducing the disciplines of law, education, and psychiatry and the experience of volunteers into the process.

The elimination of bias was not, in the nature of things, as readily solved in the areas of observation and discussion. The author had to rely perforce on his professional background and experience and on the recognition of the fact that he began without any fixed view about the issues at stake or the relative merits of various parts of the Court. Careful detailed recording made it possible for consultants and members of the Advisory Committee to check inferences drawn from observational material and record reading. Such material is also presented in the text proper, to enable the reader to form his own opinions. The accuracy of the reporting perhaps is measured best by the extent to which the observational and interview material yield conclusions similar to those derived from record analysis and reached by other experienced individuals who have come into contact with court practice. Further confirmation was obtained by checking courtroom observations with a group of more than twenty Citizens' Committee members who, not as part of this study, had occasion at various times to be guests of the Children's Court in the three largest boroughs. Finally, early drafts of this study have been submitted for review by individuals on various levels of practice in the Court, and there is agreement that the picture presented is a valid one.

THE FORMULATION OF RECOMMENDATIONS. In the writing of each section of this report, the attempt has been made to enable the reader to distinguish between findings (fact), conclusions (inference), and recommendations. In stating recommendations, the emphasis has been, first, on basic suggestions and principles, in the hope that clarity of principle will assist implementation. What is more, to the extent that basic premises can be agreed upon, it should be possible to apply the findings to new contingencies and circumstances. Because one purpose of the study was to outline those actions which might be presented to the public for immediate support, the recommendations do contain specific detail, and indicate short-range solutions as well as a full long-range program.

BIBLIOGRAPHY

Abbot, Grace. The Child and the State. 2 vols. Chicago: University of Chicago Press, 1938.

Ackerman, Nathan. "The Adaptive Problems of the Adolescent Personality," in Community Service Society of New York, The Family in a Democratic Society. New York: Columbia University Press, 1950, pp. 85-120.

Addams, Jane, et al. The Child, the Clinic and the Court. New York: New Republic, Inc., 1927.

Alexander, Franz, and Thomas M. French. Psychoanalytic Therapy. New York: Ronald Press, 1946.

Alexander, Franz, and Hugo Staub. The Criminal, the Judge and the Public. New York: Macmillan, 1931.

Allegheny County Juvenile Court. Focus the Child. Pittsburgh: Juvenile Court of Allegheny County, 1947.

American Association of Social Workers. Social Work Year Book, 1951. New York, 1951.

American Bar Association. Report of the Committee on Problems of Juvenile Delinquency, Gustav L. Schramm, chairman. N.d. Mimeographed.

Archibald, Dorothy. "Some Services for London's Difficult Boys," in K. R. Eissler, ed., Searchlights on Delinquency. New York: International Universities Press, 1949.

Association of the Bar of the City of New York, Committee on Law Reform. Report on Consideration of New Methods to Select Judges. New York, 1952.

Austin, Lucille. "Basic Principles of Supervision," Social Casework, XXXIII, No. 10 (December, 1952), 411-419.

Barnes, Harry E., and Negley K. Teeters. New Horizons in Criminology. New York: Prentice-Hall, 1949.

Beaser, Herbert Wilton. "Law and Its Relation to Healthy Personality Development." Report on a symposium, prepared by the Fact Finding Staff for the Midcentury White House Conference on Children and Youth, 1950. Mimeographed.

Beck, Bertram. Simple Arithmetic about Complex Children: a Study of Temporary Shelter for Dependent and Neglected Children in New York City, Prepared for the Commission on the Foster Care of Children. New York: Community Service Society of New York, 1951.

Beck, Bertram, and Leonard V. Harrison. While Children Wait: Report on Temporary Detention of Delinquent and Allegedly Delinquent Children. New York: Community Service Society of New York, 1949.

Bernard, Viola. "Adolescence in Its Implications for Family and Community," in Community Service Society of New York, The Family in a Democratic Society. New York: Columbia University Press, 1949, pp. 121-140.

Blenkner, Margaret. "Obstacles to Evaluative Research in Casework," Social Casework, XXXI, No. 2 (February, 1950), 54-60; No. 3 (March, 1950), 97-105.

Boswell, Charles H. "Citizens Help a Juvenile Court," The Child, XV, No. 7 (March, 1951), 127-129.

Bovet, Lucien. Psychiatric Aspects of Juvenile Delinquency. Geneva: World Health Organization, 1951.

Brennan, Marion M. "Probation in the Children's Courts as a Constructive Approach to the Treatment of the Delinquent." A paper read at the New York State Conference of Social Work, New York City, November 29, 1950.

Brick, Morris D. "A Study of Twenty Boys Who Were Committed to the New York State Training School for Boys through the Manhattan Children's Court." Unpublished master's thesis, New York School of Social Work, 1949.

Bruno, Frank J. Trends in Social Work. New York: Columbia University Press, 1948.

California, Board of Corrections, Special Commission for Study of Adult Correction and Juvenile Justice. Final Report of the Special Crime Study Commission on Juvenile Justice. Sacramento: Board of Corrections, 1949.

—— Probation Services in California. Sacramento: Board of Corrections, 1949.

Carr, Lowell J. Delinquency Control. New York: Harper, 1950.

Chaskel, Ruth. "Impact of Community Needs on Casework Policy," Social Casework, XXXII, No. 3 (March, 1951), 114-119.

Chute, Charles L. "Fifty Years of the Juvenile Court," in National

Probation and Parole Association, Current Approaches to Delinquency, Yearbook, 1949. New York, 1950, pp. 1-20.

Connecticut Commission on Children and Youth. Report on Juvenile Court. Hartford: General Welfare Committee, 1950. Mimeographed.

Consulich, Gilbert. Juvenile Court Laws of the United States. New York: National Probation and Parole Association, 1939.

Cook County, Circuit Court, Executive Committee. Report of a Special Committee; Report Respecting the Juvenile Court of Cook County. Chicago: Circuit Court of Cook County, 1947.

Crystal, David. "Family Casework in Probation," *Federal Probation*, XIII, No. 4 (December, 1949), 47-53.

Dich, J. S., *et al.* Social Denmark. Copenhagen: Socialt Tidsskrift, 1947.

Dressler, David. Probation and Parole. New York: Columbia University Press, 1951.

Eissler, K. R., ed. Searchlights on Delinquency. New York: International Universities Press, 1949.

Elmott, Charlotte. Aspects of a Community Program for Delinquency Control and Youth Protection. Sacramento: California Youth Authority, 1945.

Federal Probation: a Journal of Correctional Philosophy and Practice. Particularly Special Issue Commemorating the Fiftieth Anniversary of the Juvenile Court, Vol. XIII, No. 3 (September, 1949).

Federal Security Agency, Children's Bureau. Child Welfare at the Crossroads. Publication No. 327. Washington: Government Printing Office, 1949.

—— Controlling Juvenile Delinquency. Publication No. 301. Washington: Government Printing Office, 1943.

—— Helping Children in Trouble. Publication No. 320. Washington: Government Printing Office, 1947.

—— The Juvenile Court of the District of Columbia; Report of a Special Committee. Washington: Children's Bureau, 1951. Mimeographed.

—— Juvenile Court Statistics. Statistical Series, Report 8. Washington: Government Printing Office, 1951.

—— Understanding Juvenile Delinquency. Publication No. 300. Washington: Government Printing Office, 1943.

Feldman, Yonata. "The Teaching Aspect of Casework Supervision," *Social Casework*, XXXI, No. 4 (April, 1950), 156-161.

The Field Foundation. A Review of Activities for the Year Ended September 20, 1951. New York: The Field Foundation, Inc., 1952.

Flexner, Bernard, and Roger N. Baldwin. Juvenile Courts and Probation. New York: Century Co., 1914.

Flynn, Frank T. "Probation and Individualized Service," *Federal Probation*, XIV, No. 2 (June, 1950), 70-76.

Frank, Jerome. Courts on Trial. Princeton, N.J.: Princeton University Press, 1949.

Garrett, Annette. Interviewing: Its Principles and Methods. New York: Family Welfare Association of America, 1942.

Giles, F. T. The Juvenile Courts. London: Allen and Unwin, Ltd., 1946.

Glueck, Sheldon, ed. Probation and Criminal Justice. New York: Macmillan, 1933.

Glueck, Sheldon, and Eleanor T. Glueck. After-conduct of Discharged Offenders. London: Macmillan, 1945.

—— Unraveling Juvenile Delinquency. New York: The Commonwealth Fund, 1950.

Goldberg, Harriet. Child Offenders. New York: Grune & Stratton, 1948.

Greene, Richard D. "Probation—Philosophy, Function and Fact." Paper presented at the Annual Conference of the New York State Association of Judges of Children's Courts, New York City, December 1, 1950. Mimeographed.

Hamilton, Gordon. "Helping People—the Growth of a Profession," in Community Service Society of New York, Social Work as Human Relations. New York: Columbia University Press, 1949, pp. 8-18.

—— Theory and Practice of Social Case Work. 2d ed. rev. New York: Columbia University Press, 1951.

Herlands, William B. Juvenile Delinquency in New York City; a Report to the Mayor's Committee on Juvenile Delinquency. 1944. Mimeographed.

Hess, Loren J. "A Graduate School and Court Coöperate in Training for Probation Work," *Federal Probation*, XV, No. 2 (June, 1951), 28-32.

Hill, John Warren. "Limiting Unofficial Casework," in National Probation and Parole Association, The Community and the Correctional Process, Yearbook, 1951. New York, 1952, pp. 75-88.

Hoey, Jane. "Social Work: Its Base, Skills and Relation to Other Fields," *Social Casework*, XXXI, No. 10 (December, 1950), 399-410.

Hogan, Frank S. Report of the District Attorney, County of New York, 1946-1948. New York, 1949.

Hollis, Florence. "The Relationship between Psycho-social Diagnosis and Treatment," *Social Casework*, XXXII, No. 2 (February, 1951), 67-74.

Hunt, J. McV., Margaret Blenkner, and Leonard S. Kogan. Testing Results in Social Casework. New York: Family Service Association of America, 1950.

Hyatt, Alice Scott (Nutt). "The Future of the Juvenile Court as a Case Work Agency," in National Conference of Social Work, Proceedings, 1939. New York: Columbia University Press, 1939, pp. 370-380.

—— "Juvenile and Domestic Relations Courts," in Social Work Year Book, 1949. New York: Russell Sage Foundation, 1949.

—— "The Juvenile Court in Relation to the Community: an Evaluation," *Social Service Review*, XVII (March, 1943), 1-7.

—— "Juvenile Courts and Services to Delinquents." Prepared for the Midcentury White House Conference on Children and Youth. Washington: Children's Bureau, 1950. Mimeographed.

—— "The Responsibility of the Juvenile Court and the Public Welfare Agency," in National Probation and Parole Association, Redirecting the Delinquent, Yearbook, 1947. New York, 1948, pp. 206-223.

"Juvenile Delinquency," *The Annals*, American Academy of Political and Social Science, Vol. CCLXI (January, 1949).

Kahn, Alfred J. "The Functions of Police and Children's Courts," in National Probation and Parole Association, The Community and the Correctional Process, Yearbook, 1951. New York, 1952, pp. 60-74.

—— "Functions of Youth Police in an Integrated Community Plan for Helping Children in Trouble," *Journal of Educational Sociology*, XXIV, No. 9 (June, 1951), pp. 534-543.

—— Police and Children. New York: Citizens' Committee on Children of New York City, Inc., 1951.

—— Proposals for the Development of a Statistical and Research Service in the Domestic Relations Court (Children's Court). New York: Citizens' Committee on Children of New York City, Inc., 1951. Mimeographed.

Kahn, Alfred J., Trude W. Lash, *et al.* Children Absent from School. New York: Citizens' Committee on Children of New York City, Inc., 1949.

Kaplan, Nathaniel. "Youth Services." Paper delivered at the New York State Conference of Probation Officers, New York City, October 10, 1950. Mimeographed.

Keith-Lucas, Alan. "Social Work and the Court in the Protection of Children," *Child Welfare*, XXVIII, No. 7 (July, 1949), 3-6.

Kenney, John P., ed. A Study of Juvenile Control by the Police Department, Oakland, California. Sacramento: California Youth Authority, 1948. Mimeographed.

——— A Study of the Juvenile Bureau of the San Francisco Police Department and Its Relationship to the Juvenile Probation Department. Sacramento: California Youth Authority, 1949. Mimeographed.

Killian, Frederick W. "The Juvenile Court as an Institution," *The Annals*, American Academy of Political and Social Science, CCLXI (January, 1949), 89-101.

Klein, Philip.. "Next Steps in Dealing with Delinquency," in *Bulletin*, New York School of Social Work, Columbia University, July, 1945.

——— "Reformation: Principles and Methods." Unpublished MS, New York, 1912.

——— "The Treatment of the Delinquent Child in the United States." Unpublished MS, New York, 1914.

Landry, Herbert H. "The Prosecution of School Non-attendants." Unpublished MS. New York: Board of Education, 1948.

Leeds, Clarence M. "Probation Work Requires Special Training," *Federal Probation*, XV, No. 2 (June, 1951), 25-28.

Levine, Norma D. "Educational Components of Supervision in a Family Agency," *Social Casework*, XXXI, No. 6 (June, 1950), 245-250.

Lou, Herbert H. Juvenile Courts in the United States. Chapel Hill: University of North Carolina Press, 1927.

Lowrey, Lawson G., ed. Orthopsychiatry, 1923-1948: Retrospect and Prospect. New York: American Orthopsychiatric Association, 1948.

Lukas, Edwin J. "More on the Children's Court, and Cognate Matters," *The Record*, Association of the Bar of the City of New York, III, No. 8 (November, 1948), 331-347.

Lundberg, Emma O. Unto the Least of These. New York: D. Appleton-Century, 1947.

McKinney's Consolidated Laws of New York. Book 66, Part 3, including the "Children's Court Act of the State of New York" and the "Domestic Relations Court Act of the City of New York." Brooklyn: Edward Thompson Co., 1945.

Maeder, Leroy. "Generic Aspects of the Intake Interview," *Social Casework*, XXIII, No. 1 (March, 1942), 14-23.

Michael, Jerome, and Mortimer J. Adler. Crime, Law and Social Science. New York: Harcourt, Brace & Co., 1933.

Midcentury White House Conference on Children and Youth. For Every Child a Healthy Personality: a Digest of the Fact Finding

Report. Washington: Midcentury White House Conference, 1950.
—— Proceedings. Raleigh, N.C.: Health Publications Institute, Inc., 1951.
National Conference on Prevention and Control of Juvenile Delinquency, Washington, D.C., November 20-23, 1946. Reports Nos. 1-18. Washington: Government Printing Office, 1947.
National Probation and Parole Association. A Standard Juvenile Court Act. Rev. ed. New York: National Probation and Parole Association, 1949.
—— Yearbooks. New York: National Probation and Parole Association, 1939-1951.
—— "Probation Service in Rural Areas." Typewritten memorandum. New York, 1952.
Neumeyer, Martin H. Juvenile Delinquency in Modern Society. New York: D. Van Nostrand Co., Inc., 1949.
New York Academy of Medicine. The Domestic Relations Court; Report of the Subcommittee of the Committee on Public Health Relations, Bernard Sachs, M.D., Chairman. New York: New York Academy of Medicine, 1935. Mimeographed.
New York City, Department of Welfare. Report of the Mayor's Committee on Child Care. New York: Department of Welfare, 1949. Mimeographed.
New York City, Domestic Relations Court. Annual reports, 1933-1952. Mimeographed after 1939.
—— Manual of Procedure for Statistical Recording and Tabulation in the Children's Division of the Domestic Relations Court. 1941. Mimeographed.
—— "Minutes of the Meeting of the Special Committee on the Bureau of Adjustment, January 20, 1942." Typewritten record.
—— Rules of Practice. 1950.
New York City, Mayor's Committee on Juvenile Delinquency. First Interim Report, Analysis of the Statistics of the Children's Court Division of the Domestic Relations Court of the City of New York. 1943. Mimeographed.
New York City, Mayor's Committee on Management Survey. Classification and Compensation of the Service of the City of New York. 2 vols. New York: Griffenhagen and Asociates, 1951.
New York City Youth Board, Central Registration Project. Review of First Year's Operations. New York: New York City Youth Board, 1952. Mimeographed.
—— Review of Second Year's Operations. New York: New York City Youth Board, 1953. Mimeographed.

New York County Lawyer's Association. A Colloquium on Juvenile Delinquency and Its Socio-legal Aspects. New York, 1948.

—— Report of the Proceedings of Conference on Preventive Law to Safeguard the Children of Unstable Families. New York, 1950.

New York State, Department of Correction. Annual Report, 1948. Albany, 1949.

New York State Division of Probation. Manual for Probation Officers. Rev. ed. Albany: Division of Probation, 1945.

New York State, Joint Legislative Committee to Examine into, Investigate, and Study the Existing Facilities for the Care and Treatment of Children, Fred A. Young, Chairman. Young People in the Courts of New York. Albany: Williams Press, 1942.

New York State Citizens' Committee of One Hundred for Children and Youth. The Four Million. Albany: New York State Citizens' Committee, 1951.

Norman, Sherwood. "New Goals for Juvenile Detention," Federal Probation, XIII, No. 4 (December, 1949), 29-35.

Norman, Sherwood, and Helen Norman. Detention for the Juvenile Court. New York: National Probation and Parole Association, 1946.

Peck, Harris B. "Principles and Techniques in the Integration of Psychiatric Services in a Juvenile Court with a Community Youth Program," American Journal of Orthopsychiatry, XXII, No. 2 (April, 1952), 277-285.

—— "Relationship of a Court Clinic to Plans for the Mental Health Needs of Children in New York City," Journal of Educational Sociology, XXIV, No. 9 (May, 1951), 544-550.

Peck, Harris B., and Virginia Bellsmith. Individual and Group Therapy in a Court Setting. To be published by Family Service Association of America.

Pennsylvania, Children's Commission. The Legal Foundations of the Jurisdiction, Powers, Organization and Procedures of the Courts of Pennsylvania in Their Handling of Cases of Juvenile Offenders and of Dependent and Neglected Children. Philadelphia, 1926.

Perlman, Helen H. "The Caseworker's Use of Collateral Information," Social Casework, XXXII, No. 8 (October, 1951), 325-333.

Pigeon, Helen D. Probation and Parole in Theory and Practice. New York: National Probation and Parole Association, 1942.

Planning for the Mental Health Needs of New York City Children. A special issue of Journal of Educational Sociology, Vol. XXIV, No. 9 (May, 1951).

Polier, Justine Wise. Everyone's Children, Nobody's Child. New York: Charles Scribner's Sons, 1941.

—— "Psychiatry and the Court Offender." Paper delivered at the

Massachusetts Conference of Social Work, Boston, November 28, 1951.

—— Review of Sheldon Glueck and Eleanor T. Glueck, "Unraveling Juvenile Delinquency," *Harvard Law Review*, LXIV, No. 6 (1951), 1036-1038.

—— "The Role of a Juvenile Court in 1948." Address delivered at the 64th Annual Meeting of the Illinois Children's Home and Aid Society, Chicago, January 30, 1948. Privately published.

Pound, Roscoe. Criminal Justice in America. New York: Henry Holt & Co., 1930.

—— "The Juvenile Court and the Law," in National Probation and Parole Association, Cooperation in Crime Control, Yearbook, 1944. New York, 1945, pp. 1-22.

Pray, Kenneth. Social Work in a Revolutionary Age. Philadelphia: University of Pennsylvania Press, 1949.

Rappaport, Mazie F. "Social Work and the Court," *Child Welfare*, XXVIII, No. 9 (November, 1949), 15-17.

Reckless, Walter. "Training Probation and Parole Personnel," *Focus*, XXVII, No. 2 (March, 1948), 44-48.

Regensburg, Jeanette. "Utilizing the Contribution of Psychiatric Staff within an Agency," *Social Casework*, XXXII, No. 6 (June, 1951), 231-236.

Richmond, Mary. Social Diagnosis. New York: Russell Sage Foundation, 1917.

Robinson, Virginia. Dynamics of Supervision under Functional Controls. Philadelphia: University of Pennsylvania Press, 1949.

Rubin, Sol. "The Legal Character of Juvenile Delinquency," *The Annals*, American Academy of Political and Social Science, CCLXI (January, 1949), 1-8.

—— "Protecting the Child in Juvenile Court," *Journal of Criminal Law, Criminology and Police Science*, XLIII, No. 4 (November-December, 1952), 425-440.

Schneider, David M. The History of Public Welfare in New York State, 1609-1866. Chicago: University of Chicago Press, 1938.

Schramm, Gustav L. "The Judge Meets the Boy and His Family," in National Probation and Parole Association, Social Correctives for Delinquency, Yearbook, 1945. New York, 1946, pp. 103-104.

—— "Philosophy of the Juvenile Court," *The Annals*, American Academy of Political and Social Science, CCLXI (January, 1949), 101-108.

Seliger, Robert V., Edwin J. Lukas, and Robert M. Lindner, eds. Contemporary Criminal Hygiene. Baltimore: Oakridge Press, 1946.

Sicher, Dudley F. "Divorce Procedure Reform." Reprint from *Virginia Law Weekly*, March, 1950.

—— "Socialized Procedure of the Domestic Relations Court of the City of New York: the Lawyer's Role in Its Children's and Family Court Divisions." New York: Privately printed, as rev. May 15, 1951.

Simon, Caroline K. "Racial and Religious Democracy: Its Effect on Correctional Work," in National Probation and Parole Association, The Community and the Correctional Process, Yearbook, 1951. New York, 1952, pp. 205-217.

Smith, A. Delafield. "The Child and the Law." Report prepared for the use of the Technical Committee on Fact Finding, Midcentury White House Conference on Children and Youth, 1950. Mimeographed.

Stott, D. H. Delinquency and Human Nature. Dunfermline, Fife, Scotland: Carnegie United Kingdom Trust, 1950.

Sussman, Frederick B. Law of Juvenile Delinquency. New York: Oceana Publications, 1950.

Tappan, Paul W. "Children and Youth in the Criminal Court," *The Annals*, American Academy of Political and Social Science, CCLXI (January, 1949), 128-136.

—— Delinquent Girls in Court. New York: Columbia University Press, 1947.

—— Juvenile Delinquency. New York: McGraw Hill, 1949.

Teeters, Negley K., and John Otto Reinemann. The Challenge of Delinquency. New York: Prentice-Hall, 1950.

Thurston, Henry W. Concerning Juvenile Delinquency. New York: Columbia University Press, 1942.

Timasheff, Nicholas S. One Hundred Years of Probation, 1841-1941. 2 vols. New York: Fordham University Press, 1941 and 1943.

—— Probation in the Light of Criminal Statistics. New York: Fordham University Press, 1949.

United Nations, Department of Social Affairs. Probation and Related Measures. New York: Columbia University Press, 1951.

Van Waters, Miriam. "Adult Offenders," in Social Work Year Book, 1951. New York: American Association of Social Workers, 1951.

Welfare Council of New York City, Conference Group on Correctional and Allied Services. Standards of Probation Services. New York: Welfare Council of New York City, 1951. Mimeographed.

—— Report on Conference on Better Services to Children. New York, 1949. Mimeographed.

Winters, Glenn R. "A Better Way to Select Our Judges," *Journal of the American Judicature Society*, XXXIV (April, 1951), 166-173.

Witmer, Helen L. Social Work. New York: Rinehart & Co., Inc., 1942.

Wylegala, Victor B. "Children's Courts, an Effective Aid to Social Agencies," *Child Welfare*, XXVIII, No. 7 (July, 1949), 6-9.

Young, Kimball. "Social Psychology and Social Casework," *American Sociological Review*, XVI, No. 1 (February, 1951), 54-61.

Youth House, New York City. Fifth, Sixth and Seventh Annual Reports of the Executive Director. New York: 1949, 1950, 1951. Mimeographed.

INDEX

Administration, 217-20, 318-21
Adult proceedings, 45, 46(*tab.*), 125
Advisory committee for Children's Court, 317-18, 324
Allocation Unit, 248
Attendance officers, 125
Augustus, John, 137

Bar associations, responsibility for aid in improving Children's Court, 326
Big Brothers, 173, 240, 242, 243
Big Sisters, 240, 242, 243
Boys House, 257
Bronx: Children's Court schedule in, 36; new Children's Court cases (1949-1952) in, 45(*tab.*); relative proportion of cases terminated by petition (1949-1952) in, 68(*tab.*); physical facilities of Children's Court in, 96; number of rehearings in, 120; Court reporting officer in, 131; problems of probation officers in, 206, 207; probation offices and clerical facilities in, 211
Brooklyn: Children's Court schedule in, 36; new Children's Court cases (1949-1952) in, 45(*tab.*); relative proportion of cases terminated by petition (1949-1952) in, 68(*tab.*); petition desk in, 91; physical facilities of Children's Court in, 95-96; pressure of court calendar in, 120; Court reporting officer in, 131; number of rehearings in, 206, 207; probation offices and clerical facilities in, 210
Budget for Children's Court, 320

Buffalo, New York's first juvenile court in, 30
Bureau of Adjustment of Children's Court, 54-56, 60-88; statistics on new cases in, 42, 67; type of cases handled by, 61, 65-67; cases terminated by, (1948-1952), classified by disposition, 64(*tab.*); new applications (1938-1952) in, 64(*tab.*); receptionist in, 64; relative proportions of cases terminated by petition (1949-1952) in, 68(*tab.*); representative cases classified by borough and source of referral, 69(*tab.*); cases reviewed in study of, 69*n*; representative cases, classified by problems presented on referral, 71(*tab.*); representative cases, classified by borough and disposition, 73(*tab.*); evaluation of, 74-83; function of, 83-84; personnel needs of, 84-88; physical facilities in, 88; summary of findings, 266-67; proposal for incorporation into a Bureau of Applications, 285-89; case analysis in study of, 334-35
Bureau of Adjustment Record as summarized in probation case studies, 150-52
Bureau of Applications: need for, in Children's Court, 93-94; possible effect on treatment of witnesses, 102-103*n*; proper functioning of, 282; recommendations for, 285-89; as related to Court's demonstration-research project, 322; potential contribution of Youth Board, 325